Polar Politics

A volume in the series

Cornell Studies in Political Economy

EDITED BY PETER J. KATZENSTEIN

A full list of titles in the series appears at the end of the book.

Polar Politics

CREATING INTERNATIONAL ENVIRONMENTAL REGIMES

EDITED BY

ORAN R. YOUNG and
GAIL OSHERENKO

CORNELL UNIVERSITY PRESS

Ithaca and London

Contents

Preface

What would it take for states to work together to achieve a comprehensive ban on nuclear testing, reduce the threat of global climate
change, or create a body of international law to protect the atmosphere
more generally? Why have governments not yet forged agreements to
deal with pressing global and regional problems that cannot be solved
in the absence of cooperation among nations? Can we predict when and
under what conditions states will agree to restrict their sovereign authority and abide by new international rules that constrain and channel
their subsequent actions?

Why do actors in international society succeed in forming institutional arrangements or regimes to cope with some transboundary problems but not with other, seemingly similar, problems? Both scholars and
practitioners engaged in international negotiations have offered a wide
range of responses to these questions. Yet efforts to conduct sustained
empirical tests of the principal hypotheses dealing with the process of
regime formation have been few and far between. This book, the culmination of a multinational research project, begins to fill this gap.

Scholars from four countries collaborated in composing a template of
hypotheses based on the literature relating to international cooperation
and in conducting five comparative studies of the formation of regimes
dealing with Arctic issues to test these hypotheses. Chapter 1 introduces
the cases and the hypotheses. Chapters 2 through 6 contain the five
case studies. The final chapter returns to the template of hypotheses to
assess the findings of the project and identify areas that we believe
merit priority in future research.

Three distinctive attributes mark this project: a focus on the Arctic as a source of case materials, the use of focused, comparative case studies as a methodology for testing hypotheses formulated in advance of the empirical work, and the formation of a multinational team to carry out the research.

The Arctic is emerging as an international region of military, economic, and environmental importance. The area is a major theater for the deployment of strategic weapons systems. The impact of extraction of nonrenewable resources on Arctic eco- and socioeconomic systems will require long-term monitoring and regulation. The struggle of indigenous peoples to maintain the integrity of their cultures and achieve a measure of self-determination will continue in the face of the militarization and industrialization of the Arctic. Accordingly, we now face a growing need to devise arrangements to manage ongoing conflicts of interest arising in connection with transboundary Arctic issues. Perhaps the most promising approach involves the formation of international regimes for the Arctic.

Functionally specific or geographically limited regimes have emerged in the Arctic during the twentieth century, ranging from bilateral arrangements to regimes with many parties. Additionally, geographically broader regimes address problems prevalent in the Arctic as elsewhere. We examined in this volume three regimes specific to the Arctic and two broader multilateral regimes of great importance to the region.

The Arctic is experiencing considerable ferment with regard to the formation of international regimes. The International Arctic Science Committee, a nongovernmental body formed in 1990, could become a catalyst for regime formation in the region. In 1991, the eight Arctic states—Canada, Denmark/Greenland, Finland, Iceland, Norway, Sweden, the Soviet Union, and the United States—agreed to an Arctic Environmental Protection Strategy, which has already led to one concrete step—creation of the Arctic Monitoring and Assessment Program (AMAP). Interest is also growing in a proposal to establish an international Arctic Council modeled after the Conference on Security and Cooperation in Europe (CSCE) and encompassing several "baskets" of issues, including economic, security, environmental, and cultural concerns.

While the need for enhanced international cooperation in the Arctic is easy to document, the region also illustrates the significance of impediments to sustained cooperation, even when joint gains are feasible. Despite the several initiatives currently under way, the road to effective international cooperation in the Circumpolar North may well be long and rocky. Thus the Arctic offers an important arena for applying existing knowledge of regime formation as well as an attractive testing ground for new ideas about the politics of regime formation.

We used structured or focused case studies to test and refine theory-based arguments. This practice is not without its limitations or, for that matter, its critics. There is a danger of skewing the results through a biased selection of cases, producing ad hoc or biased reconstructions of historical events, and manipulating information to conform to theoretical expectations. Carefully selected case studies, however, have substantial advantages. Although the results of a single case may be suspect, the opportunity to compare conclusions across several well-chosen cases increases our ability to test specific hypotheses and to refine theories of regime formation. When hypotheses state necessary or sufficient conditions, single contrary cases suffice to disconfirm the hypothesized relationships. For hypotheses framed as measures of association, the evidence from the case studies can only be characterized as more or less consistent with the expected results. Overall, we believe it is reasonable to treat the findings of this project as a challenge to those seeking to refute, refine, or extend our conclusions in their own research on regime formation.

Our research team met as a group in two workshops and presented preliminary results of the politics of international regime formation at the 1990 and 1991 annual meetings of the International Studies Association. The first workshop, in June 1989, yielded the template of hypotheses that all team members agreed to employ in their case studies; it also afforded an opportunity to discuss issues regarding methodology.

The second workshop, held immediately before the International Studies Association meeting in April 1990, provided a unique opportunity for individual authors to work together; indeed, team members working on the same case agreed to integrate their written products rather than produce several separate essays. Three of the five empirical chapters are coauthored and thus have the advantage of looking at a single regime from several national perspectives as well as drawing upon the historical record available in different countries. The individual authors of Chapters 5 and 6, both Americans, have tried to broaden their perspective by relying on written and oral accounts of the formation of the relevant regimes prepared by non-Americans.

Perhaps the most remarkable feature of this project is the composition of the research team. Fourteen scholars developed the research design and ten of these conducted the individual case studies. The participants hold advanced degrees in such varied fields as political science, geography, economics, law, and engineering as well as international relations. Moreover, the team included individuals from four countries: Canada, Norway, the former Soviet Union, and the United States.

The multinational nature of the team allowed us to examine materials in Russian and Scandinavian languages as well as English, to gain access to the files of different foreign ministries and other government agencies, and to overcome cultural biases that afflict many efforts to develop and test theoretical ideas about international cooperation. Cultural differences and geographical distance, however, presented obstacles: divergences in intellectual cultures and epistemologies, language differences, and practical problems of communication.

We selected researchers to conduct the case studies who, for the most part, have not been contributors to the body of theory under consideration and who accordingly had no particular biases or predetermined reasons to espouse one theoretical framework or set of hypotheses over another. This procedure required the participants to comprehend a large body of theory with which they had little familiarity.

Despite these numerous obstacles, the case studies provide an ample basis for testing a broad set of hypotheses. More important, comparing and analyzing the case studies enabled us, in the final chapter of this book, to initiate the development of a multivariate model for understanding and predicting regime formation and to offer some practical advice to researchers and to practitioners regarding international and transboundary regime formation.

We have received assistance from numerous sources. The Ford Foundation made the initial grant that enabled us to embark on an ambitious research program. Small grants from the International Research and Exchanges Board and the Soros Foundation helped defray the costs of travel for several members of our research team from the former Soviet Union. Other organizations provided in-kind assistance by granting members of their professional staffs the freedom to participate in our project. They include the John Sloan Dickey Endowment for International Understanding at Dartmouth College, the Canadian Institute for International Peace and Security in Ottawa, the Nansen Institute in Oslo, and the Institute for World Economy and International Relations and the Institute for Systems Studies (since renamed the Institute for Systems Analysis) of the Soviet (now Russian) Academy of Sciences in Moscow.

We are grateful as well for help provided by individuals. Chrystel Buell and Nicki Maynard, our project secretaries, kept the entire operation going smoothly. Karen Poage, copyeditor for the project, transformed a diversity of drafts into comprehensible and comparable English. We had help along the way from Dartmouth students, including Peter McDonald, Megan Ryan, Benjamin Kwakye, Himraj Dang, and Natasha Brown. We thank the staff of the Stefansson Collection in Dartmouth College's Baker Library for help in retrieving information related to the Svalbard case. Others who supplied information and reviewed drafts are too numerous to name, but they played a major role in helping the researchers reconstruct complex stories. Olav Schram Stokke of the Nansen Institute actively participated in our workshops, contributing significantly to the research design as well as critiquing drafts. Roger Haydon of Cornell University Press energized us during the final phase of our work with his enthusiasm for the project. Trudie Calvert edited the final manuscript in a professional manner. A detailed review by M. J. Peterson at the University of Massachusetts, Amherst, helped us to clarify and improve the entire manuscript.

Most of all, we express our gratitude to the members of the research team. They tackled the challenging task of linking theory and practice with vigor, found ways to communicate effectively across language and cultural barriers, and responded to our repeated suggestions for improvements in successive drafts of their case studies. Much of the merit of this book is attributable directly to the ability of this diverse group of researchers to work together as an effective team.

ORAN R. YOUNG
GAIL OSHERENKO

Wolcott, Vermont

Polar Politics

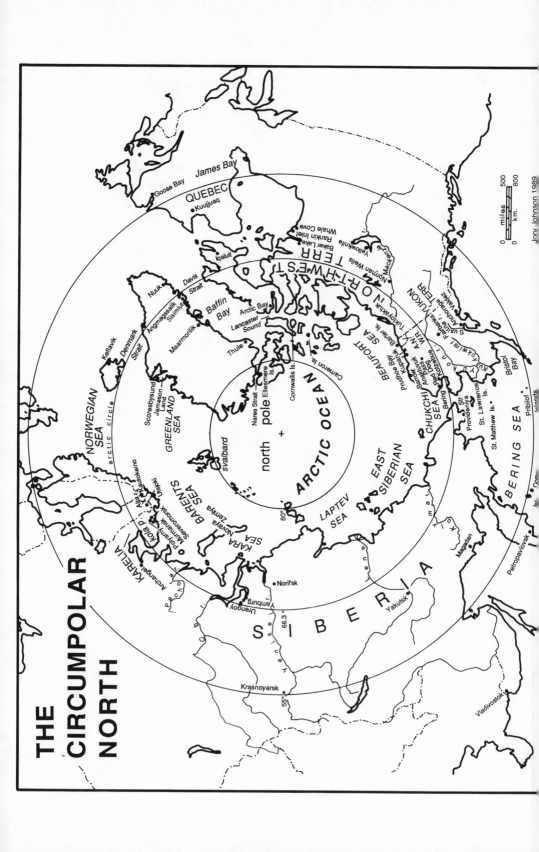

THE
CIRCUMPOLAR
NORTH

Jory Johnson 1989

0 miles 500
0 km. 800

QUEBEC

James Bay
Goose Bay
Kuujjuaq

NORTHWEST TERR.

Whale Cove
Rankin Inlet
Baker Lake
Norman Wells
Yellowknife

YUKON TERR.
W.N.W.T.
Tuktoyaktuk
Inuvik
Fairbanks
U.S.A. KOYUKUK
Anchorage
Valdez

Iqaluit
Davis Strait
Nuuk
Angmagssalik
Sismiut
Maarmorilik
Baffin Bay
Arctic Bay
Lancaster Sound
Thule
Cameron Is.
Banks Is.
BEAUFORT SEA
Kuparuk
Prudhoe Bay
Barrow
Amderma
Kotzebue
Bering Str.
St. Lawrence Is.
Providnniya
St. Matthew Is.

CHUKCHI SEA

Keflavik
Denmark Strait
Scoresbysund
Jameson Land
GREENLAND SEA
Nares Strait
Ellesmere Is.
Cornwallis Is.
north pole
ARCTIC OCEAN

NORWEGIAN SEA

arctic circle

svalbard
80°

BARENTS SEA
KARA SEA
Novaya Zemlya
LAPTEV SEA
EAST SIBERIAN SEA

BERING SEA
Pribilof Islands
Bristol Bay

Polyarny
Murmansk
Severomorsk
Kola P.
Alta
Kautokeino
Ustoki
Apatity
Arkhangel
KARELIA

Pechora

Noril'sk

Urengoy
Yamburg
66.3°
Yakutsk
Magadan

SIBERIA

Yenisey
Lena
Kolyma

55°
Krasnoyarsk

Petropavlovsk

Vladivostok

CHAPTER ONE

The Formation of International Regimes: Hypotheses and Cases

GAIL OSHERENKO AND ORAN R. YOUNG

Regimes are social institutions composed of agreed-upon principles, norms, rules, and decision-making procedures that govern the interactions of actors in specific issue areas.[1] They are the rules of the game that determine the character of recognized social practices. Whereas some international institutions are broad and encompassing (for example, the international economic order), most regimes deal with a limited set of well-defined activities or a specific geographical area of interest to some subset of the members of international society. Often regimes are limited both functionally and geographically.

The importance of international regimes is growing in a world in which increasing interdependence heightens the impact of the actions of individual states (or of those operating under the jurisdiction of individual states) on the welfare of other states and their inhabitants. The proliferation of regimes dealing with the control of arms (for example, the nuclear nonproliferation regime), international commerce (for example, the General Agreement on Tariffs and Trade system), and human rights (for example, the Helsinki Accords) illustrates this proposition. Natural resource and environmental regimes play an increasingly

---

1. This definition was agreed on at a meeting of fifteen scholars representing four large-scale, multi-year research projects on international regimes at Minary Center, Dartmouth College, 22–24 November 1991. See also Oran R. Young, *International Cooperation: Building Regimes for Natural Resources and the Environment* (Ithaca: Cornell University Press, 1989).

important role in structuring international relations as transboundary air and water pollution, the protection of migratory or endangered species, and other environmental issues have come to the attention of policy makers and the public. International regimes already regulate human activities in Antarctica, the dumping of oily wastes at sea, transboundary air pollution, whaling, trade in endangered species, and the preservation of natural and cultural heritage sites, to name a few. The framework conventions on climate change and biological diversity, signed during the United Nations Conference on Environment and Development in June 1992, initiated a process of regime creation regarding these global environmental concerns.

We began our research with a single question: what are the determinants of success or failure in efforts to form regimes dealing with specific issues? This question is familiar to both scholars and practitioners. Like others who have sought answers to it, we have been motivated in our search by both explanatory and prescriptive concerns.[2] In our view, those seeking to foster international cooperation on behalf of states, intergovernmental organizations, and even nongovernmental organizations stand to benefit from improvements in our understanding of the process of regime formation and, especially, of initiatives likely to increase the probability of success in this process. Naturally, questions arise about the relationship between regime *formation* and regime *effectiveness*. To engage in an in-depth analysis of the numerous hypotheses concerning regime formation, we set aside questions of effectiveness for later exploration. A sequel to this project, now in progress, will focus on the effectiveness of international regimes.

As our project developed, we came to understand that the concept of regime formation requires unpacking if it is to be analytically tractable as a dependent variable. Three aspects of regime formation are particularly worthy of differentiation. First is the simple question of whether a regime forms, in other words, whether the efforts of those involved in the process of regime formation succeed or fail. A second aspect deals with the issue of timing. How long does it take to reach closure on the terms of a constitutional contract establishing a regime, and why does the process take much longer in some cases than in others?[3] Finally,

2. Kenneth A. Oye, ed., *Cooperation under Anarchy* (Princeton: Princeton University Press, 1986), 1.

3. A constitutional contract is an agreement setting forth an interlocking system of behavioral prescriptions expected to remain operative over an indefinite period. Such contracts may, but need not, be codified in legally binding instruments such as conventions or treaties. See James M. Buchanan, *The Limits of Liberty: Between Anarchy and Leviathan* (Chicago: University of Chicago Press, 1975).

there is the matter of a regime's substantive content—not only whether and when a regime forms but also how its principal provisions are arrived at. These are analytic distinctions; it does not make sense to deal with any one of these concerns to the exclusion of the others. Still, in considering the analyses set forth in our case studies, one should bear in mind these distinctions.

The cases we have chosen for study all involve the formation of international regimes dealing with Arctic issues. Chapters 2, 3, and 4 examine the formation of multilateral, geographically limited, and functionally specific regimes that are or have been operative in the Arctic: the regime for the conservation of North Pacific fur seals, the Svalbard regime, and the regime for the conservation of polar bears.[4] Chapter 5 deals with a functionally specific regime that is broader in geographic scope, extending far beyond the Arctic but certain to have a significant impact on the Arctic: the regime for the protection of stratospheric ozone. Chapter 6 seeks to test our hypotheses by considering a case in which no regime has yet formed to address a significant problem in the Arctic: haze produced by a combination of air pollutants originating far to the south of the Arctic region. The chapter contrasts the failure to form a specific regime to cope with Arctic haze with the successful establishment of a regime for long-range transboundary air pollution among industrialized nations of the Northern Hemisphere.

There is nothing sacred about these cases from the point of view of testing hypotheses about regime formation; other cases can be and are being used by interested scholars.[5] Yet the Arctic has several attractions as a testing ground for such study. Physical and biological systems do not vary much from one part of the region to another, but the human experience in the Circumpolar North has varied considerably both spatially and temporally. The Arctic has been a focus of attention for those interested in regime formation under the substantially different circumstances prevailing in the pre–World War I era, the interwar period,

---

4. Some notable bilateral regimes are also Arctic-specific. Examples include the various agreements concerning migratory birds, the Canada–Denmark/Greenland agreement on the marine environments of the Davis Strait and Baffin Bay, and the informal agreement between Norway and the Soviet Union on uses of the disputed area in the Barents Sea (the so-called gray zone agreement).

5. Volker Rittberger led a collaborative project employing a similar methodology but focusing on European cases at the University of Tübingen. Results of the project are summarized in Volker Rittberger and Michael Zurn, "Regime Theory: Findings from the Study of East-West Regimes" (paper presented at the annual meeting of the International Studies Association, Vancouver, March 1991). See also Rittberger, ed., *International Regimes in East-West Politics* (London: Pinter, 1990).

the post–World War II era, and the post–Cold War period.[6] The five cases we have chosen are sufficiently diverse with respect to participants, functional scope, and context to be interesting. Yet they have enough in common to facilitate controlled comparisons aimed at testing ideas about the determinants of regime formation. Additionally, we believe that the cases examined here constitute an attractive source of lessons for those now working on the development of new Arctic regimes.[7]

Prized for several centuries by human users for the quality of its skin, the northern fur seal, at issue in our first case, experienced severe stock depletions as a result of the rapid growth of pelagic (at sea) harvesting toward the end of the nineteenth century. Unilateral efforts on the part of the United States to regulate the harvest resulted in a sharp conflict with Great Britain (acting for Canada) over marine jurisdiction in the Bering Sea and eventuated in a well-known case of international arbitration which, however, failed to provide a mechanism for protecting the fur seals. By the early years of the twentieth century, the consequent decline in the fur seal population had reached crisis proportions, a situation that led to the negotiation of an international regime for the protection of the North Pacific fur seal in 1911 among Great Britain, Japan, Russia, and the United States. In essence, this regime banned pelagic sealing and placed all harvesting operations under the control of the United States on the Pribilof Islands and Russia on the Commander Islands in return for a guaranteed share of the annual harvest of sealskins for Canada and Japan.

The regime is widely credited with halting the depletion of fur seals

6. For a more complete picture of international cooperation in the Arctic, consult the listings of international agreements in Gail Osherenko, "Environmental Cooperation in the Arctic: Will the Soviets Participate?" *International Environmental Affairs* 1 (Summer 1989): 203–221; and Oran R. Young and Osherenko, "International Cooperation in the Arctic: Soviet Attitudes and Actions," in *The Soviet Maritime Arctic*, ed. Lawson Brigham (London: Belhaven, 1991), 258–283, 321–327. The U.S. Arctic Research Commission compiled a listing of 450 cooperative agreements for the conduct of Arctic research, logistical support, and access to Arctic sites. Some of these arrangements involve the establishment of international regimes. An abstract of the commission's report on this listing appears in *Arctic Research of the United States* 4 (Fall 1990): 63–64.

7. For a survey of new initiatives relating to international cooperation in the Arctic see Oran R. Young, "The Arctic in World Affairs," a lecture delivered 10 May 1989 at the University of Washington and published in the pamphlet series *The Donald L. McKernan Lectures in Marine Affairs* (Seattle: University of Washington Sea Grant Program, 1989); Gail Osherenko, "Developments in International Environmental Law: Will They Help or Hinder Arctic Peoples?" *Nordic Journal of International Law* 58 (1989): 332–338; and Osherenko and Young, *The Age of the Arctic: Hot Conflicts and Cold Realities* (Cambridge: Cambridge University Press, 1989), chap. 9.

and establishing conditions allowing for recovery of the fur seal population. This pioneering effort to foster international cooperation to protect a shared resource functioned for over seven decades, with a hiatus in the 1940s occasioned by the war between Japan and the United States. The regime finally collapsed in 1984, when the United States Senate, influenced by lobbying on the part of antiharvesting organizations opposed to arrangements sanctioning any consumptive use of wild animals, refused to extend it, even with modifications.[8] In recent years, the fur seal population has declined again amid considerable controversy in the scientific community about the causes of this trend.[9] Efforts to manage this highly migratory species today are confined to the actions of individual states within their fishery conservation zones or exclusive economic zones. There are no institutional arrangements providing for international cooperation or even coordination regarding the northern fur seal.

The Svalbard Archipelago is a collection of islands located 600 miles northwest of the north coast of Norway and covering 62,400 square kilometers (about the size of Belgium and the Netherlands combined). Interest on the part of actual or potential users from several countries led to the international regime that is our second case under the terms of the 9 February 1920 Treaty Relating to Spitsbergen. This treaty originated as an element in the larger settlement of issues outstanding at the close of World War I (even though the fate of the archipelago was not an issue during the war). In essence, the Svalbard regime couples a recognition of Norwegian sovereignty over the archipelago with a series of significant commitments by Norway to respect previously acquired rights in the area, to allow nationals of all the signatories (currently forty in number) access to the natural resources of the island on non-discriminatory terms, to tax activities in the area solely to raise revenue needed to cover the costs of administering the archipelago, and to maintain the archipelago in a permanently demilitarized state. Legally, therefore, the Svalbard Archipelago is a part of Norway. But the Norwegian government has relinquished the authority to exclude others from using the resources of the area, including both minerals and fish, and Norway has accepted an international obligation to act as a

---

8. The U.S. Senate failed to ratify a 1984 Protocol to the Interim Convention on the Conservation of North Pacific Fur Seals, which would have extended the life of the regime for an additional four years.

9. For a glimpse of the range of opinion within the scientific community see "North Pacific Fur Seals—Pribilof Island Population: Designation as Depleted," National Marine Fisheries Service, 52 *Fed. Reg.* 49450–49456 (31 December 1987).

steward charged with preventing any use of the archipelago for warlike purposes.

Despite the disruptions of World War II and pressures of the Cold War, the Svalbard regime has remained intact for more than sixty-six years. The regime is not free of controversy. Norway and the former Soviet Union dispute application of the treaty to the adjoining outer continental shelf, and they engage in recurrent conflicts over Norway's efforts to implement rules promulgated under the terms of the regime in the Russian communities of the archipelago. The continuing conflict may be a sign of the regime's success in conflict management rather than of its instability. The arrangement continues to be a major source of order in an important segment of the Arctic. Its success stands as a monument to the proposition that state sovereignty need not constitute a barrier to effective international cooperation when individual states (in this case, Norway) are willing to accept explicit restrictions on the exercise of their sovereign authority.

Our third case concerns the regime for the conservation of polar bears. The polar bear, in many ways the quintessential symbol of the Arctic, has long been a prime target of trophy hunters from affluent societies around the world. By the 1960s, the rising value of polar bear hides coupled with the practice of using snowmobiles and light aircraft to hunt bears led to unprecedented increases in the number of polar bears killed.[10] Animal protection organizations drew public attention to the unsportsmanlike use of modern technologies in trophy hunting as well as the continued use of unmanned set-guns and traps. Polar bears ranged widely in the Arctic without regard to political boundaries, but remarkably little was known about the population dynamics of this species. Concern about the status of polar bear stocks led to a remarkable set of initiatives among scientists interested in the polar bear, operating within the umbrella of the International Union for the Conservation of Nature and Natural Resources (IUCN), which eventuated in the signing of an agreement in 1973 establishing an international regime for the conservation of polar bears. The resultant regime, whose members are Canada, Denmark/Greenland, Norway, Russia, and the United States, focuses on conservation rather than on any effort to eliminate the consumptive use of polar bears.

The heart of this regime is a set of commitments by each of the parties to prohibit the killing or capturing of polar bears except under clearly delimited circumstances, to limit commercial trade in

10. Ian Sterling, "Research and Management of Polar Bears *Ursus Maritimus*," *Polar Record* 23 (1986): 168.

polar bear skins and other products, to take steps to protect ecosystems located within their jurisdictions of which polar bears are a part, and to engage in a substantial program of coordinated research. The regime has not only played an important role in conserving polar bears, whose numbers probably do not exceed twenty thousand throughout the Circumpolar North, but it also stands as testimony to the feasibility of cooperation involving both of the superpowers and several lesser powers with regard to Arctic issues of mutual concern. Additionally, this regime offers important lessons concerning the role of scientists, advocacy groups, and the media in the politics of regime formation.[11]

The ozone protection regime, our fourth case, is concerned with an issue that lies beyond the Arctic as well as within it. In the 1970s, scientists became concerned that certain chemicals contained in chlorofluorocarbons (CFCs) could deplete the thin layer of ozone in the stratosphere that filters ultraviolet light from the sun's radiation before it reaches the earth. These scientists warned that increased ultraviolet radiation reaching the earth's surface would result in public health problems such as increases in cataracts and skin cancer, possible declines in agricultural productivity, and lower yields from marine fisheries. Growing commercial applications of CFCs in air conditioning, refrigeration, installation of plastic foam and foam insulation, cleaning solvents, aerosol propellants, and fire extinguishing heightened concern. In mid-1985, a dramatic report announced a rapid and unexpected thinning of the ozone layer over Antarctica during the austral spring. Scientists have since documented a similar seasonal thinning of the ozone layer in the Arctic, though it is not as pronounced as the annual Antarctic "ozone hole."

While scientists continued to debate the causal links between the use of CFCs and the ozone hole, the United Nations Environment Programme (UNEP) initiated discussions aimed at reaching agreement on an international convention to control the use of CFCs. Chapter 5 analyzes the development of the international ozone protection regime formed in stages and encapsulated in the 1985 Vienna Convention for the Protection of the Ozone Layer, the 1987 Montreal Protocol on Substances That Deplete the Ozone Layer, and the 1990 London Amendments to the protocol. This case offers a rich source of empirical data

---

11. Chapter 4 constitutes the first and only detailed case history of the regime formation process culminating in the 1973 Agreement on the Conservation of Polar Bears. For this reason, the chapter is somewhat longer than our other case studies, whose authors were able to draw on prior historical accounts.

on the role of science and scientists, intergovernmental organizations such as UNEP and the European Community (EC), and individual leaders in processes of regime formation. The author, an important contributor to the development of knowledge-based theories, explores the relative importance of such theories in contrast to power-based and interest-based theories.

The final case study deals with an atmospheric phenomenon known as Arctic haze, which is prevalent over the north polar region during the winter and early spring months. It has received little attention outside the scientific community, in contrast to the problems of acid rain, depletion of stratospheric ozone, and global climate change. Scientists first recognized what is now known as Arctic haze as early as the 1950s, but scientific study of its components and sources began in earnest only in the mid-1970s. The components of Arctic haze range from relatively benign particles of soil dust and sea salt to traces of heavy metals, soot, sulfate, and compounds originating in pesticides and fungicides. The deposition of these particulates on land and at sea may explain the increasingly high levels of toxic substances found in polar bears, seals, and even humans residing in the Arctic.

This case makes use of the theories of regime formation considered in this volume to determine how well they explain the failure to form a regime explicitly addressing the Arctic haze problem. To enrich the analysis, the author contrasts this lack of progress on international cooperation regarding Arctic haze with the significant progress that has been made in establishing the regime for transboundary air pollution embodied in the 1979 Geneva Convention on Long-Range Transboundary Air Pollution (LRTAP) and its supplemental protocols on sulfur emissions (1985), nitrogen oxide emissions (1988), and volatile organic compounds (1991). This case provides a unique opportunity to test our hypotheses and to use the findings to suggest a promising strategy for addressing the Arctic haze problem.

INDEPENDENT VARIABLES: DETERMINANTS OF REGIME FORMATION

In thinking about the determinants of success or failure in efforts to form international regimes, students of international relations have generally directed their attention to the exercise of power, the interplay of interests, the role of knowledge, and (to a lesser extent) the impact of various exogenous forces. For the most part, they have produced explanations of regime formation highlighting the role of one or another of these sets of factors. To test the adequacy of these explanations, we began by distilling a set of explicit hypotheses from the existing literature on regime formation. The resultant theoretical template has guided the work of those conducting the case studies that form the heart of this book.[12] We have grouped these explanatory arguments into four broad categories: power-based hypotheses, interest-based hypotheses, knowledge-based hypotheses, and contextual arguments (the full template can be found in the Appendix).[13]

Power-Based Hypotheses

Political scientists and others who accept the tenets of realist or neo-realist perspectives on international relations have long looked to the distribution or configuration of power in international society as a key to explaining collective outcomes. They assume that international institutions, including issue-specific regimes, are structured by and reflect the interests or preferences of the dominant member(s) of the international system.

The most analytically developed and widely espoused hypotheses of the power theorists stress the role of a single state possessing a preponderance of material resources (in the current vocabulary of international relations, a hegemon) in the process of regime formation. Theorizing about the role of hegemons arose and has been applied most systematically to explain the formation of a group of economic regimes—for example, the international trade and monetary arrangements—that emerged during the post–World War II period when the United States played a dominant role in the promotion of world economic order. Responding to perceptions of (relative) decline in the power of the United States during the 1970s and 1980s, power theorists have begun to focus also on the stability of such regimes in a period of hegemonic decline. The cases examined in this book provide an important opportunity to test the robustness of the theory by looking at cases outside the realm of economics.

The strongest and most widely discussed hypothesis of the power theorists states that the presence of a hegemon is a necessary condition for the emergence of institutional arrangements at the international

---

12. Individual case studies do not necessarily discuss each of the hypotheses in detail, but each author used the template in structuring the case materials.

13. For a similar, though not identical, categorization of the theoretical literature on regime formation see Stephan Haggard and Beth A. Simmons, "Theories of International Regimes," *International Organization* 41 (Summer 1987): 491–517.

level.[14] The hegemonists regard the dispersion of power or the presence of a number of parties possessing substantial bargaining strength as a barrier to regime formation because it can drive up transaction costs to a level that precludes agreement. Thus they see concentration of power in the hands of a single, dominant state or hegemon as a key ingredient in the recipe for success in regime formation.

Two schools of thought have developed to explain how a hegemon uses its preponderant material resources (superiority in military power, natural resources, trade, or finance) to create the regimes it prefers. The benign hegemon exercises positive leadership, inducing others to accept its preferences regarding institutional arrangements by agreeing to shoulder a disproportionate share of the costs of supplying regimes treated as public goods.[15] The hegemon is not acting altruistically. Nor is it acting to exploit the other members of the regime. Rather, as Charles P. Kindleberger has put it, "Realists maintain that international public goods are produced, if at all, by the leading power, a so-called 'hegemon,' that is willing to bear an undue part of the short-run costs of these goods, either because it regards itself as gaining in the long run, because it is paid in a different coin such as prestige, glory, immortality, or some combination of the two."[16] The coercive hegemon, by contrast, uses its power to impose the institutional arrangements it prefers on a group, regardless of the preferences of other members. Whereas others, acting as free riders, may acquiesce voluntarily in the actions of the benign hegemon, they tolerate the regimes imposed by the coercive hegemon because they have no other choice.

Although the theoretical literature linking configurations of power other than hegemony to the process of regime formation is sparse, our research team agreed to consider what role power considerations may have played in the formation of regimes in the absence of a hegemon.

---

14. Robert Gilpin, *The Political Economy of International Relations* (Princeton: Princeton University Press, 1987). For more specific discussions of the role of hegemons in regime formation, see Robert O. Keohane, *After Hegemony: Cooperation and Discord in the World Political Economy* (Princeton: Princeton University Press, 1984), chap. 3; and Duncan Snidal, "The Limits of Hegemonic Stability Theory," *International Organization* 39 (Autumn 1985): 579–614.

15. The benign variant of the hegemony hypothesis is closely associated with the work of Charles P. Kindleberger, although he prefers the terms "dominance" and "leadership" to "hegemony." See especially Kindleberger, "Dominance and Leadership in the International Economy," *International Studies Quarterly* 25 (June 1981): 242–254; and Kindleberger, "International Public Goods without International Government," *American Economic Review* 76 (March 1986): 1–13.

16. Kindleberger, "International Public Goods," 3, describes the realist school of thought on hegemony and contrasts it with the views of the "moralists" or "institutionalists."

Other possible distributions of power that might enhance the prospects for regime formation, we felt, include a bipolar or bimodal distribution of power, symmetry or equality among the parties with regard to power, or the existence of a small group of great powers (or even middle powers) interested in a given issue area. Our template also suggests that the role of power in international society is not limited to structural power exercised by states. Individuals may also become leaders by acting to translate the structural power of states into bargaining leverage applicable to specific instances of regime formation (we revert to this theme in our general discussion of leadership in the section on interest-based hypotheses).

Interest-Based Hypotheses

The fundamental premise of interest-based arguments concerning regime formation is that social institutions, including international regimes, arise when self-interested parties engaged in interactive decisionmaking approach a problem in contractarian terms and seek to coordinate their behavior to reap joint gains. The institutional bargaining that results may encompass both tacit bargaining and efforts on the part of individual parties to bring power to bear in the form of bargaining leverage. An agreement is struck and a regime forms when the participants reach closure on the terms of a mutually acceptable constitutional contract.

The theoretical literature on bargaining has taught us that the presence of a (potential) contract zone or zone of agreement constitutes a necessary condition for success in institutional bargaining.[17] But such a zone is not sufficient to ensure that a regime will form in a given issue area. Both theories of bargaining and the literature on actual cases of institutional bargaining at the international level are replete with accounts of collective-action problems and impediments to bargaining that block the efforts of actors to form international regimes, even when all participants acknowledge that a contract zone and, therefore, a range of feasible joint gains exist. As a result, interest-based hypotheses about regime formation generally deal with conditions over and above the existence of a contract zone that can be expected to facilitate

---

17. For a review of the major theories of bargaining see Oran R. Young, ed. and contributor, *Bargaining: Formal Theories of Negotiation* (Urbana: University of Illinois Press, 1975); and Young, "The Politics of International Regime Formation: Managing Natural Resources and the Environment," *International Organization* 43 (Summer 1989): 349–375. For a broader account of recent thinking about negotiation see Howard Raiffa, *The Art and Science of Negotiation* (Cambridge, Mass.: Harvard University Press, 1982).

or obstruct the efforts of parties to reach agreement on provisions to be included in the constitutional contracts laying out the terms of the relevant regimes.

The approach of this project diverges significantly from a series of well-known utilitarian arguments stressing factors such as the number of participants, the character of the payoff structure, and the role of recurrent interactions or "the shadow of the future" as determinants of success or failure in bargaining relating to regime formation.[18] These arguments are not without merit in some contexts, but we find them inadequate to explain or predict the formation of international regimes.

The argument about *numbers of participants* rests on the intuitively appealing idea that transaction costs rise (perhaps geometrically) as the number of actors engaged in interactive decision making increases. But this idea runs into trouble immediately when applied to actual processes of regime formation in international society. There are numerous cases in which sizable groups of actors have succeeded in reaching agreement on the terms of regimes (for example, the nuclear nonproliferation regime, the LRTAP regime, and the regime dealing with trade in endangered species). And bilateral efforts to reach agreement on the terms of regimes (for example, arms control arrangements involving the Soviet Union and the United States) frequently fail.

The problem with the argument about the *payoff structures* associated with specific instances of regime formation, by contrast, arises because those endeavoring to work out the terms of international regimes seldom know at the outset or subsequently make a concerted effort to delineate the contours of the contract zone or "utility possibility set" associated with their interactions. Rather, they exhibit a marked tendency to focus on a few key issues and then to begin work on the development of a negotiating text setting forth proposed provisions relating to these issues.

For its part, the *shadow of the future* may influence efforts to form international regimes but not in the manner envisioned in the standard utilitarian arguments relating to interactive decision making. Those engaged in regime formation do not ordinarily see themselves as engaging in an iterative game. They seek, instead, to agree on the provisions of regimes expected to last for an indefinite time period. Under the circumstances, they may well think hard about the long-term as well as the

---

18. For a clear exposition of these arguments see Kenneth A. Oye, "Explaining Cooperation under Anarchy: Hypotheses and Strategies," in Oye, ed., *Cooperation under Anarchy*, 1–24.

short-term consequences of the operation of the regimes they devise (a point to which we revert below). But this is not equivalent to thinking about the impact of current behavior on future plays of an iterative game.

We come, then, to the interest-based hypotheses that informed the work of the research team working on the case studies included in this volume. Our template contains ten distinct, and occasionally conflicting, hypotheses pertaining to regime formation envisioned as a process of interactive decision making.

Integrative bargaining and the veil of uncertainty. The first of these hypotheses states that institutional bargaining can succeed only when the parties approach the process in contractarian terms. Partly, this means that participants must be able to expend a significant portion of their energy on integrative or productive bargaining rather than distributive or positional bargaining.[19] This does not require that parties refrain from staking out definite positions on major issues or avoid questions regarding distribution. Yet it does imply that success in the process of regime formation can occur only when integrative bargaining or a search for mutually beneficial solutions assumes a prominent role in the process.

A distinctive element of this hypothesis suggests that the thicker the veil of uncertainty, the easier it will be for parties to approach the problem under consideration as an integrative exercise. The veil of uncertainty refers to all those factors that make it difficult for individual participants to foresee how the operation of institutional arrangements will affect their interests over time.[20] Individual parties' inability to predict a regime's impact on their welfare increases incentives to formulate provisions that are fair or equitable, which raises the probability that the parties can come up with institutional arrangements that are acceptable to all. Under the circumstances, those engaged in regime formation may consciously or unconsciously act to thicken the veil of uncertainty by lengthening the time that the regime is expected to remain operative, enlarging the set of issues at stake, changing the membership of the group engaged in the search for mutually agreeable provisions, or devising ambiguous provisions open to later interpretation.

---

19. For a seminal account of the distinction between integrative and distributive bargaining see Richard E. Walton and Robert B. McKersie, *A Behavioral Theory of Labor Negotiations: An Analysis of a Social Interaction System* (New York: McGraw-Hill, 1965), chaps. 2–5.

20. See Geoffrey Brennan and James M. Buchanan, *The Reason of Rules: Constitutional Political Economy* (Cambridge: Cambridge University Press, 1985), 28–31.

Equity. A second hypothesis states that the articulation of institutional options that all participants can accept as equitable is necessary for institutional bargaining to succeed. Economists and others who approach the problem of regime formation from the perspective of social welfare tend to focus on the achievement of allocative efficiency in thinking about the relative merits of alternative institutional arrangements for any given issue area.[21] They are critical of arrangements that are inefficient because they appear to misallocate scarce resources. Yet this perspective fails to give sufficient weight to the importance of focusing on equity (even at the expense of efficiency) to forge regimes that all the participants are prepared to accept. To state it more bluntly, institutional bargaining in international society can succeed only when all the major parties and interest groups feel that their primary concerns have been treated fairly.

In some cases an equitable outcome is also efficient so that the emergence of regimes whose provisions are designed to achieve efficiency does not in itself disprove the hypothesis.[22] Yet allocative efficiency is an abstract matter that is difficult to measure until a regime has operated for some time, whereas equity is an immediate and passionately felt concern. This suggests that satisfying identifiable community standards of equity is likely to be a precondition for success in international regime formation. The real question to be explored in empirical research, therefore, is whether the parties pay greater attention to equity than to efficiency in the bargaining process or lean toward the pursuit of equity when the two goals are difficult or impossible to achieve simultaneously.

Salient solutions. The emergence of salient solutions or focal points that have the power to shape expectations increases the probability of success in institutional bargaining.[23] Success is often linked to the ability of those formulating proposals to draft simple formulas that are intuitively appealing or to borrow formulas or approaches from prior cases with which negotiators may already be familiar. The influence of salience lies in its capacity to facilitate the convergence of expectations in international bargaining involving numerous parties operating un-

---

21. This paragraph draws heavily on the discussion in Young, "Politics of International Regime Formation," 368–369.

22. Nor does the setting aside of certain options that are obviously inferior in allocative terms violate the hypothesis.

23. Ibid., 369–370.

der a consensus rule.[24] This hypothesis regarding salience may appear initially to conflict with the hypothesis concerning integrative bargaining and the veil of uncertainty. But it is possible for the two hypotheses to be valid simultaneously. While a salient solution must be formulated in a simple manner that is easy for everyone to grasp and remember, its very simplicity may also cause it to be ambiguous or uncertain, leaving much to be resolved after the regime is in place.

Exogenous shocks or crises. The occurrence of a shock or crisis that is exogenous to the process of regime formation (though not necessarily to the issue area) increases the probability of success in efforts to reach closure on the terms of an international regime. Events such as the nuclear accident at Chernobyl or the discovery of the ozone hole over Antarctica engender a sense of urgency that spurs quick action to conclude international agreements, such as the arrangements agreed to in 1986 for nuclear accidents or the 1987 protocol on stratospheric ozone. In the absence of any event triggering a sense of urgency or crisis, states appear to be in no hurry to reach agreement on the substance of a regime to prevent or respond to global climate change.[25]

Policy priority. Our template contains two contrasting hypotheses relating to the place of the issue or problem on the policy agendas of the parties. Success in regime formation can occur, on one account, only when an issue is of high priority on the policy agenda of each of the participants. Alternatively, some analysts argue that it is easier to form a regime when the subject matter does not loom large on the political agendas of the parties. To evaluate these contrasting hypotheses about the determinants of regime formation, we looked for individual leaders or organizations in each state with powerful political incentives to arrive at a solution to the problem. We also considered whether it is necessary for all the parties to exhibit a strong desire to find a solution in contrast to one or a few states providing leadership, either enticing or pressuring the others into following.

The common good. The growing need to manage conflicts in areas that have traditionally been treated as open-to-entry common property has led to an increasing interest in the role of values or ethical systems in

---

24. For the role of salience in international bargaining see Thomas C. Schelling, *The Strategy of Conflict* (Cambridge, Mass.: Harvard University Press, 1960), chap. 4.

25. Young, "Politics of International Regime Formation," 371–372.

the development of international institutions.[26] Some advocates of international cooperation in managing commons, such as the oceans, Antarctica, outer space, the geostationary orbit employed by communications satellites, and the stratospheric ozone layer, have come to believe that states must set aside narrow national interests in favor of some broader conception of the common good if they are to succeed in forming international regimes. A fuller treatment of the role of values appears in the next section where we focus on knowledge-based hypotheses. In this section, we confine our attention to the question of whether self-interested actors engaging in interactive decision making regarding the provisions of international regimes must alter the way they define their interests, adopting a larger conception of the common good, for institutional bargaining to succeed.

Science and technology. We have also reserved most of our discussion of the role of science and the scientists who develop and deploy scientific knowledge for the section on knowledge-based hypotheses. Yet several arguments relate science and technology to the prospects for success in regime formation conceptualized as a process of interactive decision making. Three of these arguments are noted here. According to the first of these arguments, the greater the propensity of the parties (or those who negotiate on their behalf) to focus on scientific or technical considerations, the higher will be the probability of success in the process of regime formation. A related argument states that the greater the role of negotiators with a scientific or technical background, the better the prospects for success in regime formation. And a third argument suggests that it is easier to form international regimes to deal with issues that are highly technical in contrast to issues that are openly political.

Relevant parties. Our eighth interest-based hypothesis states that all stakeholders—parties with an interest in the problem or issue area—must participate in the negotiation process for regime formation to succeed. The literature on alternative dispute resolution places considerable emphasis on having all those likely to be affected by the handling of a competitive/cooperative or mixed motive interaction represented

---

26. See Marvin S. Soroos, "The International Commons: A Historical Perspective," *Environment Review* 12 (Spring 1988): 1–21; and Soroos, "Conflict in the Use and Management of International Commons" in Jurki Käkönen, ed., *Perspectives on Environmental Conflict and International Politics* (London and New York: Pinter Publishers, 1992), 31–43.

at the negotiating table. This is necessary, scholars and mediators argue, to achieve a lasting settlement, thereby avoiding an outcome that an excluded party might, at best, refuse to join or, at worst, sabotage.[27] Are these ideas applicable to institutional bargaining regarding the formation of international regimes? To test this hypothesis, we asked whether key parties were missing at critical stages in the negotiations, whether the roster of interested parties changed over time, and whether changes in the composition of the group impeded or hastened regime formation.

Compliance mechanisms. A common obstacle to regime formation is a concern that other participants will fail to comply with the terms of any arrangement established.[28] Doubts about verification have often impeded progress toward the establishment of arms control regimes. Similarly, a preoccupation with enforcement has raised questions about accords designed to address transboundary pollution, fisheries management, and other topics. This suggests that the probability of success in institutional bargaining is a function of the availability of compliance mechanisms which the parties regard as clear-cut and likely to be effective.[29]

Efforts to elicit compliance need not involve the creation of a supranational organization or the delegation of responsibility to a preexisting international body. In fact, recent studies stress the practicality of relying on available national institutions[30] and suggest that "regime formation in international society is most apt to succeed when the participants can rely on relatively simple, non-intrusive compliance mechanisms which municipal governments can operate without undue effort

---

27. On the identification of parties to participate in negotiations and other matters arising during prenegotiation see Janice Gross Stein, ed., *Getting to the Table: The Processes of International Prenegotiation* (Baltimore: Johns Hopkins University Press, 1989).

28. Schelling, *Strategy of Conflict*, and Robert Axelrod, *The Evolution of Cooperation* (New York: Basic Books, 1984).

29. Challenging the orthodox perspective, some scholars have argued that enforcement is not the only important basis of compliance. See Young, "Politics of International Regime Formation," 370–371; Abram Chayes and Antonia Handler Chayes, "Compliance without Enforcement: State Behavior under Regulatory Treaties," *Negotiation Journal* (July 1991): 311–330; and Abram Chayes, "An Enquiry into the Workings of Arms Control Agreements," *Harvard Law Review* 85 (1972): 905–969.

30. Peter H. Sand, *Lessons Learned in Global Environmental Governance* (Washington, D.C.: World Resources Institute, 1990).

or the need to expend scarce political resources."[31] Likewise, compliance in international arenas is not merely or even primarily tied to the use of legal sanctions; the activities of governmental and nongovernmental bodies in raising a hue and cry in the face of violations may do more to ensure compliance than any threat of legal action.[32] To explore this hypothesis, we asked whether there were strong incentives to cheat or, conversely, to comply in the relevant issue area, whether decentralized compliance mechanisms were available, and whether there were ways to verify compliant behavior without intruding too far into the domestic affairs of individual states.

Individuals as leaders. The final hypothesis in this set states that success in institutional bargaining is likely to occur when effective leadership emerges; it will fail in the absence of such leadership. In the course of our research, we have come to realize that leadership by individuals differs from leadership by states, a topic that is addressed for the most part under the rubric of power-based arguments. Thus leadership as we use it in our case studies refers to the actions of individuals who endeavor to solve or circumvent the collective-action problems encountered by parties seeking to reap joint gains through the formation of new regimes.[33]

Leadership, in this sense, is a behavioral phenomenon that can take any of the following forms: structural leadership, entrepreneurial leadership, or intellectual leadership. A *structural* leader is an individual who acts in the name of a party (usually a state) in a bargaining process and leads by bringing that party's structural power (based on the possession of material resources) to bear in the form of bargaining leverage in specific interactions. An *entrepreneurial* leader (who may, but need not, represent a major stakeholder) uses negotiating skills to influence the way issues are presented and to arrive at mutually acceptable solutions. An *intellectual* leader (who may or may not be affiliated with a party to the process of regime formation) relies on the power of ideas to shape the way participants in institutional bargaining understand the issues and conceptualize options available to deal with these issues.

---

31. Young, "Politics of International Regime Formation," 371. For a general discussion of compliance in decentralized social settings see Oran R. Young, *Compliance and Public Authority: A Theory with International Applications* (Baltimore: Johns Hopkins University Press, 1979).

32. Sand, *Lessons Learned in Global Environmental Governance.*

33. Oran R. Young, "Political Leadership and Regime Formation: On the Development of Institutions in International Society," *International Organization* 45 (Summer 1991): 281–308.

While several types of leadership may come into play at the same time in institutional bargaining, the hypothesis states only that the emergence of some type of leadership is crucial to success in regime formation.

Knowledge-Based Hypotheses

Some students of international institutions, dissatisfied with mainstream power- and interest-based explanations of regime formation, have developed an alternative view centered on the premise that ideas matter too.[34] On this account, knowledge and values not only affect power and operate as determinants of interests, they also play a more direct role in regime formation. Two alternative, though not necessarily contradictory, sets of ideas about the role of cognitive forces in regime formation are discernible in the literature.

The first alternative involves scientific convergence. Exemplified with particular clarity in Richard Cooper's analysis of the establishment of an international public health regime to deal with communicable diseases, cooperation is relatively easy to achieve once a common or widely shared (though not necessarily accurate) understanding of the problem, its causes, and its solutions arises. Focusing primarily on the case of cholera in the nineteenth century, Cooper describes the failure to agree on the terms of an international public health regime so long as the conflict between the contagonists and the miasmatists remained unresolved. He then documents the rapid progress toward international cooperation to eradicate the disease when a consensus emerged toward the end of the century regarding the mechanism of cholera's transmission and appropriate steps to prevent its spread.[35]

More recent cases involving environmental issues lend credence to the importance of scientific consensus on cause-and-effect relationships. As scientific consensus emerged not only on the existence of an ozone hole over Antarctica but also on the causal role of chlorofluorocarbons, international cooperation to phase out the production and consumption of CFCs and related chemicals followed rapidly. Conversely, the absence of consensus on key issues relating to global climate

---

34. For a sustained presentation of this point of view see Ernst B. Haas, *When Knowledge Is Power: Three Models of Change in International Organizations* (Berkeley: University of California Press, 1990).

35. Richard N. Cooper, "International Cooperation in Public Health as a Prologue to Macroeconomic Cooperation," in Cooper et al., *Can Nations Agree? Issues in International Economic Cooperation* (Washington, D.C.: Brookings Institution, 1989), 178–254.

change constitutes a problem for those currently seeking to establish an effective international regime dealing with the issue of climate change.

A second line of reasoning supplements the argument concerning scientific convergence first by stressing the importance of shared values as well as knowledge of causal connections and then by suggesting a particular mechanism through which new ideas, causal beliefs, and values lead to regime formation. For a regime to form, according to this hypothesis, a network (an international organization or some less formal arrangement) must arise to link the community of those who share a common understanding of the problem and its solution and to allow them to communicate their ideas persuasively to policy makers. This network, whose membership generally includes both scientists and government officials and which is often characterized as an epistemic community, becomes a significant force in the process of regime formation. Its members offer authoritative and concordant advice in areas in which policy makers are poorly informed or plagued by uncertainty. By creating a common set of interpretations, the epistemic community reduces uncertainty and influences the form and range of the options considered in regime formation. Such a community may also become influential enough to prevent opposing views and values from gaining currency at the domestic level in each of the relevant states.[36]

Contextual Factors

We come finally to the idea that international regimes form only when events and conditions seemingly unrelated to the issue under consideration provide a window of opportunity or are in some other way conducive to regime formation. On this account, larger national and world events play a critical role in determining if and when international cooperation to address a particular problem or issue area occurs and in shaping the content of any regime that forms.

In our project, this set of considerations surfaced when Russian members of the research team articulated what they thought was missing from the preceding three sections of the template. Once the category of contextual factors made its way into our thinking, the research teams found it useful in alerting them to the relevance of larger national and world events which, though far removed from the subject matter involved in specific cases of regime formation, can and do sig-

---

36. Emanuel Adler and Peter M. Haas, "Conclusion: Epistemic Communities, World Order and the Creation of a Reflective Research Program," *International Organization* 46 (Winter 1992): 367–390.

nificantly affect both the timing and content of regime formation. Because this is an area that students of regime formation have not considered systematically, we ultimately chose to include this category without attempting to state explicit hypotheses about the role of contextual factors in advance of the empirical research.

The chapters that follow take us back initially to the end of the nineteenth century, when jurisdictional concepts prevalent today (for example, the idea of an exclusive economic zone) were not even on the horizon, the idea of *terra nullius* (land outside any state's jurisdiction) remained influential, and the notion of placing restrictions on the sovereignty of individual states seemed alien. They then bring us up to the present, when regimes for some international problems, such as the depletion of stratospheric ozone, are evolving rapidly, while attempts to come to terms internationally with such other problems as Arctic haze, continue to encounter serious impediments. The stories these chapters have to tell are critical building blocks in our pursuit of a general understanding of the determinants of sustained international cooperation. They are, at the same time, intriguing accounts of the complexities of international affairs treated as self-contained case studies.

Chapter Two

North Pacific Fur Seals: Regime Formation as a Means of Resolving Conflict

Natalia S. Mirovitskaya, Margaret Clark,
and Ronald G. Purver

The international regime articulated in the North Pacific Sealing Convention of 1911 remained in place until the 1980s. Although this agreement was elaborated long ago, it nevertheless offers lessons and insights for contemporary negotiators. That there is no longer a large market for seal furs in no way diminishes the importance of the factors that contributed to formation of a regime in this case. The individuals who negotiated the regime to protect the northern Pacific fur seal—not unlike negotiators of today—had to be responsive to the demands of state leaders, indigenous people, public opinion, the scientific community, and representatives of the industry.

In this chapter we examine the 1911 fur seal convention and the resulting regime from the perspectives of the four parties to it: Russia, Great Britain/Canada, the United States, and Japan.[1] In addition to identifying the primary components of the treaty, we consider to what degree each of the theories of regime formation applicable to this Arctic cooperation project influenced the creation of this regime.

The first step in understanding the fur seal regime is to look at the long history of trade in fur seal skins and the prolonged international

---

1. For Russia, Great Britain/Canada, and the United States, we have used official archival data in both Russian and English together with other appropriate resources. For the perspective of the Japanese delegation, we have been limited to previously translated material.

negotiations that led to the 1911 treaty. The negotiating process provides evidence of how the regime emerged.

Hunting of fur seals in the Bering Sea began in the eighteenth century with the Russian colonization of the Pacific coastline. In 1755, Stepan P. Krashenninikov described fur sealing in the waters off Kamchatka.[2] Although the colonists at first hunted exclusively for their own needs, within only a few years sealing had become a profitable business.

In 1799 the Russian government authorized the formation of the Russian-American Company to conduct all commercial activities in Alaska and the Aleutian and Commander island groups. The family of the tsar was the largest shareholder in this company, whose charter defined "the fur animal's harvest as its primary aim."[3] With the help of indigenous inhabitants, the company quickly developed a large-scale sealing business with a reported annual harvest of 200,000 to 400,000 seals (from a stock estimated to be between 2,500,000 and 4,000,000).[4] Over the next sixty years, the Russian-American Company harvested more than 2,560,000 seals from the Pribilof and Commander island herds.[5] The Russian sealers, however, killed only bachelor seals on land. This practice, governed by various unilateral regulations, posed no threat to the survival of the herd.

Under the 1867 Convention for the Cession of the Russian Possessions in North America to the United States (the Alaska Treaty),[6] the United States acquired the Pribilof Islands, home of the world's largest fur seal herd. Shortly thereafter, officials from the U.S.-based Hutchinson, Kohl & Company attempted to obtain exclusive rights to hunt these seals. After extensive debate in the U.S. Congress, the govern-

---

2. Stepan P. Krashenninikov, *Description of Kamchatka Land* (St. Petersburg: Imperial Academy of Sciences, 1755).

3. Semion B. Okun, *The Russian-American Company* (Leningrad: M. L. Socekgiz, 1939).

4. There were four main fur seal herds in the Bering Sea. They were differentiated by their rookeries, their paths of migration, and some physical differences. *Callorhinus ursinus* bred on the Commander Islands, *C. alascanus* lived on the Pribilof Islands, and *C. curilensis* rookeries were on the Robben and Kurile islands. See Nikolai V. Sliunin, *Natural Resources of the Kamchatka, Sakhalin and the Commander Islands*, Report to the Department of Agriculture (St. Petersburg, 1895); and Voloshinov, *The Fur Seals* (St. Petersburg: Erlich, 1899). The differentiation of the herds was not important when Russia had exclusive sovereignty and hunting was exclusively by Russian citizens, but when four states became active in sealing, problems over regulating the stocks became acute. The differentiation of the individual herds became an important factor in negotiating an agreement.

5. P. Tikhmenev, *The Historical Description of the Russian-American Company and Its Activities up to the Present Time* (St. Petersburg, 1863).

6. 1867 Convention for the Cession of the Russian Possessions in North America to the United States, in *Complete Statute Book of the Russian Empire* (1867).

ment in 1870 granted a Hutchinson subsidiary, the Alaska Commercial Company, a twenty-year lease for fur sealing on the Pribilof Islands. The terms of the lease included both monetary and conservation provisions: an annual rental payment to the government of $55,000, an annual tax of $2.62 per pelt, limitation of the seal harvest to 100,000 male seals during an annual four-month season, and the furnishing of certain necessities to the islands' inhabitants.[7] A year later Hutchinson, Kohl & Company arranged a similar twenty-year lease with the Russian Department of Internal Affairs for fur sealing privileges on the Commander and Robben islands. The firm agreed to pay the Russian government an annual rent of 5,000 rubles and a tax of two rubles per pelt. The inhabitants of the islands were to receive fifty kopecks for each skin.[8]

During the twenty-year duration of these leases, Hutchinson, Kohl & Company killed more than 760,000 seals from Russian herds and at least 1,900,000 seals from the Pribilof Islands without severely depleting the stocks.[9] With market prices ranging from three to four hundred rubles per pelt, the total income of the Hutchinson Company can be estimated in billions of rubles. The company guarded its monopoly of this profitable industry, leading the governors of both Alaska and Siberia to note that lack of competition prevented economic development in the region.[10]

Pressure on the fur seal herds increased substantially in the 1880s, when Canadian, American, and Japanese schooners began to engage in pelagic sealing (hunting in open waters).[11] The combination of pelagic sealing—which was legal under the principle of freedom of the high seas—and the encroachment of sealing into the rookery areas threatened the very existence of the herds. Japan's newly discovered Kurile Island rookeries were nearly exterminated by Canadian sealers. The

---

7. *Report of the Fur Seal Investigations, 1896–1897*, U.S. Treasury Department doc. no. 2017, pt. 1 (Washington, D.C., 1898), 236–237.

8. History of Leasing Fur Seal Privileges on the Commander and Robben Islands, file no. 1129, 1897, Pacific Department, Archives of Russian Foreign Policy Documents, Moscow.

9. Untitled article, *New Age*, 28 January 1911, 2.

10. *Report of the Governor of Alaska*, 50th Cong., 2d sess., Senate Ex. Doc. 74 (Washington, D.C., 1889), 1–13; also History of Leasing Fur Seal Privileges, Archives of Russian Foreign Policy Documents.

11. Pelagic sealing endangered the health of the herd because it killed not only the mother but also the fetus she might be carrying, the nursing pup left behind, and any future pups she might have delivered. Furthermore, because the market price for skins of females was not as high as that of males, nearly twice the number of females had to be killed to make the same profit.

American and Russian governments also predicted rapid depletion of their herds: between 1874 and 1890, the Pribilof fur seal herd population was reduced by an estimated 80 percent, and the Commander Island yield was also greatly diminished.[12]

In 1884, Japan issued a proclamation forbidding the killing of fur seals except by persons licensed by the government. Laws were introduced stipulating the duration of the hunting season, the areas for hunting, and the instrument for capture. At the same time, the Japanese government encouraged sealing by paying a bounty for fur seal pelts. These policies, coupled with low labor and equipment costs, resulted in the establishment of a large Japanese sealing fleet,[13] which in turn led to a rapid reduction in the size of the Kurile and Robben herds.[14] In 1850, Russian experts had estimated these combined herds to comprise approximately 25,000 individuals. By 1890, this number had dropped to 17,000, and a decade later only 1,000 seals were thought to exist.[15]

In 1886, the Russian government created a special commission to determine the value of seal herds and to make recommendations—for example, a specific hunting season and recognized hunting areas—for regulation of the Russian fur seal industry. In 1892 a state commission was formed to act on the special commission's recommendations. The following year legislation was passed prohibiting pelagic sealing, under threat of imprisonment and confiscation of equipment. Treating the existing state of the herds from the legal perspectives of *cas de force majeure* and *cas de défense légitime*, the Russian government imposed a complete ban on pelagic sealing in two areas: a zone of ten nautical miles out from Russian coastlines along the Bering Sea and a zone of thirty nautical miles around the Commander and Robben islands.[16]

---

12. File no. 1125, 1889, Pacific Department, Archives of Russian Foreign Policy Documents; 54th Cong., 1st sess., House Ex. Doc. 175, vol. 54 (Washington, D.C., 1895–1896).

13. According to Japanese sources, in 1910 the sealing fleet consisted of fifty-one vessels. Russian estimates put the number of Japanese vessels at only thirty-five. From file no. 1130, 1911, Pacific Department, Archives of Russian Foreign Policy Documents.

14. The Robben Islands were acquired by Japan in 1906. See James Thomas Gay, *American Fur Seal Diplomacy: The Alaskan Fur Seal Controversy* (New York: Peter Lang, 1987), 122. Gay's book is a particularly detailed history of the international interactions and diplomatic endeavors connected with the hunting of North Pacific fur seals and has been of considerable help to the authors.

15. File no. 1130, 1911, Pacific Department, Archives of Russian Foreign Policy Documents.

16. Note from State Counselor Shimkin to the Ambassador of Great Britain, 12/2/1893, file no. 1132, 1912, no. 509, Pacific Department, Archives of Russian Foreign Policy Documents.

In the United States, measures designed to manage the fur seal herds such as catch quotas and seasonal limits were in vain as long as pelagic sealing continued. One of the first attempts at limiting pelagic sealing was through a narrow interpretation of Section 1956 of the U.S. Revised Statutes stating that "fur bearing animals shall not be killed within the limits of the Alaska Territory, or in the waters thereof."[17] This interpretation was used against an American citizen in 1876, when the schooner *San Diego* was seized in Alaskan waters.[18] Great Britain and other states perceived the attempt by the United States to apply *mare clasum* (closed sea) status to the Bering Sea to be in violation of international law.[19] During this period, the U.S. government also faced strong pressure from the Alaska Commercial Company and the United States Treasury Department, both of which were afraid of losing revenue if the hunting of fur seals were restricted.

The unilateral attempts to manage the fur seal population reinforced the necessity for international cooperation. Not only had efforts to stop pelagic sealing failed, but events had escalated into near violence. In 1887, therefore, the U.S. government took the first step toward international agreement, requesting that the governments of France, Germany, Great Britain, Japan, Russia, and Sweden/Norway make arrangements to prevent their citizens "from killing seals in the Bering Sea, which threatened the speedy extermination of those animals and consequent serious loss to mankind."[20] This was the first in a long series of attempts to achieve international cooperation for protection of the northern fur seal (see Table 2.1). Although it received a generally positive response from the other governments, this attempt finally failed because of British opposition on legal, economic, and political grounds.

Great Britain regarded the limitation of pelagic sealing as an illegal infringement on freedom of the high seas. Britain was also committed to protection of Canadian interests, which necessitated coordination of

---

17. Americans asserted that under the terms of the Alaska treaty, the United States gained jurisdiction over certain waters (as much, even, as most of the North Pacific and the Bering Sea) surrounding Alaska. This contention was at the heart of many of the disputes associated with the fur seal issue, particularly those with Great Britain. The matter was not resolved until the Paris Tribunal Arbitration decisions in 1893. For a fuller discussion of the ongoing controversy, see Gay, *American Fur Seal Diplomacy*, 25–94.

18. Gay, *American Fur Seal Diplomacy*, 24–25.

19. A closed sea is a marine area in which the major coastal state has succeeded in asserting jurisdictional claims extending beyond those associated with the territorial sea or the exclusive economic zone.

20. 50th Cong., 2d sess., House of Representatives Ex. Doc., vol. 1 (Washington, D.C., 1888–1889), 1824. The immediate catalyst for this action was the seizure by United States authorities of three Canadian seal schooners in the Bering Sea in August 1886.

Table 2.1 Chronology: North Pacific fur seal regime

1887–1888	U.S. proposal for multilateral cooperation supported by Russia, rejected by Britain (on behalf of Canada); Japan snubbed
March 1889	bilateral American-Russian agreement aborted
1889–1890	United States rejects Anglo-Canadian draft convention
1891	Anglo-American *modus vivendi* agreed
1892	Anglo-American *modus vivendi* agreed
1893	bilateral Anglo-Russian agreement on western Bering Sea
1893–1894	bilateral Anglo-American adoption of Paris Arbitration Tribunal regulations
1894	bilateral Russian-American agreement on western Bering Sea
1894–1895	Britain rejects U.S. proposals (supported by Russia) for four-power agreement extending Paris regulations to entire Bering Sea
1897	Japanese-Russian-American agreement founders on British refusal to accede
1897	Anglo-American conference of experts fails to agree
1898–1899	Anglo-American Joint High Commission reaches agreement on fur seals but deadlocked over Alaska boundary
1903–1906	repeated proposals by the United States for Anglo-American revisions rebuffed by Britain (on behalf of Canada)
1910–1911	bilateral Anglo-American agreement covering eastern Bering Sea
11 May–7 July 1911	four-power convention results in acceptance of North Pacific Sealing Convention

British actions with those of Canada. For its part, the Canadian government strongly opposed the American proposals. The 1890s were the most prosperous period in the Canadian seal business, which employed nearly two thousand people and involved more than one hundred vessels.[21] Moreover, termination by the United States in 1866 of the 1854 Reciprocity Treaty between the two neighbors—resulting in the emergence of bilateral disagreements over tariffs, fisheries, and other questions—had not disposed the Canadian government to comply with American requests.[22]

Nearly all the skins taken in the Bering Sea were prepared for market and sold in London, and the British position further reflected the potential destruction of this important enterprise. Monopolized by Lampsen & Company, a powerful trade firm with close connections to

---

21. File no. 1129, 1910, Pacific Department, Archives of Russian Foreign Policy Documents.

22. Gay, *American Fur Seal Diplomacy*, 41.

political and financial interests in both Britain and Canada, the London fur seal skin business in the mid-1890s represented an investment of more than U.S. $5 million and employment for twenty-five hundred people.[23] Concerned with stabilizing its trade, much of which came from pelagic sealing, Lampsen & Company appeared as a vigorous, although "diplomatically mute," opponent.

In 1890, the United States made another attempt to achieve international agreement. But because the United States claimed jurisdictional powers beyond the agreed-upon limit of territorial waters, the Russian government declined to participate in these negotiations.[24] Anglo-Canadian-American meetings had begun in Washington in October 1889, propelled by Canadian agitation over the continued seizure of its vessels in the Bering Sea by the United States. In a December 1889 memorandum to the British Foreign Office, the Canadian government presented four preconditions for the renewal of formal negotiations with the United States.[25]

Throughout the winter and spring of 1890, the British minister in Washington, Sir Julian Pauncefote, the American secretary of state, James G. Blaine, and the Russian minister, Baron Pyotr Struve, continued to hold talks on the possibility of a closed season for the hunting of fur seals. It was proposed that an expert commission study the situation and make recommendations and that a temporary closed season be in effect until it reported. This suggestion was rejected by Blaine, who took particular exception to the extension of such a closed season to land as well as sea. Consequently, this attempt at a multilateral settlement ended.[26]

Nevertheless, two *modi vivendi*, setting temporary regulations on hunting for a specific year, were signed, one in 1891 and a replacement in 1892, by the United States and Great Britain. Although neither of these agreements resolved issues of fur seal management, the process of arranging them gave the negotiators knowledge and skill in dealing with each other. Probably the most important outcome of these exchanges between British and American diplomats, however, was the

23. File no. 1129, 1910, Pacific Department, Archives of Russian Foreign Policy Documents.

24. Ibid.

25. These preconditions were (1) the United States would renounce its claim to the "closed sea" concept regarding the Bering Sea, (2) Canada would be represented in any Joint High Commission regarding fur seals, (3) the proceedings of any commission would need Canadian approval, and (4) an agreement would need to compensate British subjects seized by American revenue cutters (Gay, *American Fur Seal Diplomacy*, 47).

26. Ibid., 51.

formally agreed-upon decision to submit Bering Sea sealing questions (for the most part, jurisdictional questions) to international arbitration. The British foreign secretary, Lord Salisbury, had proposed arbitration as early as August 1890, but it was not until 18 December 1891 that an agreement was signed. After considerable procedural squabbling, a panel of seven arbiters was chosen, and both sides began to prepare their cases.[27]

Before the arbitration tribunal convened in Paris in February 1893, the British and Russians entered into negotiations that resulted in the 1893 Anglo-Russian Agreement for West Bering Sea. This agreement prohibited pelagic hunting for one year within thirty miles of both the Commander and Robben islands as well as within ten nautical miles of the Russian continental coastline. Russian land kills were limited to 30,000 seals per year. According to the Russian Treasury, this meant an annual loss of 80,000 rubles, but the agreement was nevertheless extended in 1894 and 1895. In addition, bilateral negotiations between the United States and Russia, begun in 1892, led to comparable agreement on a *modus vivendi* in relation to fur seal fisheries in the Bering Sea and the North Pacific Ocean.

After preliminary meetings in which the two parties presented their cases, the first full session of the Paris Arbitration Tribunal was held on 23 March 1893. Six months of deliberations followed, and the decisions of the tribunal were announced on 15 August 1893. All five jurisdictional points were decided against the United States.[28] The principal conclusion drawn by the tribunal was that beyond the internationally recognized three-mile limit, the United States had no "right of protection or property of the fur seals." The tribunal also proposed regulations to conserve the seals, calling for a prohibition on pelagic sealing within sixty miles of the Pribilof Islands, a closed season (from 1 May to 31 July) for pelagic sealing in the eastern Bering Sea, and restrictions on the method of killing (covering both weapons and boats) during the open season. These regulations were to be reconsidered after five years. The tribunal also urged domestic legislation to achieve the goals of the

---

27. Ibid., 55-63.

28. Briefly, the five jurisdictional questions were (1) What exclusive jurisdiction in the Bering Sea and what exclusive sealing rights belonged to Russia before the cession of Alaska? (2) To what extent were these claims recognized by Great Britain? (3) In the Treaty of 1825 between Russia and Great Britain was the Bering Sea included as part of the Pacific and did Russia retain any exclusive rights to the Bering Sea? (4) Did all the jurisdictional rights of Russia pass to the United States? (5) Has the United States any rights of protection or property of the fur seals frequenting the Bering Sea islands when the seals are beyond the three-mile limit?

regulations.[29] In April 1894 both the British Parliament and the American Congress passed appropriate legislation.[30]

On the whole, the regulations proposed by the tribunal, which provided a measure of protection for the fur seals, were to the benefit of the fur seal industry, but they did not affect Japanese and Russian activities. In compliance with provisions of the Paris arbitration, however, the United States requested the governments of Russia and Japan to adhere to them. Secretary of state Walter Q. Gresham knew that the Russians, whose seal herds were suffering from unregulated foreign hunting, were interested in multilateral controls for the entire Bering Sea area. He used this knowledge to gain Russian support for an agreement among the four powers (Canada/Great Britain, Japan, Russia, and the United States) that would extend the Paris regulations to the entire Bering Sea. Because of the economic impact such measures could have on the Canadian sealing industry, however, the British resisted this idea. They also refused to join a four-power expert commission, together with a proposed *modus vivendi* prohibiting all pelagic sealing in the Bering Sea.[31]

Over the next few years, American diplomats continued their attempts to establish international cooperation for the management of fur seals. Japanese, Russian, and American representatives met again from 23 October to 6 November 1897.[32] The British, still unwilling to consider any agreement that might include the entire Bering Sea, would consent to participate only if the Russians and Japanese were excluded. The Japanese were in a complicated political and economic situation because of the problem of extraterritorial jurisdiction, their need for American support, their profitable pelagic sealing industry, and the depletion of their own herd. Proposals made at this time by the Japanese delegates would have resulted in complete protection of the Pribilof herds while permitting unlimited pelagic sealing of Russian herds.[33] Japan appears to have been more interested in the fact of ne-

---

29. John Bassett Moore, *History and Digest of International Arbitrations*, vol. 1 (Washington, D.C.: U.S. Government Printing Office, 1898), 948.

30. The regulations suggested by the tribunal covered an area it defined as "High Sea." This area was north of 35° north latitude and east of 180° longitude and included only the eastern Bering Sea.

31. Over the next several years, the British and Americans tried continually to negotiate short-term agreements at the last minute to protect the herds for the sealing season that was upon them. This *modus vivendi* was one such proposal. See Gay, *American Fur Seal Diplomacy*, 58–65.

32. Ibid., 105.

33. File no. 1124, 1897, Pacific Department, Archives of Russian Foreign Policy Documents.

gotiations than in their actual success. Canada, with economic interests at stake, refused either to suspend or to abolish pelagic sealing without a formula for compensation.[34]

In 1898, when an Anglo-American Joint High Commission convened in Québec (it was to meet again in Washington, D.C., in 1899) to review bilateral problems, the fur seal question was among the most important. By this time the economic situation had changed. Regular patrolling of the coast, undertaken by the Royal Navy under the Paris regulations, was expensive. Furthermore, low harvests in recent years had caused Canadians to believe that pelagic sealing was becoming unprofitable.[35] The Canadian sealing fleet was reduced, further diminishing the catch. These factors worked to change the attitude of the London market toward the problem of fur seal preservation and contributed to the will of the British government to find other ways to protect its interests. The Joint High Commission reached a tentative agreement on the fur seal question: in return for cessation of pelagic sealing, compensation was to be provided to Great Britain (and therefore Canada) for the sealing fleet and for relinquishing its "national right" of sealing in the open sea. (This compensation would have involved payments to Canada of a portion of the annual receipts derived from land killing.) But the work of the commission eventually broke down over the failure to resolve the unconnected Alaskan boundary dispute. Between 1903 and 1906, Canada, perennially dissatisfied with the compensation proposed, rebuffed further attempts by the United States to establish regulations for the Bering Sea.

By the early 1900s, the Bering Sea fur seal population had reached its lowest level in recorded history: the Pribilof herd had shrunk to 130,000 seals and the Commander Islands herd was estimated at only 4,500 seals.[36] Data obtained by American and Russian scientists, together with diminishing income from the fur seal industry, demonstrated the ineffectiveness of current protective regulations, including the conditions imposed by the 1893 Paris Arbitration Tribunal. Scientists and the media in each country were expressing shock over the depletion of the stocks and the apparent inability of their governments to protect the seals. Following a similar proposal by the governor of Alaska—and desperate to stop the rapaciousness of foreign sealers—the governor of Kamchatka in 1910 went so far as to propose elimina-

---

34. Gay, *American Fur Seal Diplomacy*, 104.

35. Ibid., 107–108.

36. File no. 1129, 1910, Pacific Department, Archives of Russian Foreign Policy Documents.

tion of the entire herd from the Commander Islands, with the income to be used to resettle the aboriginal people.[37]

During the early years of the twentieth century, diplomatic dealings among the four interested powers continued at a slow pace and in strict confidence. Several bilateral and multilateral contacts resulted from preparation of a Russian-Japanese agreement (not signed) and conclusion of a United States–Canada agreement (signed 7 February 1911). Under the terms of the latter agreement, the United States agreed to pay to Canada one-fifth of the proceeds from the annual harvest from the Pribilof Islands as well as a fixed annual sum if land killing were suspended, in exchange for suspension of pelagic sealing in the eastern Bering Sea and the North Pacific (north of 35° north latitude and east of the 180th meridian).[38]

The final period in the long process that ended with conclusion of the 1911 fur seal convention began on 21 January 1909, when U.S. secretary of state Elihu Root proposed a four-power conference to deal once again with the northern fur seal question. Britain proved unable to gain Canadian approval until early the following year but finally informed the United States on 4 March 1910 that Canada agreed to support suspension of pelagic sealing in return for appropriate compensation (formalized in the 7 February 1911 agreement). British assent to the four-power conference (Great Britain/Canada, Japan, Russia, and the United States) quickly followed.

The conference was opened by the United States in Washington, D.C., on 11 May 1911. The Americans proposed total prohibition of pelagic sealing in the waters of the North Pacific Ocean, including the Bering, Okhotsk, and Kamchatka seas. The Russian delegation, led by Ambassador Pierre Botkine, immediately declared that the imperial government approved all of the American proposals. The Japanese and British/Canadian delegations demanded proper compensation before they would consent.[39]

---

37. Notification from the Governor of Kamchatka to General Governor of the Heilundzian (Amur) area, 28 March 1910. Doc. N610 from the File 1129, 1910, Pacific Department, Archives of Russian Foreign Policy Documents, Moscow.

38. U.S. Department of State, *Foreign Relations of the United States* (Washington, D.C.: U.S. Government Printing Office, 1911), pp. 256–259.

39. The Canadian delegation requested 17.5 percent interest from the United States and 20 percent from Russia, leaving to Japan 7.5 and 10 percent respectively. The Japanese delegation claimed half of the American and two-thirds of the Russian sealskin income. See *Report of the Governor of Alaska*, 1–13; also History of Leasing Fur Seal Privileges, Archives of Russian Foreign Policy Documents.

Even before the conference began, the Russians and Americans had some knowledge of the British/Canadian and Japanese negotiating positions. The British/Canadians were not going to accept terms that gave them less than they received under the Anglo-American agreement. The Japanese, for their part, believed that the size of their sealing fleet entitled them to greater compensation than the Canadians, whose fleet was much smaller. When a deadlock arose over the issue of "reasonable" percentages of income from fur seal skin sales, it was broken by a personal appeal from President William Howard Taft to the emperor of Japan, who was persuaded to accept 15 percent of the gross interest in the American seal herd instead of the 17.5 percent the Japanese had been demanding.[40] The principal scheme of harvest distribution was accepted by all the parties, and after the settlement of such related issues as control, conservation, and the form of payments, the North Pacific Sealing Convention was signed on 7 July 1911. The participating parties ratified the agreement and it entered into force on 12 December 1911.

The 1911 fur seal convention was relatively simple. It was geographically confined to the northern Pacific Ocean and functionally limited to conservation and management of the fur seal stocks at the maximum sustainable yield, the highest level of productivity a resource can maintain indefinitely. The parties to the convention were Canada, Japan, Russia, and the United States (with Great Britain acting on behalf of Canada). No supranational organizational apparatus was proposed.[41]

The convention stipulated that the citizens and subjects of the parties to the convention (and all other persons subject to their laws) be prohibited from engaging in pelagic sealing in the northern Pacific Ocean, including the Bering, Okhotsk, and Kamchatka seas. The only exception was subsistence sealing practiced by the region's indigenous people. Ports or territories belonging to the signatories could not be used for purposes connected with pelagic sealing. A system of guarantees

---

40. Although the amount in dispute was only 2.5 percent, or approximately 160 skins, it held the negotiation process at a standstill for some time.

41. In 1957, when the convention was renegotiated (as the Interim Convention for the Conservation of North Pacific Fur Seal Herds) after the lapse begun by the Japanese at the start of World War II, a North Pacific Fur Seal Commission was established, primarily to coordinate scientific research.

against foreign pelagic sealing was established to discourage this practice.[42]

According to the terms of the treaty, each signatory would have managerial authority over the herd for which it regulated the harvest: Russia managed the Commander Islands herds, Japan the Robben Island herds, and the United States the Pribilof Islands herds. The Kurile Islands herds were extinct and so were not included in the convention. Each party was to put in place appropriate regulations to ensure compliance with the treaty.

Canada and Japan were each to receive from the United States 15 percent of the sealskins taken from the Pribilof Islands. The United States further agreed to pay immediately to Canada and Japan $200,000 each as compensation to their sealers in place of payment of skins. If at any time land killings were suspended for any reason, the United States was to make an annual payment of $10,000 each to Japan and Canada while the prohibition was in effect.

Whenever the Russian herds numbered no less than 18,000 seals, Russia was to assign 15 percent of its harvest to Canada and 15 percent to Japan. To establish a recovery period for the Russian herds, however, Russia had the right to prohibit all killing of its herds for the first five years of the treaty's existence. During this period Russia was not required to make compensation payments to Canada and Japan. The Japanese were obliged to give 10 percent of the skins from their herds to each of the other three parties. The terms of harvesting for Japan were the same as those for Russia, but Japan was to suspend land killing and cease payments if its herd appeared to number less than 6,500 individuals. If any fur seal herd were to initiate a rookery on Canadian territory, Canada would have to surrender 10 percent of the harvest to each of the other three parties. So as not to give states incentive to do additional or illegal sealing, the terms of the convention ensured that no state would be obligated to pay as compensation under the agreement more than it gained as profits from legal sealing.

The treaty was to remain in force for fifteen years, or as long after that as no nation asked for termination (which required twelve months' written notice). In October 1940, with war approaching, the Japanese government gave such notice. Although it was not until 1957 that a renewed convention for fur seal conservation was formally agreed upon,

42. Among the guarantees, obligating parties were to claim the skins and forbid the import of pelts provided by illegal hunting (Article 3), water patrols would be done along the routes of fur seal migrations (Article 7), and interest would be forgiven when herds became depleted (Articles 11, 12, 13).

the principles of the 1911 convention continued as the basis for the new agreement. It is in this sense that we can say the regime remained essentially in place for more than seventy years.

The stability of the regime that came into being in 1911 with the signing of the North Pacific Sealing Convention is a sufficient basis for studying it as an important example of successful negotiation. This treaty marked the first instance in international maritime law when access to the wealth derived from a resource was separated from access to harvesting of the resource. This convention, characterized by unique environmental factors, relatively simple government regulations, and an absence of new entrants, not only functioned satisfactorily for all of the participants but also resulted in the restoration of both the Asian and the American northern fur seal herds.[43]

The early attempts at international regulation of the harvest of fur seals should not be viewed as unmitigated failures. Although they did not halt depletion of the fur seal stocks, they did result in the successful negotiation and implementation of several bilateral agreements. Sufficient progress was made toward cooperation that one cannot say that the fur seal regime can be identified solely with the 1911 convention. At the very least, events during the quarter-century preceding that convention provide important clues in our endeavor to explain the successful conclusion of the final agreement.

ANALYSIS AND HYPOTHESIS TESTING

In our effort to discover which factors contributed to the successful formation of the North Pacific fur seal regime, we considered three broad theoretical categories—hypotheses based on power, interest, and knowledge—as well as contextual arguments.

Power-Based Hypotheses

Power-based theory has had an important place in contemporary political studies. In seeking to explain the process of regime formation, the focus has been either on the distribution of power in the international system as a whole or on the balance of forces in an issue area. A fundamental element in this body of theory is the presence of a hege-

---

43. Having secured not only financial compensation for the cessation of pelagic sealing but also a significant and permanent share of the harvest, both the Canadians and Japanese became actively interested in the conservation of all northern fur seal herds.

mon or dominant actor. A simple hegemonic explanation is not supported in the fur seal case. No single hegemon of either a coercive or a benign nature can be identified. Each of the four major parties to the negotiations was recognized in international society of the time as a Great Power. Furthermore, each was predominant in a particular area of the fur seal issue: Russia had the longest history of commercial fur seal activity; the United States had sovereignty over the largest northern fur seal rookeries; Great Britain held a monopoly on the fur market and therefore could influence the incomes of the other parties; Japan possessed the world's largest sealing fleet. Unilateral attempts by each state to take advantage of its position to impose a particular solution could be, and were, met by strong responses from the other states. No state could be forced to enter into a relationship that was not to its benefit.

There were, of course, differences in military power, economic "weight," and political status. Canada was a British dominion; Japan was subject to extraterritorial jurisdiction. This asymmetry was not sufficient, however, to allow a single participant to act as either a coercive hegemon or a Kindlebergian power in the four-power structure of the fur seal negotiations.[44]

Great Britain/Canada, Japan, Russia, and the United States all possessed considerable military capabilities in the North Pacific, although shifts in the regional balance of military forces occurred over the period. American naval capabilities were gradually challenging traditional British predominance at sea, and the Russo-Japanese War of 1904–1905 occasioned a sudden growth in Japanese naval power. Furthermore, the fur sealing issue itself generated both threatened and actual hostilities. The American seizure of Canadian vessels in the Bering Sea elevated the fur seal problem to senior decision-making levels. Russians later seized both American and Canadian schooners off the Commander Islands, and several Japanese citizens were killed while poaching in Russian and American rookeries. These and similar incidents kept the atmosphere surrounding the fur seal issue tense for more than two decades.

In spite of a certain degree of tension, the prospects for warfare over the fur seal issue were slight. Conflicts tended to occur in one of two

---

44. The fur seal case is an example in which power distinctions did not result in political shifts in the existing international arena. Among the participants in the 1897 conference, Japan was the weakest from the political point of view because of extraterritorial jurisdiction, but the Japanese delegation used this fact in demonstrating their inability to agree with other participants. All the attempts of the Russian government to force Japan to enter into bilateral negotiations in the 1880s on the fur seal issue were unsuccessful.

groupings—between Great Britain/Canada and the United States or between Russia and Japan—but however fierce the discussions between
governments became, war as a method of conflict resolution appears
never to have been seriously considered (except possibly shortly after
the American seizure of Canadian ships).[45] With the exception of the
seizure of sealing vessels on the high seas, the threat or use of armed
force played little if any role in the creation of the fur seal regime.

Another use of possible coercive power might be seen in threats
made by American and Russian authorities to exterminate their herds
unilaterally as a protest against continued pelagic sealing. Because
these threats appear to have had no immediate effect on the willingness
of pelagic sealing states to compromise, however, they apparently were
not viewed as credible.

It is interesting to speculate on whether these unilateral attempts to
bring pressure to bear may actually have impeded progress toward an
agreement by creating new animosities and mutual perceptions of ex-
tremism. Rather than contributing to the successful formation of a regime, this exercise of power may instead help to explain why it took
nearly a quarter of a century to resolve the issue.

A second hypothesis derived from power-based theories states that
the greater the degree of symmetry in the distribution of power, the
greater the likelihood that efforts at regime formation will succeed. In
this case, the primary actors were relatively equal in overall power resources throughout the entire period of negotiations and consultations
on the fur seal issue. Symmetry cannot account, however, for the success in achieving agreement in 1911. Comparative military capabilities
began to shift during this later period, and the move away from approx-
imate equality appears to have coincided with resolution of the fur seal
issue.[46]

Although traditional power-based theory is not confirmed by the fur
seal case, the dynamics of the process nevertheless illustrate certain
power-related considerations. Changing the specific parties in an inter-

---

45. According to Gay, "It is probable the [U.S.] administration felt a clash with the British
navy was highly possible" in mid-1890, after the seizure of Canadian vessels (*American Fur
Seal Diplomacy*, 54). U.S. secretary of state John Foster later suggested that armed hostilities between the United States and Britain had not been inconceivable when he lauded
the Paris arbitration on the grounds that "it was far better that we should submit our
rights and interests in the seal-herd to the arbitrament of an impartial tribunal than risk
the horrors of a war between the two kindred peoples" (although Gay believes that Foster
may have exaggerated this latter aspect; ibid., 89).

46. Russia was slowly recovering from the Russo-Japanese War of 1904–1905, and the
1905 revolution was a result of economic and political crisis in Russia.

national negotiation, either by expansion or reduction, can cause shifts in the balance of power at the negotiating table. Such shifts can in turn allow decisions to be taken that might otherwise have been impossible. In the 1890s, for example, the United States and Russia were able to conclude several agreements by excluding other participants from the process of negotiation. This success probably resulted because the interests of these two states were similar, based on sovereignty over large herds of seals, whereas the interests of Great Britain/Canada and Japan rested in the profits to be made from the commercial hunting of seals. And to consider an example in the other direction, whereas Canada and Japan had been reluctant to resolve the fur seal issue through bilateral and trilateral negotiations, the conference in 1911 that included all four powers was able to achieve success. It is probable that the addition of parties in 1911 mitigated, or diluted, the tension between the pairs of historical adversaries.

Interest-Based Hypotheses

The basic premise of the interest-based theory of regime formation is that regimes arise from the interactions of self-interested parties who coordinate their behavior to reap joint gains. Joint gains in this case might be increase of the fur seal herds through proper management and subsequent enhancement of each party's revenues from the sale of skins. To realize such joint gains, parties engage in what has been termed institutional bargaining.[47] In our analysis of interest-based conditions, we have in some instances grouped together factors that appear to have functioned as a unit in the fur seal case.

The first combination of conditions we will discuss brings together integrative bargaining and/or a veil of uncertainty and the concept of equitable as opposed to efficient institutional options. The 1911 fur seal regime was not created from whole cloth. It was the result of negotiations based on prior bargains (the 1897 tripartite conference, the 1898 Anglo-American Joint High Commission, and informal Russo-Japanese talks in 1909–1911) and on preexisting agreements (the Paris Arbitration Tribunal regulations, and the Anglo-American agreement of 7 February 1911). The participants in the 1911 conference could easily predict the range of possible gains and losses: they knew their roles and the interests of their own states in the fur seal case (or conflict); they could define the positions of other actors; and the status of the inter-

47. Oran R. Young, "The Politics of International Regime Formation: Managing Natural Resources and the Environment," *International Organization* 43 (Summer 1989): 349–375.

national fur market as well as the sealing industry in each country were also known to them (archival records attest to this, although in the course of negotiations some discrepancies appeared in the various estimates).

Nonetheless, uncertainties remained. Knowledge of the population dynamics of the northern fur seal was much less advanced in 1911 than it is now (and it still leaves much to be desired). It was unclear to the negotiators whether and at what point all sealing might have to be suspended in the interest of survival of the species. This uncertainty was acknowledged in the treaty in the form of monetary guarantees to the pelagic sealing states in the event of suspension of land harvesting. Thus, although individual participants may have been able to calculate their own share of the harvest under various assumptions, they could not predict with any assurance the future size of the herd and hence the magnitude of the harvest or their respective returns. In this sense, a veil of uncertainty—albeit a thin one—can be said to have existed.

The other part of the first hypothesis focuses on integrative bargaining. The development of the fur seal regime is an example of mixed bargaining, as described by Richard E. Walton and Robert B. McKersie, in which both distributive and integrative bargaining are present. Distributive bargaining involves competition to influence the distribution of limited resources, whereas integrative bargaining aims to increase the joint gains available to the negotiating parties. In integrative bargaining, interests common to all parties are identified, enlarged, and acted upon.[48]

In its early stages, the fur seal debate was distributive in nature. Each of the actors at first concentrated on protecting its individual rookeries, sealing industry, or both. When the decline of the worldwide fur seal population was acknowledged by the international scientific community, integrative bargaining became more prominent. Realization of the economic effect that fur seal extinction (or significant depletion) would have on each of the major actors provided a collective incentive to engage in bargaining, which became distributive as the participants sought to decide the economic future of the industry.

The scientific consensus that the fur seal population was declining was the dominant factor in integrative bargaining. Several factors contributed to the distributive bargaining. First, Britain acted on behalf of Canada, the only actor without any rookeries of its own, which depended entirely on pelagic sealing. Consequently, initial American pro-

---

48. Richard E. Walton and Robert B. McKersie, *A Behavioral Theory of Labor Negotiations: An Analysis of a Social Interaction System* (New York: McGraw-Hill, 1965), 4–10.

posals seeking to eliminate pelagic sealing held no attraction for Canada. To be considered equitable by the Canadians, an agreement would have to cover both pelagic and land-based hunting. This cleavage, which pitted the three rookery-owning states against the pelagic sealer (Canada, and therefore Britain), stalled negotiations for some time, reinforced by debates over equitable compensation and protection against such possible but unpredictable contingencies as suspension of land harvests.

Second, it is safe to say that all of the actors in the fur seal issue were motivated primarily by economic concerns. Thus, although the United States always presented its case in terms of seeking to preserve the "noble race" of fur seals and mitigating cruelty to animals, it is difficult to fault the Canadians for seeing these sentiments as a thinly veiled attempt to preserve the monopoly of the Alaska Commercial (and later the North American Commercial) Company. This perspective is reinforced when we consider the close ties of these enterprises to leading American public figures and senior officials. Canada's interests in the fur seal question were definitely economic. It should not be surprising, therefore, that as the Canadian sealing fleet declined precipitously in the early years of the twentieth century,[49] Canada appeared to become more amenable to compromise on the fur seal issue.

Great Britain also had an economic interest in the fur seal question. As U.S. secretary of state Thomas F. Bayard hastened to remind the British in February 1888, at least ten thousand people in London depended for their employment on the dressing, dyeing, and marketing of North Pacific fur seal skins. Britain never lost sight of this particular economic interest,[50] which may help explain a certain sympathy for the conservation cause (as well as British willingness to pressure Canada from time to time in this regard). But Britain's economic considerations appear to have been subordinated to two other factors. The first was to ensure the continued unity of the British Empire by placating the Canadians and safeguarding their interests, and the second was to preserve and enhance friendly relations with the United States. Britain was in an awkward position because the Canadians constantly suspected—

---

49. Gay, *American Fur Seal Diplomacy*, 50, 122–123.

50. See, for example, "Report of the Behring Sea Seal Fishery Patrol" (13 September 1909), in *Documents on Canadian External Relations (DCER)*, vol. 1: *1909–1918* (Ottawa: Queen's Printer, 1967), 519, in which the commanding officer of HMS *Algerine* evoked the "necessity for making every effort at the next conference to preserve and if possible increase this herd to its normal size owing to the great profit and large employment of labour derived from preparing the skins in London (from where the retailer still insists upon obtaining the finished article)."

and occasionally accused—the home country of poorly representing Canadian interests and appearing overly eager for an agreement to mollify the Americans. The United States, for its part, professed a total inability to understand why the mighty British Empire should be beholden to its puny Canadian "colony."[51]

Turning to the hypothesis concerned with equity and efficiency, we find that all of the actors in this case were concerned that fur seal herds be managed efficiently so as to protect the fur seal industry and the revenues to be derived from it. The regime that was proposed in 1911— prohibiting pelagic sealing and introducing state regulations for land hunting while viewing the fur seal herd as (restricted) common property and sharing the profits—met this criterion. Actual bargaining in the course of the 1911 conference, however, turned on the principles of equity and fairness. Both Canada and Japan were particularly eager to make sure that their compensation was equitable, and negotiations succeeded only when the parties to be compensated agreed on a formally equal sharing of assigned resources.[52] Thus the issue of protection of North Pacific fur seals was resolved in a manner that was both efficient and equitable.

Clearly, both elements—equity and efficiency—played an important role in ensuring a successful negotiation. If the hypothesis is that equity (and not simply efficiency) is critical to success, then it is indeed confirmed. But if it is a question of equity being emphasized *over* efficiency (as in some versions of the theoretical template), then the fur seal case cannot be said to confirm the hypothesis because the very essence of the agreement was to ensure an end to pelagic sealing, largely on the grounds of its inefficiency (to the point of endangering the very survival of the resource). A purely equitable agreement—regardless of considerations of efficiency—would presumably have allowed some pelagic sealing to continue.

Two other interest-based factors that worked in tandem in the formation of the fur seal regime were the availability of compliance mechanisms and the emergence of salient solutions. The first of the two rele-

51. As U.S. secretary of state Bayard put it in a memorandum of 17 May 1888, he found it "difficult to see why Great Britain should permit one of her colonies to thwart a plan intended to preserve the race of seals from extermination. Why should Canada any more than India assume to control the treaty-making power of the EMPIRE on the subject?" (quoted in Charles Callan Tansill, *The Foreign Policy of Thomas F. Bayard, 1885–1897* [New York: Fordham University Press, 1940], 474).

52. The final solution was considered equitable by the parties even though Japan had the most to lose by stopping pelagic sealing and the United States had to cede more than any other state to reach an agreement.

vant hypotheses states that the probability of success in institutional bargaining rises when compliance mechanisms are available that the participants perceive to be clear-cut and effective. The concern here is with the availability of such compliance mechanisms, not the degree to which they are actually used. Corollary questions refer to the existence of strong incentives (and means) to cheat and whether there are ways to verify compliant behavior without intruding too deeply into the domestic affairs of the states.

Throughout the period under review, there were continual suspicions and allegations of noncompliance with the various bilateral sealing regulations such as seasons and quotas. Nevertheless, in the final negotiations, the fact that all sealskins were processed in London made compliance seem more probable because the opportunities to cheat were limited. Concerns had been expressed about the possibility that other (nonsignatory) states might engage in sealing under their own flags in the North Pacific—thereby defeating the purpose of the convention—and the danger that signatories would circumvent their obligations by having their nationals seal under the flags of other states. This problem was solved by the simple mechanism of including a provision (Article III) that excluded nonauthenticated sealskins from the ports of the parties to the agreement. As a Canadian delegate observed, "London is the only place where . . . seal skins are dyed, and if they are shut out of London, there would be no object in capturing them."[53] Fur seals in the North Pacific differ in both genus and species from southern fur seals (which were not regulated under this convention), which also helped to verify compliance. Skins could be readily identified as being from either northern or southern species upon inspection in port.

In a sense, these compliance mechanisms reflected the salient solution arrived at over this long period. A salient solution or focal point— which must be formulated in terms that are simple and easy to understand—facilitates the convergence of expectations and may increase the success of institutional bargaining. In this case, the salient solution was accomplished by a simple ban on pelagic sealing while treating the fur seal herds as (restricted) common property: although management was the responsibility of individual states, the harvest, and therefore the profits from the harvest, were shared among the signatories according to a clear and equitable set of rules. Well-defined procedures for modifying these rules was one of the keys to success in these

---

53. Canadian Delegate to Secretary of State for External Affairs, 5 July 1911, in *DCER* 1:586.

negotiations. The salient solution hypothesis suggests that an approach may sometimes be borrowed from prior cases with which the negotiators may already be familiar. The final fur seal convention negotiations in 1911 certainly benefited from the precedent set by the Anglo-American Joint High Commission of 1898–1899 and the 1911 bilateral American-Canadian agreement. In exchange for cessation of pelagic sealing, Canada, a pelagic sealing state with no rookeries, had been compensated with a portion of the land-based harvest of the rookery-owning state. The application of this principle to the other major actors (Japan and Russia) in the closing stages of the 1911 negotiations helped to assure the commitment of all five actors (including Canada). The series of previous bilateral agreements provided the actors with both experience and confidence that aided in the successful conclusion of the 1911 agreement.

The inclusion of all interested parties is the sixth interest-based condition. The prehistory of the convention shows that whenever interested parties were deliberately excluded, or when the exclusion was self-imposed, progress could be made only toward very limited, specific, and temporary goals, rather than toward an effective regime for the conservation of the fur seal. Although several bilateral agreements were achieved during this period, the American attempt at a bilateral deal with Russia in March 1889 broke down in part because of the absence of British participation; the Paris arbitration regulations suffered from the noninclusion of Japan and Russia; and the tripartite conference of 1897 ultimately failed in part as the result of British nonparticipation. It was not until all of the parties came together, perhaps with a greater realization of the importance of the herd to all of them, that real progress could be achieved.

The seventh interest-based hypothesis states that the occurrence of an exogenous shock or crisis increases the probability of success in achieving agreement. Although the fur seal regime was created in an atmosphere of crisis that was emphasized by the media in the various countries, its extension over a lengthy period makes it difficult to characterize it as a shock. Discrete shocks occurred at times: the initial seizure of British vessels by the United States, various reports of drastic reductions in the size of the herds, and the killing of Japanese poachers in the early 1900s. There does not, however, appear to have been a particular shock that brought about the final settlement in 1911.

An eighth interest-based hypothesis states that greater concentration on scientific and/or technical considerations, rather than on political issues, increases the likelihood of regime formation. The lack of consensus during the first half of the period under review about the degree to which survival of the herds was threatened helps to explain the failure to achieve agreement earlier. The technical approach to the issue, as reflected in the convening of numerous expert commissions, proved to be of little avail as long as the "experts" continued to disagree about the magnitude of the threat to the herd. Once the scientists were able to reach a consensus or agreement as to the overall health of the fur seal population, they were able to agree on a remedy. Although after a scientific consensus was reached, the more political issues of equity and adequate compensation continued to play an important role in the negotiations, scientific convergence was essential to bring the parties to the realization that fur seal populations were declining and that pelagic sealing was the primary cause.

A ninth interest-based hypothesis contends that success in regime formation can occur only when the specific issue has high-priority status on the domestic policy agenda of each of the participants. In retrospect, the extent to which the fur seal issue achieved high political status in the late nineteenth century appears remarkable. It engaged the keen interest of some of the world's leading political powers and, at least occasionally, was dealt with at the highest levels by those states.[54] The various states certainly had incentives to arrive at a solution to the problem. Canada had to safeguard an important and politically significant economic interest, while at the same time asserting its independence vis-à-vis both Britain and the United States. Great Britain was striving to satisfy Canadian aspirations while improving relations with the United States. The United States and Russia both sought to safeguard their sealing industries.

Nevertheless, any issue that is under consideration for a quarter of a century is unlikely to be of consistently high priority for each of the interested parties. This was particularly true for the fur seal issue on the domestic Russian agenda. In the early 1900s Russian public opinion was preoccupied with the failure of democratic reforms, the 1905 Revolution, the Russo-Japanese War, and other serious internal problems. Likewise, on several occasions the fur seal issue appeared to be crowded off the Anglo-American agenda by more pressing concerns, perhaps most notably at the turn of the century when, for the United States, "an Isthmian canal and the Alaskan boundary controversy were the main objects of interest."[55] Canadian leaders, who placed perhaps the highest consistent priority on the issue in the early years, had obviously rel-

---

54. A partial explanation could also be the absence of large bureaucracies to deal with such issues at the time.

55. Gay, *American Fur Seal Diplomacy*, 115.

egated it to secondary importance by the time of the Joint High Commission (1898–1899), when they held it hostage to a settlement of other outstanding bilateral issues, in particular the Alaskan boundary dispute.

Thus in the fur seal case, the converse of the stated hypothesis appears to hold true: it was only after the issue had lost its priority on the domestic policy agendas of the parties and ceased to be considered an issue of high politics that it became possible to settle it rationally and coolly.

There was substantial discussion within the fur seal regime research team about the influence of a government on the observed leadership ability of an individual employed by that government. We attempted to determine when an individual was acting on behalf of the government and when on his or her own initiative. In some situations, acquiring the information necessary to make such a determination would require access to information that was not available to us. In considering the twenty-five years during which the fur seal regime developed, Young's leadership typology[56] has been useful in understanding the leadership abilities of both individuals and states. Young identifies three possible kinds of leadership used by individuals in regime formation: structural, entrepreneurial, and intellectual.

Structural leadership was not a continuous influence on bargaining in this case, although it was evident on some occasions. One such example occurred during the final four-power conference in 1911. After a month of debate, the conference was deadlocked over the amount of compensation due to those states that practiced pelagic sealing. The Japanese were holding out for 17.5 percent interest from both the United States and Russia. Acting as the most senior agent for the United States, President Taft exercised structural leadership by making a personal appeal in a letter to the emperor of Japan. James T. Gay concludes that "this unusual appeal from one Head of State to another made a positive impression on the Japanese Emperor."[57] (It is unclear whether Taft acted on his own initiative or on the advice of others.) Throughout the twenty-five-year period under study, each of the states was able to function confident of its own influence and status as a world leader. Therefore, any individual acting as an agent of the state in a

---

56. Oran R. Young, "Political Leadership and Regime Formation: On the Development of Institutions in International Society," *International Organization* 45 (Summer 1991), 281–308.

57. Gay, *American Fur Seal Diplomacy*, 127.

sense brought into the process structural leadership, or the weight or "baggage" of a world leader.

An entrepreneurial leader has three functions: to draw attention to the importance of issues at stake, to invent innovative policy options, and to broker deals and garner support for salient options.[58] Among the fur seal treaty negotiators, two in particular seem to have acted as entrepreneurial leaders. One, Lord Salisbury, was the British foreign secretary. The other, David Starr Jordan, represented the interests of the United States throughout the period under study. Jordan, a noted fur seal expert, headed the U.S. investigation team to assay the northern fur seal population in 1896 and participated in the 1897 conference as one of the American representatives.

Both of these men were tenacious in trying to find a solution to the fur seal issue, but each had specific priorities. Salisbury wanted to find the best arrangement for the Canadian sealing industry and also to assure British rights to the Arctic waters. Because Canada relied heavily on pelagic sealing, Salisbury had to withhold his participation in negotiations when this practice was politically threatened. The British/Canadian position was reversed during the meeting of the Joint High Commission (23 August 1898–20 February 1899). Patrolling by the Royal Navy was becoming too costly, and it was decided that "commercial pelagic sealing would become increasingly unprofitable."[59] Salisbury then had to act as a broker with other participants on two points, first for "fair" compensation to Canada for stopping pelagic sealing, and second to assuage Great Britain's sense of loss for giving up its national right to sealing in the open sea. Salisbury was also a broker of rights and responsibilities in the evolving relationship between Great Britain and Canada during this period.

David Starr Jordan brokered an understanding (and agreement) between those who did not consider the fur seal population to be in jeopardy and the more radical fur seal protectionists. Prominent among the protectionists was Henry W. Elliott, a fur seal expert who predicted the fur seal's demise. By the start of the Joint British-American Diplomatic Commission (1897–1898), at which Jordan represented the United States, the "depletion of the fur seal herd had rendered land-killing and sea-killing alike unprofitable." As a result, a delay in negotiations seemed practical to Great Britain. During this time, Jordan was endeavoring to resolve American-Canadian differences over the Pribilof herd.

---

58. Young, "Political Leadership and Regime Formation," 293–298.

59. Gay, *American Fur Seal Diplomacy*, 108.

(According to the Paris Arbitration Tribunal, the United States had no legal claim to ownership of the herd, although it was still responsible for protecting the herd on land.) Jordan found a new perspective for seeking resolution. An arrangement with Canada was sought on behalf of the animals, emphasizing their plight over either side's political aspirations. Before this avenue could be fully explored, however, Japanese sealers—who were not party to the Paris tribunal—invaded the Bering Sea, killing seals within the three-mile limit as well as within harems.[60] Jordan maintained his commitment to the animals by contributing significantly to four large volumes about the fur seal that were later published by the government. This action, drawing attention to the importance of the issue at stake, is another characteristic of an entrepreneurial leader as defined by Young.

Jordan also exemplified the intellectual leader. Despite the long time line for intellectual thought and the relatively short time recognized by policy makers, Young believes that an individual may be both an intellectual and an entrepreneurial leader.[61] Over the twenty-five-year period during which the fur seal issue was debated, Jordan had plenty of time not only to reflect and refine his ideas about the Alaskan region and fur seals but also to use this intellectual capital to broker agreements. One example was an article written by Jordan entitled "Colonial Lessons of Alaska," which appeared in the *Atlantic Monthly* in November 1898. In this piece Jordan discussed "the nation's disastrous neglect of the Salmon, Fur Seal, and Sea Otter, and its utter disregard for the welfare of the natives."[62] The article attracted the attention of Theodore Roosevelt, who made use of such information to try to improve matters (discussed below in the section on knowledge-based theory).

Other individuals were involved as leaders in the formation of the fur seal regime. Jordan and Salisbury have been singled out for extra consideration for two reasons: their leadership contributions spanned much of the period under review, and their contributions were significantly productive. All three leadership types (structural, entrepreneurial, and intellectual) existed during the formation of this regime, although no single type of leader dominated the process.

---

60. David Starr Jordan, *The Days of a Man: Being Memories of a Naturalist, Teacher, and Minor Prophet of Democracy*, vol. 1 (Yonkers-on-Hudson, N.Y.: World Book, 1922), 604.

61. Young, "Political Leadership and Regime Formation," 300–301.

62. David Starr Jordan, "Colonial Lessons of Alaska," *Atlantic Monthly*, November 1898, p. 583.

Knowledge-Based Hypotheses

This body of theory emphasizes the direct role of shared knowledge and values in regime formation. It also considers the role of both epistemic communities and advocacy organizations. This line of inquiry seems well suited for analyzing environmental and resource issues, which tend to be international in scope.

During the late 1800s people in both Europe and the United States became increasingly aware of the impact of human activities on nature. In Great Britain three movements emerged to reflect wildlife protection, human health, and the yearning for open space in nature. This concern led to such laws as the Alkali Act of 1863, in which the central government was charged to "do something about the protection of air against pollution by noxious vapours."[63] Groups were also organized to rally on behalf of nature and against its abuse. In Britain, the Commons, Open Spaces and Footpaths Preservation Society, the world's first private environmental group, was formed in 1865. Similarly, in the United States the Sierra Club (1892), the Appalachian Mountain Club (1876), and Campfire Girls (1897) emerged and attracted followers.

In the early years of the twentieth century, a number of European states (including England, France, Italy, Germany, and Portugal) cooperated in the preparation and signing of draft articles "concerning nature protection in Africa."[64] These articles endorsed such radical actions as the regulation of hunting, closed seasons for hunting some animals, and a complete ban on the hunting of other animals. Although the agreement lasted only a few years, it did establish a precedent for both the concept of animal protection and the tools to accomplish it.

Meanwhile, during the early 1900s, the conservation movement in the United States continued to gain political influence, led by such luminaries as Gifford Pinchot and Theodore Roosevelt. Pinchot's plan was to "bring the tradition of progressive agriculture to public land management."[65] His three principles for resource management—to develop resources for the present generation, to prevent waste, and to develop resources for the many rather than the few—were to influence the use of natural resources for generations. During the Roosevelt pres-

---

63. John McCormick, *Reclaiming Paradise: The Global Environmental Movement* (Bloomington: Indiana University Press, 1989), 5.

64. Ibid., 354.

65. Ibid., 13.

idency, when Pinchot was known as the "Secretary of State for Conservation," resource management became public policy.[66]

Later, the influence of conservation in national politics may have been substantially diminished by President Taft's actions, but the conservation movement was by no means dead. The publicity and public education of the Roosevelt/Pinchot era were permanently etched not only in the American mind but also in the minds of Europeans.

The period of intense conservation activity during the first decade of the new century spawned a variety of groups that focused on the management of natural resources. Such topics began to be included on national policy agendas. Natural resource management, or conservation, became the focus of international forums. These practices created a sense of shared perceptions, beliefs, learning, and understanding about natural resources at both the national and international levels.

This shared knowledge helped to generate a scientific convergence about the status of the North Pacific fur seal population, which appears to have made a significant contribution to the formation of the regime to protect these animals. Cooper states that "international cooperation emerges quite readily when a shared understanding of the problem, its causes, and its solutions arises."[67] For a considerable portion of the time under review, these three questions were debated. Once the scientific community reached agreement that the fur seal population was diminishing at a dangerous rate, that pelagic sealing was a primary cause, and that stopping such practices would help the seal population to recover and to sustain a healthy size, the negotiation process became productive.

Likewise, once the ideas of population biology became sufficiently articulated, businessmen began to accept them. It was at this point that acceptance of regulations and mutual constraints became possible. As conservation principles became more accepted in national and international decision making they were used to supplement policy options. The conservation tools defined during the apex of the conservation movement (regulated harvesting, for example, and partial or total bans) served as guidelines in the fur seal treaty.

---

66. Among other measures, Roosevelt—at Pinchot's suggestion—created the Inland Waterways Commission in March 1907. Roosevelt believed that any plan to use the waterways needed to consider flood control, the prevention of soil and silt erosion, and the construction of dams (ibid., 15).

67. Richard N. Cooper, "International Cooperation in Public Health as a Prologue to Macroeconomic Cooperation," in Cooper et al., *Can Nations Agree? Issues in International Economic Cooperation* (Washington, D.C.: Brookings Institution, 1989).

The alternative idea about the role of cognitive factors in regime formation—the rise of an epistemic community that communicates with policy makers—does not appear to receive support in the northern fur seal case. Such a network would link those individuals who have a shared understanding of the problem and allow them (potentially) to influence policy makers. The general disagreement regarding the existence of a fur seal problem and its potential solutions prevented the formation of such a community. Even after scientific convergence occurred, the task of persuasive communication with policy makers continued to be undertaken by individuals.

Contextual Factors

At various points in the period under review, the formation of the fur seal regime appears to have been affected by factors not identifiable in terms of the theoretical approaches outlined earlier. Some of the contextual factors may have had a negative influence on regime formation in this case. One of these was the linkage of the fur seal issue to the Alaska boundary dispute. The Alaska boundary question prevented consummation in 1898–1899 of the fur seal agreement tentatively reached within the Joint High Commission. The settlement of the boundary dispute a few years later left the Canadians so dissatisfied that they were unwilling to accommodate subsequent American requests for an early settlement of the fur seal question. Despite their belated acknowledgment of the threat to the survival of the herd and their own decreased economic interest in the fur seal trade, Canadians successfully blocked resolution of the fur seal issue for several more years.

Another explanation for the lack of progress during the first decade of the twentieth century may have been Russia's inability to accord the issue a sufficiently high priority. Despite the serious threat continued pelagic sealing posed to its economic interests during this period, Russia may simply have been too preoccupied with domestic revolution and high tension with Japan (including outright war), to devote sufficient high-level attention and resources to the fur seal problem.

A final contextual factor with a negative impact may have been the decline over time in the sense of urgency surrounding the fur seal issue, as the likelihood of armed conflict between the United States and Britain over this question quickly receded after the late 1880s and early 1890s. This in turn was a result both of the rise of the U.S. Navy in the eastern Pacific (making defense of Canadian interests by the British military an increasingly dubious proposition) and the necessity for Britain to maintain good relations with the United States in the face of a growing European challenge by Germany. The reduced salience of the fur seal issue rendered it a far less urgent problem than it had been in the earlier period, thus enabling Canada to stall in the hopes of winning additional compensation.

Several contextual factors can be identified as having enhanced the prospects of a negotiated settlement in the later years. For example, the period immediately before the negotiation of the 1911 convention saw the emergence of a worldwide conservation movement, beginning in the United States but soon spreading to other Western countries, including Canada and Britain. It was also a period when the concepts of international conciliation and arbitration were in their heyday. The existence of such global trends undoubtedly helped account for the success of the 1911 negotiations. Also on the positive side, Canada's growing self-confidence as an independent actor may have increased its inclination to compromise in later years. And the desire for international legitimacy and recognition as a major power in the international arena may have accounted for initial Japanese interest in the fur seal question. The same desire may also explain Japan's willingness to compromise and to accept compensation disproportionately small in comparison to the size of its sealing fleet.

The important influence of contextual factors in helping to account for the successful achievement of a fur seal agreement in 1911 can be illustrated by considering whether such an accord could have been reached even just a year later. In all likelihood, this would not have been possible. After 1911, a succession of political crises involving states active in this case led to serious shifts in the interests of the states and the relations among them. Military crises too followed one after the other, as all the European powers were engaged in preparations for what became World War I. After the contemporary political agenda had become full of military-strategic questions, the major actors would have had neither the time nor the opportunities to deal with fur seal problems.

CONCLUSIONS

Three theoretical components appear to have had particular influence in the fur seal regime's evolution. The first is the interaction of self-interested parties who coordinate their behavior to reap joint gains (interest-based theory). The second involves the importance of ideas and the occurrence of a scientific convergence (part of knowledge-based theory). The third component is the window of opportunity provided by contextual factors.

The interest-based theory consists of several specific hypotheses, five of which have proved to be consistent with the case study—leadership, the importance of equity, salient solutions, compliance mechanisms, and inclusion of all parties. Over twenty-five years, fur seal negotiations were strengthened by structural, entrepreneurial, and intellectual leadership. Although there was no continuous influence of structural leadership, the personal letter of President Taft to the emperor of Japan was an important example of such leadership. Two men, Lord Salisbury and David Starr Jordan, were entrepreneurial leaders. Both were able to use their expertise to broker understanding and agreements with various factions. Salisbury brokered an agreement on pelagic sealing compensation, while Jordan generated agreement between the conservationists and those who questioned fur seal data and whether the population was actually in jeopardy. As a fur seal expert, Jordan was also able to act as an intellectual leader and educate people through various publications. In this case study, all three types of leadership are clearly demonstrated.

Both elements of another interest-based hypothesis—equity and efficiency—were important in the development of this regime. A truly equitable arrangement would have permitted pelagic sealing, which would have been very inefficient in managing the fur seal population. Consequently, both elements were necessary for completion of an agreement to protect this animal.

Our research acknowledged the salient solution designed by the regulators, which coupled the concept of fur seals as a restricted common property with a ban on pelagic sealing. It was not until all parties realized that they had something to lose—in other words, that without a cooperative effort neither the fur seal industry nor the fur seals themselves would survive—that they all came together and agreement became possible.

The specific compliance mechanisms designed for the 1911 convention helped to ensure that the salient solution was implemented. The task of excluding nonauthenticated sealskins from the ports of the parties to the agreement was simplified because London was the only place where skins were dyed. This fact made it easy to monitor any pelagic sealing by either signatory or nonsignatory states.

The fur seal case was also consistent with the hypothesis that the inclusion of all parties was necessary for the successful development of a regime. Although several bilateral and multilateral agreements were achieved in the course of twenty-five years, the effective management of the fur seal population necessitated an agreement that included all relevant parties.

Our results were more mixed on three other interest-based hypotheses—integrative bargaining, a veil of uncertainty, and the existence of an exogenous shock or crisis. The development of this regime is an example of mixed bargaining, involving the use of both integrative and distributive bargaining tactics. The early as well as the final stages of the negotiations were distributive, as concerns over the economics of the fur seal industry were debated. Integrative bargaining seemed to materialize most clearly when the decline of the fur seal population and what that would mean to the fur seal industry were recognized by all participants. Integrative bargaining contributed to the development of the regime but was not the primary form of bargaining.

The second hypothesis with mixed results was the existence of a veil of uncertainty. All the parties were very familiar with each other's roles and interests, as well as with the status of the sealing market, but knowledge of the population dynamics of the fur seal was either limited or disputed. This uncertainty about the actual size and health of the herds, and consequently the respective monetary returns to the actors, was a relatively minor factor in the regime's development.

The existence of an exogenous shock or crisis was also only partially consistent with the hypothesis. The decline of the fur seal population occurred over a long period of time, too long to have been a true shock. A few specific events stand out during the period of the negotiations— the killing of Japanese poachers in the early 1900s, for example—but there was no specific shock that led to the convention in 1911. Because the fur seal industry relied on the existence of a healthy, growing fur seal population, the disputed claims over the population level were perceived as an ongoing crisis, just enough to sustain interest in the debate.

The findings in this case study do not confirm two other interest-based hypotheses: concentration on scientific questions rather than political issues and high priority of the topic on the national agendas of all parties. The scientific consensus that the fur seal population was declining and that pelagic sealing was the primary cause may have helped to convince the participants that it was important to work together to form a treaty. Hence the period of integrative bargaining. But the political matter of compensation to the pelagic sealers quickly replaced the more scientific issues. On the second point, given the length of time over which the fur seal negotiations took place, it is not surprising that other topics took higher priority on the national agendas of the parties.

The second theoretical component that was significant to the regime's existence reflects two aspects of the knowledge-based hypotheses: first, that ideas and values matter, and second, that consensus must emerge. The development of the conservation movement created an environment of shared ideas and goals, which enabled parties to concentrate on a common or mutual task. This development engendered a situation ripe for acceptance of the conclusion by the scientific community that the fur seal population was rapidly diminishing and that pelagic sealing had to stop. At this stage, the business side of the fur seal issue recognized the potential financial loss and was willing to seek a solution.

It was the third theoretical component, the window of opportunity provided by contextual factors, that may have had the most significant impact. In 1911 a unique window of opportunity appeared. The theory of institutional bargaining, although helpful in identifying some of the important prerequisites for conflict settlement, still does not explain what makes all these necessary conditions join together to create a final solution. The theory of institutional bargaining is actually a structural analysis of the form of a conflict or the means of its solution (negotiations), that is, a conflict's inner logic. But this leaves aside such questions as the nature of a conflict and the context in which it exists. Each international conflict (and this case is a typical conflict over international resources) is a part of a complex interstate system and, besides its inner logic, is highly influenced by the dynamics of the entire system and its other components. International conflict over the North Pacific fur seal herds arose, had been developing, and then was resolved by means of regime creation under the strong influence of the international context.

The essence of the problem was that prosperous branches of the economies of different countries were based on the same resource, and their wealth had been diminished by their collective but unregulated efforts. These contradictions reached a critical point when depletion of the stocks endangered the very existence of this industry in the region. Thus, through the crisis in resources, economics, and relations of resource users, objective prerequisites for the solution of the problem matured. The first manifestation of crisis took place in the 1880s but was temporarily quieted by bilateral agreements on the eastern and western Bering Sea. The second and more severe crisis occurred in the early 1900s and eventuated in the 1911 convention.

Maturation (ripeness) of the problem was brought to the attention of policy makers in the relevant countries by reports of treasury and local officials and the complaints of merchants, manufacturers, and native people. As policy makers' perceptions of the problem took the form of specific state interests and became a part of national policy and politics, the "problem stream" became more influenced by subjective factors: the current international mood and political ideas, interest groups, pressure campaigns, the personal opinions of political leaders, and the necessity of their correlation with other national interests. Many examples of the subjective factors' influence on the negotiations can be cited. The role of the main state interests is predominant, being more steady and less dynamic than specific interests and less exposed to compromise and bargaining. Although specific interests may be sacrificed to ensure main political interests, the opposite variant is impossible. For instance, first, although international regulation threatened its economic interests (trade in furs), Great Britain was not going to take any steps toward regulation in the 1880s–1890s until Canadian concerns had been satisfied. Second, in the 1900s Japan had a profitable pelagic sealing business based on Russian and American herds and was not interested in the international regulation of sealing. Furthermore, the paths of migrations of Japanese herds made it possible for that country to regulate them unilaterally. Japan's specific interest in the fur seal business was solely to reinforce its relations with other Pacific countries (primarily with the United States). Third, Canada used the fur seal question in a package of other deals with the United States, but the agreement fell victim to the deadlock over the Alaska boundary dispute.

In the final, interstate stage of conflict resolution, the general state of international relations, the clash of interests, and other problem stream factors were of primary importance. A favorable political climate, the activities of devoted political entrepreneurs, and bargaining created a window of opportunity.

Although it might seem that at this stage the problem stream was affected by an element of chance, this is not true. Analogous incidents of violence to stop sealing operations had different results: in the 1880s the seizure of Canadian vessels in the Bering Sea brought the case to the attention of high-level decision makers and resulted in a temporary solution of the conflict, but incidents in 1901–1902 in which Russian officials killed nine Japanese poachers did not have significant consequences. Chance, then, became a factor of historical development only because of certain objective conditions which determined the main stream of the problem solution.

CHAPTER THREE

The Svalbard Archipelago:
The Role of Surrogate Negotiators

ELEN C. SINGH AND ARTEMY A. SAGUIRIAN

The international regime for the strategically important, resource-rich Arctic archipelago known today as Svalbard came into being as a result of the 1920 Treaty Relating to Spitsbergen, which entered into force in 1925 and continues in force today.[1] After years of squabbling among the interested nations and failed efforts at resolution, the treaty succeeded in establishing an international regime that provided simultaneously for assignment of sovereignty to a single nation—Norway—subject to explicit limitations, continuation of equal rights of access for citizens of all signatory nations for the purpose of resource exploitation, preservation of the archipelago as a demilitarized territory, and protection and renewal of the living resources of this Arctic region.

Although the Spitsbergen Treaty did not deal with a problem arising as a direct result of World War I, it was among the many agreements negotiated in the context of the Paris Peace Conference. The Spitsbergen Commission, appointed in July 1919 at the end of the conference to take up the question of the archipelago, consisted of representatives from the United States, France, Great Britain, and Italy. The "most interested" powers—Norway, Sweden, and the Soviet Union—were not members of the commission, and their participation in the process was

---

1. Svalbard, the Old Norse designation meaning "land with the cold coasts," has been the name in use for the archipelago since the assumption of sovereignty by Norway in 1925. We have used the term Spitsbergen to refer to the archipelago because that was the term used during the negotiations and prior to Norwegian administration.

limited. It was the commission members, acting as surrogates for the most interested parties, who pushed forward the conclusive negotiations that led to this regime's creation.

The purpose of this chapter is to determine whether existing hypotheses of international regime formation explain the evolution of the regime in this case. Some explanation of the Arctic location, the historical context, and the diplomacy involved in arriving at the treaty provisions is in order, however, before turning to the hypotheses concerned with international regime formation.

The area in question is a group of islands lying approximately midway between northern Norway and the North Pole. The islands have been called an Arctic Galapagos because of their unique flora and fauna. They also contain abundant reserves of coal and other minerals, including potentially significant oil and gas reserves. Because of the relatively inhospitable climate, the island group had no indigenous population. Following the discovery of the archipelago by William Barents in 1596, trappers, hunters, whalers, and fishermen from several European nations began to visit the islands on a regular basis during the summer season.[2]

By 1871–1872 an understanding had emerged, through the exchange of diplomatic notes between Sweden-Norway and Russia,[3] to treat the islands of the archipelago as *terra nullius*, or no-man's land, which had up to that time been the de facto situation.[4] And

---

2. Early Norse histories indicate, however, that at least by the twelfth century the "land with the cold coasts" was known to sailors in the far North, suggesting that Barents may have only rediscovered the islands.

3. All three of the countries most interested in Spitsbergen underwent significant political changes early in the twentieth century. Norway had come under the jurisdiction of Sweden (rather than Denmark) according to the terms of the peace of Kiel (14 January 1814) at the time of the Congress of Vienna. The joint kingdom, Sweden/Norway, dominated by Stockholm, endured until 1905, when the two sides—avoiding armed conflict—concluded a treaty of separation. Imperial Russia, as a result of the Revolution in October 1917, was replaced by a series of governments. The name most often used by the Bolshevik government at the time of the Peace Conference was the Russian Socialist Federated Republics; it was not until 1922 that the Soviet government called itself the Union of Soviet Socialist Republics. During World War I, Norway and Sweden remained neutral; tsarist Russia entered the war on the side of the Allies, but a separate peace was signed between Germany and the new Soviet Union (the Treaty of Brest-Litovsk) shortly after the Revolution.

4. Swedish note to the Powers, 17/29 March 1871, Supplement to the Report of the Ministry of Foreign Affairs, 1912, *Documents Relating to Spitzbergen, 1871–1912* (St. Petersburg: Imperial Russian Foreign Ministry, 1912), 2; and Russian Response to the Swedish-Norwegian note, 15/27 May 1871, from 850d.oo/190, decimal file, 3, Record Group (hereafter RG) 59, National Archives, Washington, D.C..

in 1906, soon after independence, the Norwegian government responded to a Russian inquiry by reaffirming this commitment to *terra nullius*.[5]

By the end of the first decade of the twentieth century, hunters, trappers, fishermen, whalers, tourists, and then miners (including claimants to coal-bearing lands), were competing for space and resources on the archipelago. The long-held assumption that no one nation should have sovereignty over the islands, but rather that the area should remain open for exploitation by nationals of any state, was both an inspiration and an obstacle to negotiators when questions of administration and regulation arose. If a private individual asserted claim to mineral-bearing land, with which government could the claim be registered? If an overlapping claim was asserted, which tribunal could handle the matter? If a Swede murdered a Dutchman on the island of Spitsbergen, did any court have jurisdiction? Once a large labor force for mining was present, what labor laws should be observed? Could laws be enforced? Questions of private ownership, legal systems, and public administration had to be addressed. Clearly the era of self-regulating *terra nullius* was coming to an end. The long process that would end in creation of an international regime for Spitsbergen was about to begin. What was needed was to provide a system of laws and administration for a large, resource-rich area in an Arctic environment with no indigenous population, while at the same time preserving the area as an "open" territory. No models existed.

In the years between 1905 and 1920, concerted, if sporadic, efforts were made to find a way to satisfy the needs of individual claimants, their respective governments, and the three northern powers—Russia, Sweden, and Norway. In addition, nationals of northern European countries expressed concern about the need to protect and renew living resources that had been depleted. During this period, Christiania (Oslo), Norway, became the center in which negotiations concerning Spitsbergen took place. Aside from diplomatic exchanges using routine channels, conference diplomacy was also employed, with *pourparlers* between Sweden, Russia, and Norway held in Christiania in 1910 and 1912. The Norwegian government then convened a full conference of interested powers in 1914.

As early as 1909, the Norwegian Foreign Ministry had begun working to organize a conference of all powers with interests in Spitsbergen, but Russia, supported by Sweden, insisted on preliminary talks between the

5. Note from the Norwegian Foreign Ministry to the Russian Legation, 6 June 1906, file P7 A 1/06, Norwegian Foreign Ministry Archives, Oslo.

three most interested powers in advance of the full conference.[6] Norway deferred to Sweden and Russia so as not to antagonize the Swedish government and surely out of regard for the earlier commitment to *terra nullius* made by the joint kingdom and reaffirmed by the Norwegian government in 1906.[7] Furthermore, the presence of a private American mining operation in Spitsbergen was, by 1910, becoming a nettlesome issue; by holding *pourparlers* among the three northern powers, Norway could postpone inviting the United States to a conference addressing the European question of Spitsbergen. The three northern powers were able to defer American participation in negotiations until the conference of 1914.

Pourparlers involving only Sweden, Norway, and Russia were held in Christiania between 19 July and 11 August 1910.[8] The result of this meeting, the final 1910 Projet de Convention, described a tripartite administration by Norway, Sweden, and Russia that nevertheless retained the commitment to *terra nullius*. Norway circulated the fifteen-chapter, seventy-five-article document to the other interested powers: Belgium, Denmark, Germany, Great Britain, the Netherlands, and the United States. The contents can be summarized in part:

1. The geographical designation of the islands was 10° to 35° east longitude, and 74° to 81° north latitude, including the surrounding waters and ice as far as eight nautical miles.

2. The archipelago was to remain *terra nullius*, and not to be annexed by any state. The islands were to remain open to citizens of all states, while nationals of noncontracting powers were to declare allegiance to one of the contracting powers in order to receive the same treatment as subjects of contracting powers in the archipelago. In case of war, the archipelago was to be considered neutral territory.

3. The islands were to be administered by an international commission, called the Spitsbergen Commission, composed of a Norwegian,

6. Ove Gude to Secretary of State Elihu Root, 26 January 1909, 3746/38–41, numerical file, RG 59, National Archives.

7. Norway had become an independent country just at the time that the question of which country or countries should regulate activities on Spitsbergen became a subject for diplomacy. Norwegian nationals were the first actually to sell land parcels on the islands, although the Norwegian Foreign Ministry denied any jurisdiction in an area designated *terra nullius*.

8. The British government gave explicit consent to this meeting, noting the desirability of the three powers "most directly concerned" to have the opportunity to discuss and propose "suitable arrangements" to the others in advance of a general conference (Memorandum, British Embassy to the State Department, 6 April 1910, 850d.00/126, decimal file, RG 59, National Archives).

a Swedish, and a Russian member, chosen by their respective governments. The commission was authorized to occupy real estate and to
levy taxes to fund the administration of the area.

4. An international police force was to be organized; the commissioner of police was to be a national of the power whose subjects
were in the majority in Spitsbergen. The police commissioner
would be competent to try minor cases involving breaches of provisions of the convention or of regulations established by the
Spitsbergen Commission, with appeal only to that commission.

5. The draft included provisions regarding civil and criminal jurisdiction, a justice of the peace, employer/labor relations, land usage, and postal and telegraph service. Provisions concerning civil
jurisdiction, with one exception, considered every person on
Spitsbergen as subject to the jurisdiction of his or her national tri-
bunals; in cases of litigation between persons of unlike nationality,
the national court of the defendant was to have jurisdiction. In
criminal cases, accused persons were to be arraigned before the
competent courts of their respective countries.

6. Land was forever to remain public property; only rights of occupancy were allowed for purposes of exploiting natural resources.
Nationals of noncontracting powers were not to be permitted to
occupy or acquire land. The text made provision for registration
of land occupied prior to the entry into force of the agreement.
Hunting was to be free everywhere, and natural harbors were not
to be included in the right of occupancy.[9]

Of the interested powers that received copies of the Projet de Convention, the United States reacted most vehemently. (The "interested
powers" were those whose nationals either historically or actually frequented the islands for resource exploitation.) The note verbale from
the State Department contained the following objections: the United
States government could not adhere to any convention without prior
recognition of the indisputable validity of the claims of American citizens as recorded in the State Department; the proposed plan was too
costly and elaborate, and it did not take into sufficient account the in-

9. Projet de Convention, Christiania, 1910, Longyear Spitzbergen Collection, Michigan
Technological University Archives, Houghton, Michigan. See also Procès-verbaux des Séances plénières à Christiania par les Délégations de la Norvège, de la Russie, et de la
Suède, et au cours desquelles fût élaboré un projet de convention concernant le Spitsbergen 19 juillet–11 août, file P7 A 1/06, Norwegian Foreign Ministry Archives. Note that
under the terms of point 4, Norway could look forward to the police commissionership's
belonging to a Norwegian national.

terests of American nationals mining coal in the archipelago; and finally, consent of the United States government would require American participation in the drafting of an agreement to cover the islands.
The United States did accept the principle of *terra nullius* for the archipelago and would not object to an administrative program agreed upon
by the other powers, so long as the principle of *terra nullius* and the
right of Americans to own land were recognized. (Previously, the State
Department had declined to participate actively in the formulation of
an administrative plan.)[10]

The German government had questions about the provisions for
land use and the proposed international jurisdiction over Spitsbergen.
Could the independence of Spitsbergen authorities be guaranteed?
Should laws that were to be applied be elaborated in the convention itself? According to Trygve Mathisen, the German government "found it
difficult to accept the rules of the draft convention to the effect that the
contracting powers should see to it that judgements and verdicts pronounced by the Svalbard legal authorities be executed in their territory."[11]

Among the other interested states, Belgium did not submit observations. The Danish government had no claims to defend in the archipelago but was interested in how the administrative plan would be
funded. The French government did not respond with specific suggestions but indicated indirectly that the draft contained "wise and satisfactory proposals."[12] The British government reported that it could not
accept the Projet de Convention. The government of the Netherlands
wished the text of the 1910 *projet* to be corrected so that Barents alone
was credited with discovery of the archipelago, eliminating mention of
discovery by nationals of the three northern powers from the preamble.
In addition, the Netherlands wanted "compulsory arbitration in dis-

---

10. Note verbale, 27 January 1911, file P7 A 1/06, Norwegian Foreign Ministry Archives.
For further discussion of the American position, see Elen C. Singh, *The Svalbard (Spitsbergen) Question: United States Foreign Policy, 1907–1935* (Oslo: Universitetsforlaget, 1980). Increased U.S. interest in formulation of the plan for Spitsbergen administration can be explained partly by the fact that since 1907 the Arctic Coal Company and Ayer and
Longyear had lobbied the State Department consistently for recognition of their claims to
coal-bearing lands (four tracts) and for protection against expected "unfair taxation" of
their infant industry in Spitsbergen. When the principal American investors got wind of
a possible conference to address the question of administration of the island, they urged
U.S. participation.

11. Trygve Mathisen, *Svalbard in International Politics, 1871–1925: The Solution of a Unique
International Problem* (Oslo: Brøggers Boktrykkeris Forlag, 1954), 85.

12. Note, Ambassador Jules Jusserand to the Secretary of State, 29 April 1911, 850d.00/
164, decimal file, RG 59, National Archives.

putes arising out of the interpretation and application of the convention whereas the draft only proposed arbitration when circumstances permitted."[13]

Considering the lack of agreement, what pressure was there to negotiate again? Between 1910 and 1912, claims to coal-bearing tracts increased in Spitsbergen, to the dismay of the Americans with mining interests there, Charles Ayer and John M. Longyear and the Arctic Coal Company (also owned by Ayer and Longyear and a few other stockholders). While the Arctic Coal Company's attorney, Nathaniel Wilson, pressed the U.S. State Department to seek resolution of existing claims based on documents filed in 1905 and on reports filed annually thereafter, the company also lobbied the department to prevent creation of a regime that would be costly to the company, that is, one under which taxes would be levied. On one hand, the company officials decried general lawlessness, strikes, claim jumping, and uncertainty over title to land; on the other, they argued for "infant industry" status and bemoaned the expected burden of taxation, especially inasmuch as their properties were the only truly productive mines operating year-round.[14]

By 1912, the Norwegian Foreign Ministry and the U. S. State Department were sending back and forth a draft agreement on arbitration of conflicting American and Norwegian citizens' claims.[15] The prospect that Norway and the United States might agree bilaterally on claims stimulated the other two northern powers to urge a second multilateral meeting. Before that second meeting began, however, a number of developments took place.

---

13. Mathisen, *Svalbard in International Politics*, 84–85. For greater detail, see "Recueil des Observations faites par les différentes puissances invitées à se prononcer au sujet du projet de convention concernant le Spitsbergen en date du 11 août 1910 et du projet de convention modifié en date du 26 janvier 1912 ainsi que du projet d'arrangement, annexé à ce dernier, concernant quelques occupations de fonds de terre au Spitsbergen," 850d.oo/262, decimal file, RG 59, National Archives.

14. "Printed copy of letter dated 28 December 1910 from the Arctic Coal Company and Ayer and Longyear to the Secretary of State relating to their coal properties in Spitsbergen and transmitting the report of their general manager for the season ending 27 October 1910, and accompanying documents," 850d.oo/156, decimal file, RG 59, National Archives. Also "Observations on the Draft of a Convention concerning Spitsbergen, agreed upon by plenipotentiaries of Norway, Russia, and Sweden, and proposed to their respective governments, submitted on behalf of the Arctic Coal Company and Frederick Ayer and John M. Longyear," filed in the State Department, 10 January 1911, 850d.oo/156, decimal file, RG 59, National Archives.

15. Norge-USA avtale om stridende okkupasjoner, 7/31/1912, BND III, P7/A, 3/10, Norwegian Foreign Ministry Archives.

In 1911, as the U.S. State Department studied the 1910 Projet de Convention, Robert Lansing (then legal counselor to the State Department) began thinking of possible solutions to the international question of Spitsbergen and writing on the subject.[16] Lansing's assumptions were that existing claims should be recognized, although he referred to exclusive and permanent use rather than to title of ownership.[17] He suggested fees for land registration rather than taxes to be levied by the proposed international commission. He also suggested a commissioner general and a police commissioner of Norwegian nationality because the work force on the islands was largely Norwegian. In addition, he recommended that Norwegian laws should apply generally in civil actions. In 1917, Lansing—who had become secretary of state in 1915— published his (modified) views on Spitsbergen in the *American Journal of International Law*. He then advocated that a neutral Scandinavian state should be awarded the islands.[18] In May of that year Lansing confided to the Norwegian minister in Washington, Helmer Bryn, that he had always thought the islands should be Norwegian,[19] which is also consistent with his instructions to the American delegates at the Paris Peace Conference in 1919, discussed below in the section on interest-based hypotheses. This idea was to become the basis for the final (1919–1920) international regime.

Meanwhile, commercial interests were lobbying in the United States for an official policy on Spitsbergen that would enhance their enterprises. The State Department was reluctant, however, to take part officially in an agreement that might prove costly in the future. Similar business-minded overtures were made by would-be mining companies in London and in Christiania; some of the companies were establishing claims that overlapped previously staked Ayer and Longyear and Arctic Coal Company lands.

The United States, as well as the other European powers with historical interests in Spitsbergen, deferred to Norway, Sweden, and Russia regarding the timing of and participants in the conference. The

---

16. See Robert Lansing, "Government over Persons within Terra Nullius: General Principles," "General Statement of Conventional Plan for Government in Spitzbergen," and "Plan of International Convention Relative to the establishment of a Government in Spitzbergen," Longyear Spitzbergen Collection, Michigan Technological University Archives.

17. Lansing, "General Statement of Conventional Plan for Government in Spitzbergen."

18. "A Unique International Problem," *American Journal of International Law* 2 (October 1917): 763–771.

19. Telegram, Bryn to the Norwegian Foreign Ministry, 6 May 1917, JN 15354, file P7 A 1/06, Norwegian Foreign Ministry Archives.

government of Norway convened a second meeting of these three northern powers in January 1912. To give an idea of the dispatch with which this meeting was arranged, observations from some of the interested powers concerning the 1910 *projet* arrived in Christiania only after the second conference was in session. The meeting resulted in a draft convention of comparable length and content to the one in 1910. The Norwegian government again circulated copies to other interested powers, and those governments registered similar observations. The British Foreign Office was especially unwilling to agree to a plan that would require its government to send representatives to Spitsbergen and bring British nationals home to try them for infractions committed on islands that were not under British jurisdiction.[20]

Between 1912 and 1914, new mining claimants arrived in the archipelago. In addition to the Norwegian claim jumpers the Americans complained about, Russian claimants also surfaced. With the addition of claims by the nationals of a third country, the idea of bilateral arbitration to resolve conflicting claims by the United States and Norway lost some of its appeal. Nevertheless, private as well as diplomatic correspondence to the U.S. State Department and to the foreign ministries of other nations frequently mentioned claims and counterclaims to mineral-bearing land in Spitsbergen. In addition, labor unrest was a problem among the Scandinavian workers employed in American mines.[21]

The Spitsbergen question was very high on Norway's foreign policy agenda. Nearly all events in the islands involved Norwegians, and because Norway had only recently become a nation separate from Sweden, the Norwegian Ministry of Foreign Affairs was eager to handle this issue effectively and in full accord with accepted diplomatic practices.

In 1914, the Norwegian government convened a meeting in Christiania of representatives from all of the interested powers: Belgium, Denmark, Germany, Great Britain, the Netherlands, Russia, Sweden, and the United States. At this conference, the delegates intended to hammer out a definitive agreement for the administration of the islands, retaining the *terra nullius* status but allowing for rotation of ad-

---

20. Mathisen, *Svalbard in International Politics*, 86–87, summarizes well the reactions of interested powers.

21. The leading American mining entrepreneur, John M. Longyear, suggested hiring more Finns or workers from England or Scotland; he even considered importing Chinese laborers to obviate the employment of the "troublesome" Scandinavians.

ministrative responsibilities among Norway, Sweden, and Russia. Due consideration would be given to the historic roles in the islands of the three northern powers, their geographic proximity, and the fact that most of the individuals frequenting the islands were Norwegian, Swedish, and Russian (although British and American mining interests were clearly present).

A meeting of the three northern powers preceded the plenary sessions, which began on 16 June, only weeks before the outbreak of World War I. The conference reaffirmed the principle of *terra nullius* but failed to provide an acceptable or practical scheme of administration. Germany advocated enlargement of the three-member Spitsbergen Commission proposed earlier to include a German representative, whereas Russia and Sweden opposed such an increase. Russian representatives were unwilling to recognize undisputed claims (including American claims) or agree to arbitration of conflicting individual claims.[22] American delegates, hampered by unclear and sometimes unrealistic instructions, were not much more cooperative, and when they did retreat from some of their early demands, it was too little or too late for an agreement to materialize.

The addition of other interested powers at the negotiating table in 1914 did not prove to be an advantage in trying to work out administrative arrangements for Spitsbergen. The conference adjourned on 30 July, with the intention of reconvening on 1 February 1915. As events turned out, however, this 1914 conference was to be the last occasion on which direct negotiations took place among all of the powers most concerned with resolving the Spitsbergen question.[23]

World War I prevented the negotiations begun in 1914 from continuing, although the conflict did not reach the Spitsbergen archipelago. Of the three northern powers, Sweden and Norway remained neutral, and only Russia was directly involved. After the October Revolution, the new Soviet government made a separate peace with Germany—formalized in the 1918 Treaty of Brest-Litovsk—in which the Soviet and German negotiators expressed their desire for creation of an international organization to administer Spitsbergen and for continuation of the Spitsbergen conference to work out the details: "The Contracting Parties will direct their best efforts to having the international or-

22. Nathaniel Wilson, Attorney for the Arctic Coal Company, to W. B. Bentinck-Smith, 8 September 1914, Longyear Spitzbergen Collection, Michigan Technical University Archives.

23. *Actes et Documents, Tome I, Recueil des procès-verbaux des séances, 16 juin–30 juillet, 1914* (Christiania: Imprimerie Grøndahl & Son), 192, 200, 233, 245.

ganization of the Spitsbergen Archipelago, which was contemplated at the Spitsbergen Conference in 1914, carried out on footing of equality for both parties. To this end the Governments of both parties will request the Norwegian Government to bring about the continuation of the Spitsbergen Conference as soon as possible after the conclusion of a general peace."[24]

At the peace conference convened in Paris in early 1919, the Norwegian minister in Paris requested that the Spitsbergen question be taken up and asked that the islands be allocated to Norway. Although the Spitsbergen issue had not arisen as a result of the war, the president of the peace conference, French premier Georges Clémenceau, did agree to consider the matter. Following a resolution adopted by the Council of Heads of Delegations on 7 July 1919, a Spitsbergen Commission was duly formed and met regularly between July and September 1919. This commission drafted a treaty by which the contracting powers recognized the sovereignty of Norway over the archipelago, subject to certain limitations, including the equal rights of access to resources for nationals of signatory powers, and provided for the demilitarized status of the islands.[25]

French, British, and American representatives played prominent roles at the Paris Peace Conference. Soviet representatives did not participate because of the earlier separate peace with Germany, and Germany participated only as a defeated power. Neutral governments—including Belgium and the Netherlands as well as Norway and Sweden—were represented in Paris but not at the actual peace conference. None of three most interested powers, therefore, was in a position to engage directly in negotiation of the provisions of the final Spitsbergen Treaty. In effect, representatives of Great Britain, France, the United States, and Italy, who made up the conference's Spitsbergen Commission, acted as de facto surrogates for the interested countries not represented at the peace conference.

In the course of its meetings, the Spitsbergen Commission heard pro-

---

24. Article 33 of the additional treaty signed 3 March 1918, at Brest-Litovsk, pursuant to Article XII of the main Treaty of Brest-Litovsk Deutsch-sowjetische Bezeihungen von den Verhandlung in Brest-Litovsk bis zum Abschluss der Rapallovertrages, *Dokumentensammlung Band I, 1917–1918* (Berlin: Staatsverlag der Deutschen Demokratischen Republik, 1957), 503; see also Handbooks Prepared under the Direction of the Historical Section of the Foreign Office, no. 36, *Spitsbergen* (London: His Majesty's Stationery Office, 1920).

25. "Préparation et signature des traités et conventions divers," *Recueil des Actes de la Conférence, Partie VII* (Paris: 1924), in General Records of the American Commission to Negotiate the Peace (hereafter GRACNP), M820, Roll 180, 181.5101/18, National Archives.

posals from the Norwegian minister, and his draft treaty suggestions were used as the basis for discussion.[26] The Swedish minister submitted a memorandum containing objections to the Norwegian minister's draft treaty and offered suggestions for the proposed convention.[27] The commission also considered a note from Russian representatives of the short-lived Kolchak regime that outlined the record of Russian commitment to the *terra nullius* principle and proposed many exceptions for inclusion in the draft treaty.[28] The Norwegian government encouraged the work of the commission, whereas the Swedish government only reluctantly agreed to Norwegian sovereignty over Spitsbergen.[29] Finally, in February 1920, representatives of Denmark, France, Great Britain, Italy, Japan, the Netherlands, Norway, Sweden, and the United States signed the Spitsbergen Treaty in Paris.[30]

Shortly after the signing of the treaty, the Soviet government protested the conclusion of this agreement without Russian participation: "The decision now reached that Norway is to have complete possession of Spitsbergen has taken place without Russia's participation, and for that reason Russia declares that the procedure is void as far as she is concerned. The Russian Government will not permit others to dispose of her international affairs without her knowledge, even

---

26. Procès-verbal no. 2, séance du 21 juillet 1919, et Procès-verbal no. 3, séance du 24 juillet 1919, ibid.

27. Annexé au procès-verbal no. 9, "Mémorandum suédois," Paris, 6 août 1919, 181.5101/9, ibid.

28. "Point de vue Russe," Annexé au procès-verbal no. 1, première séance du Commission du Spitsbergen, ibid.

29. In spite of initially strong Swedish opposition to Norwegian sovereignty over Spitsbergen, expressed in instructions from Stockholm, the Swedish minister Albert Ehrensvärd, posted in Paris, confided in a private letter to his foreign minister that Sweden should not object to a Norwegian Spitsbergen as it had previously done. If Sweden were to support Norwegian demands for Spitsbergen, Norway could support Swedish demands for the Aaland Islands, and both nations could support Danish claims to North Schleswig. (For the full text of Ehrenvärd's letter, see L. Kjellberg, "The Spitzberg Treaty of 1920," *Nordic Journal of International Law* 52 (1983): 67–68.) In the same vein, the Norwegians assured the Danish government of a settlement of the East Greenland case in Denmark's favor, in return for Danish acceptance of a Norwegian Spitsbergen. See Oscar Svarlien, *An Introduction to the Law of Nations* (New York: McGraw-Hill, 1955), 134–135, citing *PCIJ Judgement*, 5 April 1933, ser. A/B. no. 53, pp. 69–72; and Green Hackworth, *Digest of International Law*, vol. 5 (Washington, D.C.: Government Printing Office, 1940–1944), 32–33.

30. This was the same group of interested parties that had attended the 1914 conference, with the addition of Japan and Italy (as a result of World War I and the peace conference setting) and the absence of Germany and Russia as explained.

if she may not have serious objection to the proceedings as they are executed."[31]

A few months later, the Soviet government announced that it would not be bound by actions infringing on the rights of the laboring masses that were taken without Soviet participation.[32] During the early 1920s, however, gaining international recognition of the new Soviet government topped the agenda in Moscow. To attain this objective, the Soviets were willing to make numerous concessions, including yielding their position on Spitsbergen, by then undoubtedly toward the lower end of their list of priorities. They made strenuous attempts—which were ultimately successful—to trade support of the Spitsbergen Treaty for diplomatic recognition of the Soviet government by Norway. Thus in 1924, under duress of circumstances, the Soviet Union accepted the treaty provisions.[33] When the Spitsbergen Treaty entered into force in 1925, it had Soviet acquiescence but not membership.[34] The Soviet government did not formally adhere to the Spitsbergen Treaty until 1935.[35]

The area covered by the 1920 Spitsbergen Treaty is an Arctic trapezoid on the map: 10°–35° east longitude by 74°–81° north latitude. This designation includes Bear Island, which is located on the continental shelf approximately halfway between North Norway and the southern tip of Vest Spitsbergen. The entire area is about the size of West Virginia. The negotiators of 1910, 1912, 1914, and 1919 encountered no difficulty in agreeing on delineation of the area or on the territorial waters claimed by Norway (reduced to four nautical miles in 1919).

The motivation for the Spitsbergen Treaty agreed to in 1920 by

---

31. Dispatch, Minister Schmedeman to the Secretary of State, 17 February 1920, No. 1475. 850d.oo/380, decimal file, RG 59, National Archives.

32. Radiogram, Foreign Minister George Chicherin to the Norwegian Foreign Ministry, 7 May 1920, 850d.oo/385, ibid.

33. Document file note, 857h.01/12, citing 861.01/737, Telegram, Swenson to the Secretary of State, 13 February 1924, ibid.

34. The treaty entered into force when all original signatory nations had ratified, pursuant to Article 10 of the Spitsbergen Treaty.

35. Note, French Ambassador André de Laboulaye to the Secretary of State, 26 June 1935, 857h.01/103, decimal file, RG 59, National Archives. The Soviet government did not intentionally delay its adhesion once its readiness to accept the treaty's provisions was explicitly expressed. The reason the Soviet Union formally became a member of the Paris treaty system ten years after the latter was put into force could be explained by the pending de jure recognition of Russia by the states that were party to the treaty. Thus Soviet participation only became possible after the United States recognized the Soviet Union in 1933.

Denmark, France, Great Britain, Italy, Japan, the Netherlands, Norway, Sweden, and the United States was to provide the islands "with an equitable regime, in order to assure their development and peaceful utilization" (Preamble). The treaty recognized the "full and absolute" sovereignty of Norway over the archipelago and gave nationals of signatory powers equal rights to exploit living and nonliving resources (Articles I and II). Norway was to be free to undertake measures to guarantee the preservation and reconstitution of flora and fauna (Article II), which in practice has meant issuance of regulations and definition of conservation zones. All measures were to be uniformly applicable to all contracting powers, with no special favor for Norwegians (Article III). The treaty anticipated an international convention that would establish an international meteorological station on the islands and also provided for Norwegian authorization of all construction of public wireless telegraphy stations (Articles IV and V). Private claims that predated the treaty would be handled by a special commissioner (Annex), and ownership rights would be recognized by the Norwegian government (Articles VI and VII). ("Ownership" had proven to be an intractable problem in the earlier negotiations of 1910 and 1912.) Norway would be permitted to levy taxes on products extracted, but the taxes could be used exclusively for administrative costs, the rate of taxation being specified in the treaty (Article VIII). Norway undertook to draft mining regulations, which were to be subject to the examination of signatory powers before entering into force.

Significantly, Norway agreed "not to allow establishment of any naval base in the territories and not to construct any fortification in the . . . territories, which may never be used for warlike purposes" (Article IX). Claims of Russian nationals were acknowledged on an equal footing with those of nationals of the High Contracting Powers (the original nine signatories); until recognition of the Soviet government would permit adherence to the treaty, the government of Denmark lent its good offices to handle the claims of Russian nationals in Spitsbergen (Article X).

The text of the treaty indicated no time limit for the duration of the convention, nor did it stipulate "in perpetuity." The High Contracting Powers did not specify withdrawal procedures, although all original signatory powers were required to ratify the agreement before it could enter into force. Explicit "transformation rules" do not appear in the text. The French government was designated as the power responsible for inviting third parties to sign the treaty; the number of powers adhering reached twenty-five by 1931.[36] Forty states are now parties.

The treaty conferred upon Norway all the duties of sovereignty but few of the benefits. From the vantage point of Paris in 1919, either a Norwegian mandate under the expected League of Nations or full sovereignty for Norway—subject to definition of access and property rights—would have satisfied the interests of most nations in exploitation of resources on the archipelago, although the first alternative would have entailed delay in settling the question. The Norwegian government preferred careful definition of rights (limiting actual sovereignty) to a mandate, assuming that the Norwegian position would be weaker if it had to answer to the (as yet not constituted) League on questions of administration of the islands.

The treaty provisions, coupled with environmental factors—including an Arctic location with no close neighbors, a small non-native population, and specific resource endowments—provided the actors involved in this regime with fairly straightforward choices and benefits. Immediate concerns in 1919 included property rights and rights of exploitation for fishing, whaling, hunting, and coal mining. Most nations signed the treaty out of interest in possible future commercial ventures, and the Norwegians and Swedes, still smarting from the 1905 partition, finally agreed on the practicality of a Norwegian administration.[37] Although the strategic location of the islands was not of major importance in 1919, subsequent concerns have been increasingly strategic. Furthermore, the resource priority list still includes coal, as well as offshore reserves of oil and natural gas, all of which may strain existing arrangements in the future.

Analysis and Hypothesis Testing

Do existing theoretical explanations shed any light on the dynamics of the process just outlined? Or more specifically, what made agreement possible in 1919, when it had not proved possible before? We engaged in a preliminary testing of hypotheses designed to explain the formation of international regimes, as described in Chapter 1 (see also

---

36. Singh, *The Spitzbergen (Svalbard) Question*, 169–173. For texts of the Spitsbergen Treaty, the Norwegian mining code, and the royal decree asserting Norwegian sovereignty over the islands, see Willy Østreng, *Politics in High Latitudes: The Svalbard Archipelago* (Montreal: McGill-Queen's University Press, 1978), 108–116.

37. Kjellberg, "Spitzberg Treaty," 40–83.

the Appendix). These hypotheses vary widely, from assertion of the need for a hegemonic nation (power-based explanation), to institutional bargaining, regime content, and the influence of negotiators (interest-based explanations), to epistemic community actions (knowledge-based explanations), and finally, to a review of contextual issues surrounding the case.

Power-Based Hypotheses

Neither the benign dominance or leadership described by Charles Kindleberger nor hegemony as defined by Robert Keohane was present in this case.[38] We suggest that no single power possessed a "disproportionate share of resources or structural power" in this instance, but rather that the French, British, American, and Italian representatives on the 1919 Spitsbergen Commission exercised benign political dominance in formulating the Spitsbergen Treaty.[39] A group—the victors of war—exercised power not through superiority of resources but through their acknowledged role as architects of the peace. These powers were encouraged by Norway, which was willing to shoulder a disproportionate share of the costs of the new regime. Norway agreed to undertake responsibility for administration, a costly commitment, while at the same time accepting the treaty limitations on taxation of commercial enterprises in the archipelago. Rather than achieving special status among the signatories through advantages for Norwegians in the islands, Norway agreed to limitations on sovereignty so that the equal access to resources provisions could become a reality. Norway offered to provide a disproportionate share of a public good (a system of order protecting the future interests of all participants in the regime). And at no cost to themselves, the victorious powers signed on, knowing that 1919–1920, in the absence of Russian participation, was an opportune

38. Charles Kindleberger, "International Public Goods without International Government," *American Economic Review* 76 (March 1986):11–13; Robert O. Keohane, *After Hegemony: Cooperation and Discord in the World Political Economy* (Princeton: Princeton University Press, 1984), esp. chap. 3. Although our discussion of the question of hegemonic power focuses on the 1919–1920 period, during which the treaty was negotiated, it is important that we did not find hegemonic power (exercised by a single state or a group) to be a factor in the earlier negotiations (1910, 1912, and 1914) either.

39. It is unlikely that the Big Four (heads of state of France, Great Britain, Italy, and the United States) would have taken up the Spitsbergen matter in the context of the Paris Peace Conference had it not been for the entrepreneurial leadership of the Norwegian minister in Paris, Baron Wedel-Jarlsberg. Furthermore, it is clear that by 1919 the American position had changed. Robert Lansing, who became secretary of state in 1915, supported Norwegian demands for sovereignty.

time to handle the persistent international legal problem of Spitsbergen.[40]

Rather than for any particular benefit to themselves, the dominant powers on the Spitsbergen Commission and in the Supreme Council of the Allied and Associated Powers appear to have agreed on the solution for Spitsbergen to settle this persistent international question while at the same time rewarding Norway for neutral wartime shipping (avoiding the issue of compensation)[41] as well as guaranteeing their nationals equal rights of access for resource exploitation.

Because American properties in Spitsbergen had been sold by 1915, Secretary of State Robert Lansing could support the Norwegian demand when the question came up in 1919. (Before 1915, Lansing had scrupulously advised that *terra nullius* must be preserved and that the rights of American property holders must be recognized in the archipelago.) On 27 August 1919 he cabled from Washington, D.C.,

40. It is not necessarily accurate to say that in 1919 the dominance of the Allied powers was "coercive," i.e., taking malevolent advantage of Russia's absence, while observing from western Europe the sequence of fledgling Russian governments from 1917 to 1920. Provisions in the Spitsbergen Treaty allowed for protection of Russian citizens' claims and left open the way for subsequent Soviet adherence to the agreement. Some historians contend, however, that the absence of Russia from the peace conference made its results more tenuous. The following authors shed light on the Russian absence from the Paris peace talks: F. S. Marston, *The Peace Conference of 1919: Organization and Procedure* (London: Oxford University Press, 1944), 64, 107, 228–229; Arno J. Mayer, *Politics and Diplomacy of Peacemaking: Containment and Counterrevolution at Versailles, 1918–1919* (New York: Vintage Books, 1969), chaps. 13 and 14; Robert H. Ferrell, *American Diplomacy: The Twentieth Century* (New York: Norton, 1988), 147–148; and Robert D. Schulzinger, *American Diplomacy in the Twentieth Century* (New York: Oxford University Press, 1990), 116–118. Harold Nicolson gave the Russian absence one small paragraph: "There was in the first place the Russian problem. It is beyond the range of these notes to examine whether the Supreme Council dealt wisely with Russia during these months or whether such proposals as that of the Prinkipo Conference were ill considered and impulsive. The fact remains that Russia was a grave problem which had to be considered from the outset and that this problem could only have been discussed by the leaders of the world in common conference" (*Peacemaking* 1919 [1937; rpt. New York: Grosset and Dunlap, 1965]).

41. Wedel-Jarlsberg to Clemenceau, 10 April 1919, 186.95/3, M820, Roll 440, National Archives. The letter reads in part: "The Norwegian merchant marine has cruelly suffered from the German submarine warfare. I need not call your attention to the services rendered by Norwegian sailors to the cause of liberty by braving the brutalities of the war of extermination. ... But the price of this courage and devotion is 1200 Norwegians dead and the loss of 832 ships, representing 1,240,000 tons. ... The Norwegian Government addresses the Peace Conference with confidence that it will heed the interests of Norway in obtaining a just recompense for the losses of the Norwegian merchant marine and above all, the reparation of damages suffered personally by our sailors."

to the American Commission to Negotiate the Peace: "When in Paris I assured the Norwegian Minister that this Government would favor the Norwegian sovereignty. Please advise me if the subject has been discussed. If it has or if it should be raised, you should support Norway in her claims to the islands."[42]

Some members of the American delegation in Paris had doubts about the settlement, however. At a meeting of the technical delegates of the American commission to Negotiate the Peace in July 1919, Frederick K. Nielsen, the only American member of the Spitsbergen Commission, who had also served in the American delegation at the 1914 Spitsbergen conference in Christiania, reviewed the development of the treaty, noting Lansing's support for Norwegian sovereignty. He suggested that "full powers" be requested from President Woodrow Wilson so an American delegate could sign the draft treaty. In Paris, one member of the American commission, Admiral Harry Shepard Knapp, had second thoughts:

> Admiral Knapp: "It seems to me that our interests are very much more remote than are those of some neutral powers that are closer to Spitsbergen, and for the Five Great Powers to set out to regulate the world—that is the idea in my mind."
>
> Dr. James Brown Scott: "They are doing it. They are not setting out to do it. They have been doing it all the time."[43]

Failure to resolve the Spitsbergen issue in 1920 would not have led to military action—or even credible threats—by the Great Powers against smaller recalcitrant states. Similarly, in the postwar context smaller states would have spilled ink rather than blood in the event of an unsatisfactory convention. The Netherlands, for example, did question the "hegemony" of the Big Five (France, Great Britain, Italy, Japan, and the United States). When news of the drafting of a treaty for Spitsbergen reached the Netherlands, articles in leading newspapers questioned the "right" of the dominant powers to settle the question. In *Nieuws Van Den Dag*, 24 July 1919,[44] it was argued that the Supreme Council of the Allied and Associated Powers, "hardly any longer allied

---

42. Cable, no. 2963, FW 741.5714/17, 27 August 1919, GRACNP, National Archives.

43. Minutes of the meeting of Commissioners and Technical Delegates of the American Commission to Negotiate the Peace, 23 July 1919, 184.00101/121, GRACNP, M820, Roll 202, National Archives.

44. Translated and reported from a local publication in the Hague by the United States mission there: Dispatch no. 3148, 5 August 1919, from the American Mission in the Hague to the Secretary of State, FW 741.5714/16, GRACNP, National Archives.

or associated," had no right to interfere in questions such as the "sovereignty" over Spitsbergen. Spitsbergen's connection to "the termination of the war" was a "riddle." Since it was not urgent, the matter could be taken up by the projected League of Nations. The Supreme Council should not act as a "proxy" for the as yet unconstituted international organization. The British, French, Italian, and American governments, together, had in reality the "provisionally undisputed power to impose their will upon the rest of the world," even though traditional forms of international communication would have seemed appropriate in this instance.

The article continued:

> If it is desired to settle the Spitzbergen Question now, then at least a new Spitzbergen conference might have been convened. It is known that just before the outbreak of the war such a conference met at Christiania. It was opened on June 14, 1914 but adjourned after a few weeks with the intention of meeting again on February 1, 1915, this however, was prevented by the war which broke out in the meantime. With any new conference, Russia, of necessity would not participate; the remaining powers involved, England, Sweden, Norway, and Holland might be able again to discuss the question anew, if the new international idea is not designed to set up an *entre nous*. Why, however, was the invitation not sent out by the British Government instead of by a Supreme Council of the late belligerents? . . .
>
> It is a question here of more than a form, it is a question of the *hegemony* of a Power or of a group of Powers over the rest of the world that, as far as is known, has not yet been officially recognized by States that have been up till now sovereign States which, according to half a dozen official utterances of recent years will be placed upon a footing of equality.[45]

We do not in this case see overwhelming dominance by a single power, but we do see a group of victorious powers operating to solve a problem in which many states had an interest. Their role went beyond serving as intermediaries to facilitate the bargaining process among interested powers. They acted instead as third parties handing down the resolution to a long-standing controversy. The explanation for regime formation here is in large measure based on the exercise of power. That power, however, was neither hegemonic nor based on material resources. It was exercised by a group of states whose authority to act as surrogates for the interested parties was derived from their status as

---

45. Ibid.

victors in the war.[46] Once the Norwegian request to take up the Spits-bergen case had been approved, and after the treaty had been drafted, the legitimacy of the solution crafted by Great Britain, France, Italy, and the United States was difficult to counter.

Interest-Based Hypotheses

We believe a contract zone existed during the negotiations in 1910, 1912, and 1914, but various impediments to bargaining (the details of the proposed multilateral administrative system) that were present at the time of these meetings resulted in the failure of the parties to reach agreement. In the three earlier instances of negotiation, the parties were agreed on two important points: the *terra nullius* principle and the need for a multilateral administrative system that would provide law and order in an area where resource extraction and other activities collided. Although these principles provided the basis for an agreement, negotiations stalled over the substantive provisions of the administrative system.

The most problematic elements for the negotiators in 1910, 1912, and 1914 were the composition of the tripartite commission, the funding mechanism, and determination of which civil and criminal codes to apply in the archipelago.[47] These three issues were distributive in nature. The failure to reach agreement in the three early negotiating sessions appears to be attributable, at least in part, to the emphasis on distributive (positional) as opposed to integrative (productive) bargaining.

By the time of the negotiations in Paris in 1919–1920, new options appeared which had not previously been considered. World War I had intervened, and this time negotiations took place in the peace conference setting, using procedures unique to that environment. Representatives of the four Great Powers drafted the Spitsbergen Treaty on behalf of the other interested powers, although without the explicit

---

46. Historian Gordon A. Craig argues that the "Allies made no attempt to make sure that they retained enough military strength to impose their will upon recalcitrant enemies or friends. The pressure of public opinion at home led to a precipitous demobilization of American and British troops, beginning almost immediately after the armistice." Craig further argues that in addition to not providing for "possible military use," the Allies "did not have a clear, agreed procedure and agenda at the start of the conference" (*Europe since 1815* [New York: Holt, Rinehart, and Winston, 1964], 531).

47. Projet de Convention, Concernant le Spitsbergen, 1914, 850d.00/300, decimal file, 1910-29, vol. 4, RG 59, National Archives.

consent of either Russia or Germany. The treaty did not include the commitment to create a multinational or supranational organization, but both signatory and adhering nations would be governed by its provisions.

The contract zone that emerged in 1919 was based on new ideas on which the surrogate negotiators agreed: the long-held *terra nullius* principle, now seen to be impractical, should be dropped; the archipelago should become the territory of Norway; and the islands should not be used for military purposes. These new ideas were added to the earlier assumption that explicit rules should be built in to guarantee equal rights of access for resource (living and mineral) exploitation to nationals of signatory powers. The success of the bargaining process in 1919—in contrast to the earlier failures—is explained in part by some of the hypotheses discussed below.

As bargaining evolved in 1910 and in 1912 between Norway, Sweden, and Russia, and then in 1914 among the full range of interested powers, the veil of uncertainty was not thick. The draft treaties contained explicit articles incorporating the traditional open access with a complex tripartite administrative formula. In the prewar period, the attempts to translate the de facto *terra nullius* into a written agreement and to provide a specific system of governance did not bear fruit. We conclude that bargaining in the earlier meetings was at least in part distributive (because the parties differed over the provisions of an administrative system), although the continued commitment to the *terra nullius* principle demonstrates elements of integrative bargaining as well.

By the postwar period, changes had occurred: Russia was not a participant in the Paris Peace Conference, Germany was a defeated nation, and there was a new political climate in Europe. These new factors contributed to a thicker veil of uncertainty right from the start of negotiations in 1919. Furthermore, as the work of the Spitsbergen Commission proceeded, the Great Powers whose representatives were negotiating the treaty had no way of knowing exactly how administration by one country would affect the interests of their nationals. Although the negotiators may well have anticipated greater stability in law and order and more predictable conditions for investment in, and extraction of, living and mineral resources, it was not possible to spell out exactly the dividends over which to argue. Thus by the later stages of negotiation the veil of uncertainty became thick enough to permit agreement.

By agreeing to grant sovereignty to a single nation, the negotiating parties eliminated the need to make decisions on the details of administration and thereby reduced the opportunities for distributive bargaining. No longer was it necessary to determine how many and which states would sit on a governing commission, what laws would apply under what circumstances, and a myriad of other issues over which parties could at least try to calculate the costs and benefits to themselves. In 1919—when a single-sovereign solution eliminated the need for agreement on specific details—the bargaining became more integrative than it had been in the earlier meetings.

In the prewar negotiations over Spitsbergen, Norway, Sweden, and Russia—in part for reasons of historical commitment—were compelled to support equity for all nations in the form of open access (*terra nullius*), although they concurrently proposed a trilateral governing commission that appeared cumbersome and inefficient.

By 1919, it seems that equity and efficiency were intertwined. Norwegian administration of the islands was expected to be efficient, and granting sovereignty to a single nation (largely for the purpose of achieving administrative efficiency) was the major change from earlier proposals. Nonmilitarization would also be efficient: the Norwegian government would not need to place forces on Spitsbergen, and no country would have to worry, under normal circumstances, about foreign forces there. Apart from this, however, most of the rest of the provisions of the treaty spoke to equity. The treaty prohibited military use of the islands; it specified the rate of taxation on extracted resources, with tax revenues to be used only to cover administrative costs; the treaty and all rules emanating from it were to apply equally to Norwegians and to nationals of other states. Norway was to draft the mining regulations and submit them to all of the original signatories before they were implemented. In this way, nations that did not engage in the direct negotiations participated in, and had a kind of veto over, the development of the regulations.[48] In a parallel way, treaty ratifica-

---

48. "Norway undertakes to provide for territories specified in Article I mining regulations which, especially from the point of view of imposts, taxes or charges of any kind, and of general or particular labor conditions, shall exclude all privileges, monopolies or favours for the benefit of the State or of the nationals of any one of the High Contracting Parties, including Norway. . . .

"Three months before the date fixed for their coming into force, the draft mining regulations shall be communicated by the Norwegian Government to the Contracting Powers. If during this period one or more of the said Powers propose to modify these regulations before they are applied, such proposals shall be communicated by the Norwegian Government to the other Contracting Powers in order that they may be submitted to examination and the decision of a Commission composed of one representative of each of the said Powers. This Commission shall meet at the invitation of the Norwegian Government and shall come to a decision within a period of three months from the date of its first meeting. Its decision shall be taken by a majority" (Article IX of Spitsbergern Treaty). For the full text see Østreng, *Politics in High Latitudes*, 108–116.

tion too contained an equity element: for the treaty to enter into force, the original nine signatories were required to ratify the agreement (Article X). We view these provisions for equity as an evolution of the commitment to equal access, or *terra nullius*, translated into twentieth-century terms.

Provisions for equity (but not efficiency) figured in the agreements proposed in all of the negotiating sessions (unsuccessful as well as successful). The Spitsbergen case does not disprove the hypothesis that "availability of institutional options that participants can accept as equitable" is necessary for regime formation to succeed, but it does show that equity alone is not a sufficient condition for success.

For the Spitsbergen question there were no models to emulate or pre-existing regimes available for examination. There was, however, a record of previous failure in marrying *terra nullius* to a complex trilateral administration. There was also a reluctance to cancel the open access that had proved to be so beneficial to trappers, whalers, fishermen, miners, and tourists in the islands.

In the 1910–1914 period, as illustrated by the fifteen chapters and seventy-five articles of the draft convention of 1910, there were many points of negotiation. By contrast, the 1920 treaty that established the regime contains ten short articles. In 1919, the Spitsbergen Commission proposed solutions that were compelling in their simplicity: assign Norway the islands; subject Norway to some agreed-upon restrictions, limiting sovereignty, that would preserve relatively open access; allow opportunity for interested parties to register approval or make suggestions to the original mining regulations and the treaty itself; impose no real costs on treaty members, with the exception of Norway; and prohibit military bases on the islands and assert that they may never be used for warlike purposes.

Assignment of sovereignty to Norway, together with associated administrative duties and responsibilities, greatly simplified the 1920 regime by comparison with the earlier draft conventions. Creation of an administrative commission and definition of civil and criminal codes—all of which had been points of disagreement in the earlier negotiations—were no longer required. In assigning sovereignty to Norway, the Spitsbergen Commission found a salient solution, based on a long tradition of dependence on a single sovereign state for administration of a particular territory. What was innovative in this case was that the commission limited Norway's sovereignty and that Norway agreed to this limitation.

We find no specific exogenous shocks affecting the course of the Spitsbergen negotiations during either the prewar or postwar periods.

Although the international political environment changed dramatically because of the events of World War I, there was no sense of crisis over Spitsbergen that pushed the negotiators to solution of the question in 1919–1920. There were possible alternative forums for negotiating a treaty: another full conference of interested powers could have been called, or the question might have been referred to the anticipated League of Nations. A combination of power and leadership factors, rather than crisis, helps to explain why alternative forums were not used.

The Spitsbergen question had high priority on the foreign policy agenda of Norway—but not on the agendas of the other two northern powers—throughout the period studied. It did not become a high-priority item for the other interested powers that had participated in the 1914 conference. Although the Spitsbergen Commission in Paris articulated the solution to the question in 1919, the case was not a high-priority matter for France, Great Britain, Italy, or the United States, whose representatives sat on the commission.[49] In sum, the location of the item on foreign policy agendas in this instance was not uniformly high and does not explain the resolution of the question.

The alternative hypothesis states that "it is easier to form a regime when the subject matter is not high on the political agendas of the parties." In our early discussions, we also considered in conjunction with this hypothesis the number of interested parties and whether the stakes for them were high. There were only four surrogate powers on the Spitsbergen Commission, for them the stakes were not high (no country was prepared to go to war over this issue), and the question was not high on their respective political agendas. The surrogates were, however, encouraged by Norway.

In the case of the Spitsbergen Treaty, there does not appear to have been a trade-off between national interests and the common good. In this international regime, the Great Powers devised a formula to protect their own national interests (access for their nationals) and at the same time to promote the common good (resource protection and administrative stability). Of the regime's original signatories, only Norway, whose territory the archipelago became, incurred major costs. The Great Powers sacrificed nothing. Because this case did not present

---

49. Leaders—especially from the United States and France, as well as from Norway (neither a participant in the peace conference nor represented on the commission)—did use their individual positions to persuade the peace conference to take up the issue.

a situation of conflict between national interests and the common good, we can neither confirm nor disconfirm this hypothesis.

The Spitsbergen case was seen largely as a political question calling for a political solution. Although the treaty text does contain specific measures concerned with claims to land, administrative matters, telegraphy stations, protection and renewal of living resources, and taxation, provisions for some of the more technical and legal questions, such as mining regulations and claims settlement, were intentionally kept out of the treaty proper and dealt with in annexes. This simplification, in our view, facilitated the conclusion of the treaty. The technical competence of negotiators is barely relevant to the Spitsbergen case because at all of the conferences professional diplomats conducted the negotiations.[50]

Does the absence of an interested party impede regime formation? The three northern powers, called the "most interested powers," were present at the negotiations in 1910 and 1912 that yielded no solution to the Spitsbergen problem. All of the interested powers were present at the 1914 conference, which also yielded no definitive result. In 1919, all three of the most interested powers were absent from the formal peace conference, although Norway and Sweden were represented in Paris. Russia, excluded from the peace conference by virtue of the October 1917 Revolution and subsequent withdrawal from the war, was unable to participate during the meetings of the Spitsbergen Commission except to submit a note outlining the Russian point of view on the Spitsbergen question. This note was drafted by Russian diplomats in Paris representing the short-lived government of Admiral Alexander Kolchak. The leading powers, acting in a surrogate capacity, devised the regime. The commission members conducted all of the formal negotiations with participation in descending order by the Norwegian minister in Paris, the Swedish minister in Paris, and the one instance of Russian submission of a note.[51] This case tends to disconfirm the

---

50. Frederick K. Nielsen, the American representative on the Spitsbergen Commission, was the only one listed as a "technical delegate." He was in Paris as a member of the Technical Delegation of the American Commission to Negotiate the Peace.

51. The Russian diplomats, who several months later did not speak for the government in power in Russia, did not disagree in principle on Norwegian sovereignty for the islands but insisted on specific guarantees for Russian interests in the islands. See "Point de rue Russe," signed by Prince Lvoff, S. Sazonov, N. W. Tchaikovsky, and B. Maklakoff, 18 July 1919, Paris, *Recueil des Actes*, 181.5101/18, M820, Roll 180, National Archives.

hypothesis that all interested parties must participate in the negotiations in order to form an international regime.[52]

Is regime formation related to the availability of effective compliance mechanisms? The proposed compliance mechanisms for the 1910, 1912, and 1914 draft conventions were complex, involving an international commission made up of Russian, Swedish, and Norwegian members, and would have been virtually impossible to implement. In contrast, the compliance mechanisms proposed in 1919 were clear-cut and effective. Rather than creating a supranational or multilateral institution, the treaty provided for Norway to administer the islands, subject to certain limitations on Norwegian sovereignty. Because no institution was created to enforce compliance, none of the signatory powers except Norway incurred any costs. We argue that proposal of an administrative mechanism that was not only clear-cut but also efficient and fair was instrumental in facilitating closure on the Spitsbergen Treaty.

The Spitsbergen Treaty is an expression of agreement among specific nations that conferred upon Norway (without reservation) the ownership of the archipelago. The framers of this treaty anticipated that compliance questions would be most likely to arise over the way in which individual citizens of various nations respected the mining ordinances, or—on a broader scale—the way in which other nations respected the nonmilitarized status of the island group. In most of the treaty articles, Norway "undertakes" to provide administration or mining regulations in the treaty area. Because the treaty did not establish a separate international administrative structure, Norway essentially became responsible for the rule of law in the islands. We can speculate that had Russia been present in 1919, its representatives might not have agreed that Norwegian administration would provide an effective compliance

---

52. Of course, the absence of an interested party might, in some circumstances, prevent an agreement to create a regime from coming into being. In this case, the Spitsbergen Treaty did not require the signature of the absent interested party (the Soviet Union). In addition, the negotiators were careful to pay attention to Soviet interests, hoping for Soviet acceptance of the regime at a later date. In truth, however, the new Soviet Union badly needed diplomatic recognition (necessary for the reestablishment of trade) from its Scandinavian neighbor, Norway. Essentially, it was in exchange for such recognition that the Soviet Union, in 1924, dropped its opposition to the treaty, but because the Soviet Union was not recognized by the United States, Soviet adherence to the treaty was not possible until 1935. For additional discussion of the significance of Soviet absence from the peace conference, see note 40 above.

mechanism, but this does not detract from our finding that this case tends to confirm the hypothesis.[53]

What leadership elements appear to matter in the process of international regime formation? The three leaders who we believe were central to the development of the 1920 Spitsbergen Treaty were French Premier Georges Clémenceau, American Secretary of State Robert Lansing, and the Norwegian minister in Paris, Baron Fredrik Wedel-Jarlsberg.[54] Largely at their insistence, the Council of Heads of Delegations at the Paris Peace Conference established the Spitsbergen Commission which drafted the final treaty awarding the archipelago to Norway. What kinds of leadership operated in the emergence of the Spitsbergen Treaty? The picture we draw is of three resourceful men of different diplomatic and political ranks, interacting (perhaps from different motives) in the context of the Paris Peace Conference to solve one small problem among many larger ones.

Georges Clémenceau was, by most accounts, overwhelmingly interested in assuring the security of France in the postwar period. In his

---

53. The authors of this chapter differ on whether the compliance mechanisms were fair and efficient. Saguirian argues that the 1920 treaty failed to set up an international arrangement to regulate activities on the archipelago. Further, the treaty failed to introduce an appropriate mechanism to enforce compliance or to work out an effective procedure for settling disputes arising out of interpretation and application of its provisions. The states party to the treaty, therefore, have no practical way of regulating activities in the area covered by the treaty. They are also unable to bring pressure to bear on Norway should some fundamental difference of opinion arise with respect to an action taken in the archipelago. Because the Spitsbergen Treaty contains no specific provisions for such situations, any attempt made by state parties to influence Norway's legal, administrative, environmental, and other practical measures concerned with Spitsbergen may be formally objected to as encroachment on national sovereignty and interference in Norway's domestic affairs.

Singh believes that the allocation of the territory to Norway brought with it possibility for discussion and appeal through the Norwegian court system by nationals of other countries frequenting the islands. It appears that the treaty negotiators expected interaction to be between private individuals or companies on the one hand and the Norwegian administrative apparatus for the islands on the other. The emergence of state-run operations, such as Arktikugol (Soviet), may be regarded not as interaction at the intergovernmental level but rather as parallel to privately run enterprises vis-à-vis the Norwegian administration in the archipelago.

Both authors agree that the questions of regime effectiveness and fairness in operation, separate from the question here of international regime formation, are interesting and useful areas for additional study.

54. All three statesmen operated in the unique context of Paris in 1919. Clémenceau presided over the conference as premier of the host country, which, though devastated, had been on the winning side. Harold Nicolson's criticism of "shell-shocked" Paris as the site of negotiations serves to illustrate that the setting for deliberations was not a neutral one (*Peacemaking*, 76–77).

capacity as president of the peace conference, he worked unswervingly to that end, assuming that the victorious powers must settle war-related questions with an eye to limiting Germany's future war-making potential. Although he agreed to some compromises, he never strayed from his central purpose. In addition to distrust of Germany, Clémenceau was also very skeptical of the events in Russia.[55]

According to Norwegian minister Wedel-Jarlsberg, it was Clémenceau who agreed to place the non-war-related issue of Spitsbergen on the agenda of the Council of Heads of Delegations, with the result that the council created the Spitsbergen Commission to resolve the question of administration for the archipelago. How much did Clémenceau actually know about the Spitsbergen question? Did he really care?

In the absence of explicit documentation to show Clémenceau's motivations, we suggest the following: If Clémenceau knew the details of the Spitsbergen case, he could have believed that resolution of the question without Russian and German participation would be desirable. This theory is consistent with the pattern established at the peace conference: punishment for Germany for starting the war and punishment for Russia for dropping out of the war early and for subsequently falling into disorder. Clémenceau may also have believed that since smaller or neutral powers had been kept out of the decision-making circle in Paris, the Big Five could now—after the signing of the Treaty of Versailles—throw them a few crumbs by agreeing to hear some of their demands. Furthermore, it is possible that Clémenceau thought Wedel-Jarlsberg would be a less vocal proponent of compensation for shipping losses incurred by neutrals during the war if the Norwegians had the satisfaction of a Spitsbergen agreement.

Alternatively, if Clémenceau had no time for the details of the case, he might have acted out of the "right" of the Great Powers to allow the small countries their moment after the Treaty of Versailles was concluded on 28 June 1919. It is possible that Spitsbergen was swept into the conference purview along with other residual questions as a kind of epilogue. Clémenceau knew in July 1919 that with the heads of government returning home, these cases would be handled by the foreign ministers. This was a way of disposing of peripheral issues while still guaranteeing their ultimate outcome (since the foreign ministers of the

---

55. It could be said that Clémenceau literally put his life on the line at the Paris Peace Conference. An anarchist shot but did not kill him on 19 February 1919. Ten days later, with the bullet still lodged "safely" between his ribs, the elderly Clémenceau returned to his duties presiding over the peace conference. David Robin Watson, *Georges Clemenceau: A Political Biography* (New York: David McKay, 1976), 343.

Big Four would pass upon the cases). Whichever interpretation is correct, we find it significant that Clémenceau did not refuse Wedel-Jarlsberg's request, even though the Spitsbergen question had not arisen as a result of the war.[56]

We view Clémenceau's leadership as structural. As the premier of France and the president of the peace conference, he brought the influence of his government (as well as his own preferences) to bear on issues before the conference. Clémenceau definitely believed that the victorious powers—to the exclusion of the other (defeated or sidelined) interested powers—should drive the peace conference's decisions. He believed this was a matter of right: "The Five Great Powers [France, Great Britain, Italy, the United States, and Japan] . . . have lost dead and wounded that can be counted in millions, and if we had not the great question of the League of Nations before our eyes, perhaps we would have been led egoistically to consult no one but ourselves. Who can pretend that it would not have been our right?"[57] Clémenceau extended this right of the victorious but devastated powers to the Spitsbergen question, exercising his structural power to put the matter on the agenda in the summer of 1919. Without his leadership, the Spitsbergen question might have lingered, unresolved, until the League of Nations began to operate or been left to an even more uncertain fate.

Robert Lansing went to the Paris Peace Conference with considerable knowledge about the Spitsbergen question, having served as the counselor in the State Department before becoming secretary of state in 1915. Over the years he had handled documentation concerned with private American coal-mining activities in the area designated as *terra*

---

56. We have no explicit evidence to show that Clémenceau had a strong or particular interest in the Spitsbergen question. Trygve Mathisen (*Svalbard in International Politics*, 101–150) notes both the meetings between Clémenceau and Wedel-Jarlsberg and the energetic lobbying of Wedel-Jarlsberg in Paris. But we continue to seek information of just what led Clémenceau to place Spitsbergen on the conference agenda.

57. Hampden Jackson, *Clemenceau and the Third Republic* (London: English Universities Press, 1959), 193. Secretary of State Lansing also noted this phenomenon: the Allied powers proceeded, without authorization from the Plenary Conference, to form the Council of Ten composed of the "President and the British, French, and Italian Premiers with their Secretaries or Ministers of Foreign Affairs, and two Japanese delegates of Ambassadorial rank." The Council of Ten's membership was "identical with that of the Supreme War Council which controlled the armistices, their enforcement, and other military matters. It also assumed authority over the negotiations and proceedings of the Conference, though it was never authorized to do so by the body of delegates." When the Council of Four (heads of state of the Big Four) formed, it "was equally without a mandate from the conference. They (Clemenceau, Lloyd George, Orlando, and Wilson) assumed the authority and exercised it as a matter of right." See Robert Lansing, *The Peace Negotiations: A Personal Narrative* (Boston: Houghton Mifflin, 1921), 213–214.

nullius and as a result gave much thought to the concepts of sovereignty and *terra nullius*.

In 1911 Lansing drafted an internal State Department note entitled "Government over persons within *terra nullius*—General Principles." He argued that it was possible to have *political* sovereignty ("the exclusive exercise of sovereignty over particular persons without regard to the place of such exercise"), in contrast to the usual *territorial* sovereignty ("the exclusive exercise of sovereignty within a defined special sphere").[58] This reasoning, for Lansing, was the key to establishing administration over persons within *terra nullius*, or, in this case, Spitsbergen: "Since the right of sovereignty . . . is not uniformly dependent upon a special sphere for its exercise, a government can be properly established over persons within a defined territory, which forms no part of a recognized state, that is, no part of the special sphere of any established sovereignty."[59]

At the same time, Lansing also drafted a plan for State Department use in formulating objections to plans for Spitsbergen put forth by other governments and as a possible countertext in subsequent negotiations. Assuming that a trilateral commission would be central to the administration of Spitsbergen but that the *terra nullius* designation would be retained, Lansing provided for executive, legislative, and judicial powers to be exercised largely by this Spitsbergen Commission, although he allowed for the application of Norwegian laws in civil actions within the islands.[60]

---

58. Robert Lansing, "Note: Government over persons within terra nullius—General Principles," February 1911, 1, Longyear Spitzbergen Collection, Michigan Technical University Library Archives.

59. Ibid, 2. Lansing argued that government control was required in Spitsbergen to maintain public order and to regulate land-use and contractual relations between individuals. In his lawyerly manner, he spelled out the needs: "(1) *simplicity* of organization and procedure in the three necessary branches of government [legislative, executive, and judicial]; (2) an organization and procedure that will be *efficient* with the least expense; (3) an organization and procedure that will ensure *just and equitable treatment* to persons subject to such government, irrespective of their nationality, in their relations with one another; and (4) an organization and procedure that will give ample protection to persons and to established interests" (emphasis added).

60. Robert Lansing, "General Statement of Conventional Plan for Government in Spitzbergen," February 1911, 1. Although the American delegation took the Lansing draft to Christiania in 1914, it was unacceptable as a basis for discussion because it was not in French (the chief American delegate, William Collier, having failed to make a translation); it was based on Anglo-American principles of jurisprudence; and all other nations had used only the three-power *projets* as the basis for their consideration of the Spitzbergen question (Telegram, William Miller Collier and Ambassador Schmedeman to the Secretary of State, 18 June 1914, 850d.oo/288, decimal file, RG 59, National Archives).

Lansing advised the State Department that proposed international plans should recognize American private interests as long as American citizens were involved in private mining operations in the islands, and that the United States should take part in creating an international convention for the islands (which would not be the territory of any state). In 1915, however, the Americans sold their properties to a Norwegian mining consortium, and Lansing then felt free to advise that the islands should belong to Norway.

In advance of the Paris Peace Conference, Lansing wrote a long memorandum, intended as a guide for drafting instructions for future American commissioners at the expected peace negotiations. Twenty-eighth on his list of twenty-nine points was "The sovereignty of the archipelago of Spitzbergen to be granted to Norway."[61] Thus by 1919 Lansing could assure Wedel-Jarlsberg that the United States would support the idea of a Norwegian Spitsbergen.[62] In all likelihood, Lansing was also instrumental in securing a place for an American on the Spitsbergen Commission.

We think Lansing's leadership was structural: he represented one of the Big Five and used his authority in the State Department to instruct American delegates in Paris to support Norwegian demands.

Was Lansing's leadership also intellectual? He propounded a conclusion that gained acceptance among most of the interested powers, and he saw it incorporated into a treaty awarding the islands to Norway. He was not the only one advising Norwegian sovereignty, however, as the Norwegian press of the time indicates. The hypothesis concerned with intellectual leadership implies that the ideas of intellectual leaders are new, sweeping, and make breaks with past assumptions, as do the works of Karl Marx or John Maynard Keynes. Lansing provided explicit intellectual underpinnings for the development of the Spitsbergen Treaty, and his timely structural leadership was instrumental in reaching closure in 1919–1920.

Fredrik Wedel-Jarlsberg was convinced that Norway should take advantage of international negotiations going on in Paris in 1919. His recommendation was that Norway should seek compensation for neutral shipping losses in World War I, border adjustments with Russia along the Murmansk coast, a colony in Africa, and sovereignty over Spitsbergen. (His Foreign Ministry refused him permission to advocate an African colony.) Baron Wedel-Jarlsberg explained his view of Spits-

---

61. Lansing, *Peace Negotiations*, 196.

62. Cable, no. 2963, FW 741.5714/17, 27 August 1919, GRACNP, National Archives.

bergen: "The desire for Spitsbergen, in addition to being an old national goal, also had its roots in my thought that Norway should be self-sufficient in coal. During the war I saw commanders get their way by threatening reductions in coal supply, if one did not dance to their tune. I saw that by acquiring Spitsbergen with its large coalfields, we could have unlimited supply of coal for our shipping trade in the event of a new war."[63]

Wedel-Jarlsberg clearly believed in nothing ventured, nothing gained. He counseled that experience had taught him to set goals, open his eyes, and work with energy to obtain those goals.[64] He was confident enough, or brash enough, to take the initiative in making proposals and demands to other governments and then wait for instructions from his Foreign Ministry to affirm his actions.[65] Posted in Paris—where his mission was noted for its generous entertainment and fine cuisine—from 1906, Wedel-Jarlsberg had the advantage of personal acquaintance with French leaders and diplomats. He also knew Sir Arthur Balfour, the British foreign secretary, from an earlier posting as a representative of the government of Sweden/Norway in London. These contacts served him well in 1919.

Wedel-Jarlsberg held meetings with Secretary of State Lansing, as well as with representatives of the other powers on the Spitsbergen Commission. The British Foreign Office was reportedly split on the Spitsbergen question, with Lord Curzon in London opposing Norwegian sovereignty while Foreign Secretary Sir Arthur Balfour and the peace conference delegation in Paris supported Norwegian overtures. Wedel-Jarlsberg threatened to make it difficult for the British if His Majesty's government got the archipelago, and this may or may not have had an effect on the delegates in Paris.[66]

---

63. Wedel-Jarlsberg, *Reisen Gjennem Livet* (Oslo: Gyldendal, 1932), 370. All translations from Wedel-Jarlsberg's writing are by Elen C. Singh.

64. Ibid., 368.

65. Kjellberg notes, without explicit citation, that Norwegian foreign minister Gunnar Knudsen confided to Baron Ramel, Swedish minister in Oslo, that "Minister Wedel was an excellent man when he had exact instructions, but left on his own he was often erratic" ("Spitzberg Treaty," 73).

66. The Norwegian minister recounts the following exchange between himself and Arthur Balfour in Paris in 1919. Wedel-Jarlsberg assumed there was a mutual dislike between Lord Curzon and Balfour (Wedel-Jarlsberg, *Reisen Gjennem Livet*, 375–376):

Although memoirs can be self-serving, it is instructive to hear Wedel-Jarlsberg speak to the Spitsbergen Treaty development:

Throughout the spring and summer, 1919, I had much work to do, to apprise all the politicians, awaking and encouraging their interest in our demand. I had regular meetings with representatives from France, England, and America. The Peace Conference had so much to do that it was difficult to find an issue which did not fill the daily schedule of one or the other of these powers, and it was not until after I had met personally with Clémenceau that he used his very energetic and special intervention, and fortunately made them place the case on the agenda at the last minute.

Together with the French legal expert Fromageot, we quickly drafted a proposal for an international agreement concerning Spitsbergen's cession to Norway. A Commission with representatives from the interested countries was constituted and Fromageot's and my proposal regarding cession was substantially agreed upon with almost no changes by the end of September 1919.[67]

Wedel-Jarlsberg: Many times you have assured me that I could count on England's help to get Spitsbergen. I informed my Government of that and I am convinced that you still take that position.

Balfour: Naturally. I said it and I will stand by what I have said. When Norway wishes to have Spitsbergen, I will help them in every way.

Wedel-Jarlsberg: I am grateful that you say this, because the Norwegian Minister in London has just informed my Government that Lord Curzon is not of the same view.

Balfour: What is that? You have my assurances.

And, a few days after, all was arranged. Sometimes it is useful to make people angry.

Around the same time I had been with Balfour, the British Ambassador, Sir Charles Hardinge, had breakfast with us. I did not raise the Spitsbergen issue, but over coffee, he brought up the subject himself, and said according to what he had heard, that he was afraid what I wished would not be fulfilled because Curzon was against it. England wanted to have Spitsbergen for itself.

Wedel-Jarlsberg: Take it then. You have already taken so much after the war, you may as well get this also. We cannot take Spitsbergen by force, but we can deny any other state having easy possession. We can, for example, forbid shipping from Norway to Spitsbergen and forbid Norwegian citizens to work there. So please take it. If you can make something out of it, we cannot prevent it.

Hardinge: Those are strong words.

Wedel-Jarlsberg: Yes, they are. We may be a small nation, but we are a sovereign state.

Hardinge: It seems that you must absolutely have Spitsbergen. If I know you right, you will get it.

67. Ibid., 373. "Interested countries" here means those officially present at the peace conference.

We read Wedel-Jarlsberg's leadership as partly structural and as preponderantly entrepreneurial. As a structural leader he represented the Norwegian government in an official capacity in Paris, as well as on the few occasions when the Spitsbergen Commission granted him audience. His leverage as a structural leader derived largely from the obvious Norwegian presence in the islands, historical and actual. As an entrepreneurial leader, he was a successful advocate for, and promoter of, Norwegian interests, inside and outside of the conference environment and within diplomatic circles in Paris. The power he wielded was very personal, however, and he used his persuasive capacities to promote a Norwegian Spitsbergen, in some instances ahead of his government's instructions. He was clearly very fulfilled when he returned to Norway in the fall of 1919 with the draft Spitsbergen Treaty "in his pocket."[68] The reward for his efforts was public gratitude. In the case of Wedel-Jarlsberg, structural and entrepreneurial leadership occurred simultaneously.

Leadership, particularly in the person of Wedel-Jarlsberg, was more evident in 1919 than before. We can speculate that even in the absence of Lansing's support, the European powers, at Wedel-Jarlsberg's urging, might still have taken up the question and managed to conclude that Norwegian sovereignty was both practicable and acceptable after the failure record of the previous conferences.

To summarize, we can say that the conditions present in 1919 (and not earlier) that most appear to have contributed to success were as follows: absence of the Soviet Union, which changed the potential contract zone by removing one set of interests from the negotiations, making it easier to move away from the earlier tripartite commission solution; greater emphasis on integrative bargaining, including linkage of a Svalbard settlement, at least tacitly, with resolution of Swedish claims for the Aaland Islands; a clear or salient solution, the granting of sovereignty to Norway; inclusion of a modified equal access provision, reflecting in part the earlier *terra nullius* conditions; a more workable compliance mechanism than the cumbersome tripartite commission and detailed administrative provisions that characterized earlier negotiations; and a combination of entrepreneurial and structural leadership by several individuals. Thus the case tends to confirm that integrative bargaining and the presence of a veil of uncertainty, the availability of a salient solution as well as of compliance mechanisms that the parties regard as effective, and, finally, leadership are all conditions for success in regime formation. These interest-based factors—in combination with lessons learned from the earlier three failed

---

68. Ibid., 397.

efforts at devising an agreement for Spitsbergen and the unique situation at the peace conference, in which surrogates on the Spitsbergen Commission exercised authority as victorious states in World War I—begin to provide a fuller explanation of why this regime formed in 1919–1920 and not in 1910, 1912, or 1914.

Knowledge-Based Hypotheses

The assumptions found within the knowledge-based hypotheses turn on shared belief systems and mobilization of specific groups (sometimes including the scientific community) to push for the formation of international regimes.

We find no evidence of a new intellectual consensus among groups to drive the formation of the international regime under investigation here. The drafting of the Spitsbergen Treaty occurred at a time of considerable intellectual ferment, when an old world order appeared to be passing and the new one had not yet taken shape. There was an acknowledgment that the formulas for a regime which had been offered in the past were no longer adequate so the members of the Spitsbergen Commission, acting as surrogates for the interested parties, turned to a traditional device—national sovereignty—in place of the earlier *terra nullius*. The difference in 1919 was that the sovereignty was limited so as to reflect some of the open access that had obtained during the long, self-regulating *terra nullius* period. In that sense the Spitsbergen Treaty is a bridge, for which there were few models, between outright sovereignty and supranational institutions. We do not believe, however, that the conclusion of the Spitsbergen Treaty in 1920 signaled a new intellectual consensus in the Western world or elsewhere. It did successfully combine the idea of limited national sovereignty, over a defined area, with demilitarization.

Neither did an epistemic community—defined as a "cross-national advocacy group armed with convincing scientific data"—exist in the case of Svalbard. There were groups interested in scientific investigation (geographic societies, for example) that rose to the call of duty to document Dutch, British, Norwegian, and Swedish scientific and industrial activities in the islands, and they were much more apparent in 1919 than at the time of the earlier multinational negotiations.[69] Al-

69. See F. C. Weider, *The Dutch Discovery and Mapping of Spitsbergen: 1596–1829* (The Hague: Martinus Nijhoff, 1919); William C. Bruce, "Spitzbergen," *Sphere* 75 (28 December 1918): 242; *Spitsbergen's Mineral Wealth: Its Vital Importance to British Trade and Industry,*

though the surrogate negotiators were aware of the new publications, they cannot be said to have been markedly influenced by them. Among international legal experts, two Frenchmen, Louis Renault and Henri Fromageot, were already on record as favoring Norwegian sovereignty. Fromageot was personally acquainted with Minister Wedel-Jarlsberg before 1919, and he served as the legal expert in Paris for the Spitsbergen Commission. Here again, we see influence by individuals rather than by recognizable groups in the creation of the international regime for Spitsbergen. We therefore cannot confirm the two knowledge-based hypotheses with evidence from this case.

Contextual Factors

The 1910, 1912, and 1914 conferences on Spitsbergen did not succeed in creating a regime for administering the archipelago. An international regime that is still in force emerged from negotiations in 1919. In addition to the power- and interest-based conditions contributing to regime formation in 1919, were there larger world and national events (contextual factors), outside the controversy over Spitsbergen, that facilitated the agreement in 1919 and not before? Several significant developments occurred between 1914 and 1919: World War I began and ended, altering the power configurations in Europe and globally; the Russian Revolution began, and Russia withdrew from the conflict before the November 1918 Armistice, virtually assuring its nonparticipation in the Paris Peace Conference; the convocation of the conference brought forth unique procedures for handling international disputes that had not been available before the Great War; and Norwegian-Swedish relations, marked earlier by postpartition pique on the part of Sweden, improved. Each of these factors bears further examination.

As World War I consumed the brittle alliance structures in Europe, the power configuration most apparent by 1918 was the dichotomy between the victorious Allied and Associated Powers, on one hand, and

by a member of the 1918 expedition (London: Empire Printing Company, n.d.); R. N. Rudmose Brown, *Spitsbergen: An Account of Exploration, Hunting, the Mineral Riches and Future Potentialities of an Arctic Archipelago* (Philadelphia: J. B. Lippincott, 1920); William S. Bruce, "Spitsbergen Past and Present," *Journal of the Manchester Geographical Society*, parts 1 and 2 (London: Sherrot and Hughes, 1914); J. E. G. de Montmorency, "The International Legal Position of Spitsbergen," *Journal of Comparative Legislation and International Law* 18 (April 1918): 111–115; Adolf Hoel, "La Question du Spitsbergen: Une opinion norvégienne," *France-Scandinavie* 4 (1919); Charles Rabot, *A qui doit appartenir le Spitsberg?* (Paris: Masson et Cie, 1919); Charles Rabot, "The Norwegians in Spitsbergen," reprinted from *Geographical Review* 8 (October–November 1919); *Whitaker's Almanac* (1919).

the defeated Central Powers, on the other, with the Russians in an indeterminate condition as the Revolution played itself out.

The immediate postwar conditions allowed the victorious powers to conclude agreements in the context of peace-making which emasculated the former enemies, adjusted borders and populations, and assigned sovereignty in a manner unimaginable in 1914. Whereas military enforcement of the will of the victors might not have been possible because they too were demobilized and exhausted, the power vacuum created by the war was temporarily filled by the peace conference principals whose finished work was difficult to challenge.

The absence of Russia as an official participant in the peace conference, coupled with the difficulty of maintaining contact with successive new regimes under revolutionary conditions, provided an opportunity for the Big Five to tackle questions on which they had deferred to the Russians in the prewar period. Russia was in no practical position to prevent the formation of a regime to be applied to the Spitsbergen archipelago.

In the environment of the peace conference, under usual conditions, residual political questions were handled in a unique way. Issues were cleared with the Council of Heads of Delegations, which then appointed a commission to investigate and recommend resolution to the Supreme Council. This commission format was the one used for the Spitsbergen question, thus explaining why the negotiators were American, British, French, and Italian. The records of the peace conference do not show unqualified acceptance of all commission recommendations: after preliminary hearings, some questions—the Aaland Islands, for example—were deferred to the anticipated League of Nations, and the King-Crane Commission's recommendations were ignored. In the absence of initial strong objections in the Spitsbergen case, the surrogate negotiators were able to conclude an agreement that they regarded as both equitable and efficient. In addition, because the islands had been *terra nullius* before, no power lost or gained territory, as occurred in the transfer of colonial possessions from vanquished to victor. We might say that the control of the commission agenda by the victorious powers is an extension of our discussion of power after World War I. Nevertheless, the procedural effects should not be overlooked because the commission, or surrogate, format had not been in play during the prewar period.

By 1919, political relations between Norway and Sweden had improved with the lessening of Swedish irritation over the loss of Norway.[70] Both nations had been neutral in World War I, and both had common regional and domestic concerns to address once the conflict was over. Swedish leaders became more receptive to the demands for a Norwegian Spitsbergen, in part because of the decline in postpartition pique and in part because of personnel turnover in the Swedish Foreign Ministry. Although the three-way support mechanism suggested by the Swedish minister in Paris (where Sweden and Denmark would support Norway for Spitsbergen, Norway and Denmark would support Sweden for the Aaland Islands, and Sweden and Norway would support Denmark for North Schleswig) did not bear all the fruit hoped for, the sense that the Scandinavian countries could assist each other did help the Swedish decision makers accept the idea of Norwegian sovereignty for Spitsbergen.

Thus contextual factors were important in this case. It is not too much to say that changes in the world power structure, the domestic situation in Russia, the setting and procedures for negotiation, and the relations between Sweden and Norway had created a new stage onto which the players walked in 1919.

CONCLUSIONS

At the Paris Peace Conference the victorious powers from World War I determined the outcome as a function of dominant political will, but not necessarily because the Big Five could have undertaken the imposition of an economic or a military solution to the Spitsbergen issue. Thus we cannot confirm the existence of a hegemon or a hegemonic group in the Kindlebergian sense, but we do see a power configuration in which the victors (with members on the Spitsbergen Commission) acted as surrogates for the other interested powers. In this process, the Spitsbergen Commission members (British, French, Italian, and American) had the encouragement of the Norwegian government, the gradual approval of the Swedish government, and the mixed reactions (ranging from qualified acceptance in 1919 to direct opposition in 1920) from a series of Russian governments. The Spitsbergen Treaty entered into force initially without the membership of the USSR in 1925; it did adhere to the treaty in 1935.

Among the interest-based hypotheses, we can confirm that both structural and entrepreneurial leadership were important factors in the

---

70. Kjellberg, "Spitzberg Treaty."

crafting of this international regime in 1919. Especially in the context of the peace conference, the structural leadership of individuals, French Premier Georges Clémenceau, American Secretary of State Robert Lansing, and Norwegian Minister Baron Fredrik Wedel-Jarlsberg, prompted the formation of the special commission to determine the status of the archipelago. The surrogate powers on the Spitsbergen Commission finalized the treaty which recognized Norwegian sovereignty over the islands, while limiting that sovereignty to allow equal access for resource exploitation to nationals of signatory and adhering powers, thus preserving some of the spirit of the earlier *terra nullius* conditions. We think that Wedel-Jarlsberg exercised entrepreneurial leadership in his advocacy of a Norwegian Spitsbergen and that he was persuasive in the context of the diplomatic community in Paris, especially outside the official peace conference.

We argue that elements of equity and efficiency were intertwined or mixed, and that there was not a trade-off between these two elements of the agreement. We posit that the recognition of Norwegian sovereignty over Spitsbergen was a salient solution, with consensus among the negotiating parties in 1919, partly stemming from the equity content. Although the High Contracting Powers recognized Norwegian sovereignty over the archipelago, equal rights of access for resource exploitation for nationals of signatory and adhering powers applied, and original signatories had veto power over the initial Norwegian mining regulations. Since all signatories had to ratify for the treaty to enter into force, a kind of veto power also existed at the outset. The solution to recognize Norwegian sovereignty over the islands and therefore to allow the application of a single preexisting legal system was regarded as salient and efficient. Agreement on the Spitsbergen Treaty by the Spitsbergen Commission in 1919 was possible because the bargaining over the solution to the question was more integrative among the surrogates, whereas in 1910, 1912, and 1914 there had been more direct and more distributive bargaining among the interested powers themselves.

We believe that the veil of uncertainty was thick enough to facilitate agreement among the surrogate powers.

We cannot confirm the presence of an exogenous shock (specifically Spitsbergen-related) that influenced the perspectives of the negotiations in the prewar or the post–World War I periods.

We found elements of the common good, in that protection and management of resources are part of the provisions.[71] But the Spitsbergen

---

71. The Spitsbergen Treaty is an example of an early environmental treaty in which protection and renewal of living resources are clearly features of the regime.

Treaty is more an agreement of self-interested powers who crafted a so
lution that could benefit their nationals, with the administrative costs
borne only by Norway.

The Spitsbergen question was never uniformly high or low simultaneously on the foreign policy agendas of all of the interested powers (or
the surrogate powers). We cannot confirm the hypotheses regarding
placement on foreign policy agendas.

Additionally, we see the international regime for Spitsbergen as more
a political settlement than a technical agreement.[72] We also emphasize
that all interested powers did not participate in the final treaty formation, although (with the exception of Germany and Russia) the original
signatories did include all of the earlier interested powers. Thus the important element of surrogacy in this case demonstrates that all parties
need not participate in the initial regime formation.

Knowledge-based hypotheses, as currently understood, do not appear to assist in explaining the formation of this international regime.
We found no intellectual consensus or evolving epistemic communities
to focus on this issue.

Finally, we assert that contextual factors—the negotiations in 1919
taking place in Paris, dominated by the victorious powers, the use of
procedures unique to the peace conference, the gradual acquiescence
of Sweden to the practicality of a Norwegian Spitsbergen, the absence
of Germany from the commission's deliberations, and the uncertain relationship between the Western powers and Russia in 1919 (including
Russia's absence from the peace conference)—provided conditions in
which integrative bargaining successfully took place.

---

72. We worked with only a very general sense of what "technical" meant in our case.

Chapter Four

Polar Bears:
The Importance of Simplicity

Anne Fikkan, Gail Osherenko,
and Alexander Arikainen

The polar bear "is a charismatic animal: large, powerful, playful, fierce, human-like, *white* (white animals of almost any kind seem to hold a peculiar attraction for people), a survivor of the most vigorous environmental conditions in the world, *and* international in its distribution." Thus "the polar bear was an ideal 'ice breaker' for an international circumpolar agreement."[1] The polar bear regime, formalized in 1973 with the signing of the Agreement on the Conservation of Polar Bears, is unique in having brought together all five states with coastlines bordering the Arctic Ocean, even though they were divided by membership in competing military and strategic alliances. Four of them belonged to the North Atlantic Treaty Organization (NATO) and one to the Warsaw Pact. The superpowers saw in this beloved and apolitical animal an opportunity to lessen international tensions and improve circumpolar and international relations.

The polar bear regime is historically important in several ways. It is one of the first international regimes based on ecological princi-

---

1. C. R. Harington to Osherenko, 6 May 1991, p. 1. Harington was a Canadian delegate to the First International Scientific Meeting on the Polar Bear in 1965 and a member of the Polar Bear Specialist Group created in 1968. He is currently chief of the Paleobiology Division, Canadian Museum of Nature, Ottawa.

ples:[2] polar bears are viewed as part of ecosystems, and member states are called upon to protect these ecosystems as well as the bears.[3] The agreement establishing the regime is also the first international treaty to begin by prohibiting all hunting, capturing, and killing of a species and only then to enumerate specific exceptions to this prohibition.[4] Finally, this regime, like the fur seal regime (see Chapter 2), governs actions to be taken not only within the sovereign territory or jurisdiction of the parties but also in international waters. The establishment of common rules applicable in international waters, although not without precedent, was notable in an area where conflicting claims of national jurisdiction made reaching agreement more than normally difficult.

The signing of the final agreement in 1973 culminated a long process that resulted in the parties' subscribing to a strong prohibition regime eliminating the most significant threats at that time to healthy polar bear populations. Despite earlier progress among the five states in coordinating scientific research and management practices, several years of drafting and revising drafts, followed by three final days of negotiation in Oslo, were required to resolve the difficult issues still standing in the way of formalizing an international polar bear regime.

The regime for conservation of the polar bear is relatively simple. Under the terms of the agreement, membership is restricted to the five states with polar bear populations, sometimes called the ice states—Canada, Denmark/Greenland, Norway, the Soviet Union, and the United States— with the geographical limit defined by the range of the polar bear. To achieve joint gains, the five states coordinate their behavior in accord with

---

2. The Convention on Wetlands of International Importance Especially as Waterfowl Habitat (RAMSAR), which was signed on 2 February 1971 and entered into force on 21 December 1975, was the first international treaty concerned exclusively with habitat, although a few earlier treaties contained habitat protection provisions while concentrating (as did the polar bear regime) on species protection. The World Heritage Convention, adopted 16 November 1972 and entered into force 17 December 1975, aims to protect selected unique wildlife habitats and representative samples of the most important ecosystems. See Simon Lyster, *International Wildlife Law* (Cambridge: Grotius Publications, 1985), 183, 206, 237–238.

3. Agreement on the Conservation of Polar Bears, 27 United States Treaties 3918, Treaties and other International Acts Series 8409, Article II.

4. This approach was also used in the U.S. Marine Mammal Protection Act of 1972 and was employed in later national legislation in the United States and elsewhere. See, for example, the U.S. Endangered Species Act of 1973. There is, however, evidence of earlier use of the principle in Nordic states. See Resolution of the Nordic Council's Eleventh Session (1963), Nordisk Ministerrad, Copenhagen, concerning application of "the Finnish principle" to future changes in game law.

agreed-upon rules that apply within each party's jurisdiction as well as in international waters and that include regulation of trade across borders.

The members of the regime have agreed to coordinate national measures to protect the polar bear, to protect the ecosystems of which the polar bears are a part (especially denning and feeding sites and migration routes), and to manage polar bear populations "in accordance with sound conservation practices based on the best available scientific data" (Article II and Preamble). Specifically, all "taking" (defined as "hunting, killing and capturing") of polar bears is prohibited, with five exceptions: (1) for "*bona fide* scientific purposes"; (2) by the member states for conservation purposes; (3) "to prevent serious disturbance of the management of other living resources" (for example, seals); (4) "by local people using traditional methods in the exercise of their traditional rights and in accord with the laws of that Party" (the Native exemption); and (5) "wherever polar bears have or might have been subject to taking by traditional means by its [each country's] nationals" (Article III[1]). The regime rules generally prohibit the use of aircraft and large motorized vessels for taking polar bears and prohibit trade or traffic in polar bears (including parts or products) taken in violation of the rules.

The regime relies on each state to implement and comply with the agreement. The only ongoing organizational apparatus, the Polar Bear Specialist Group (PBSG) of the International Union for the Conservation of Nature and Natural Resources, is not mentioned in the agreement, although it plays an important role in coordination of scientific research, establishment of reliable data for management of polar bear populations, and exchange of information on management practices, all of which are regime functions.

The Agreement on the Conservation of Polar Bears—the legal formulation of regime rules—entered into force on 26 May 1976, ninety days after it was ratified by the third of the five member states.[5] Even before the final negotiations in November 1973, however, these member states had changed their domestic laws in accordance with the consensus among them that the polar bear needed further protection, especially from such unacceptable practices as hunting from planes and the use of set-guns. In addition, the Polar Bear Specialist Group had been holding regular meetings since 1968 to coordinate scientific research and exchange of data. Although unilateral acts and meetings of

5. The agreement entered into force ninety days after the third ratification, that of the Soviet Union on 26 February 1976. Canada ratified first on 16 December 1974, Norway second on 23 January 1975, the United States fourth on 1 November 1976, and Denmark last on 9 December 1977.

a nongovernmental scientific body do not bind states to future action, a fledgling international regime, to which the agreement gave formal expression, was already discernible by the early 1970s.

The agreement was to remain in force initially for five years. If not terminated at that time, it would continue in force indefinitely. Withdrawal by one party would require twelve months' written notice (Article X[7]). A unilateral withdrawal would not legally terminate the regime but might in practice lead to its demise. Rather than withdrawing, however, it is more likely that a party would request revision or amendment under Article X(6). At a meeting in 1981, five years after the date of ratification, the parties to the agreement formally approved its continuation, and no party has asked for withdrawal or revision.

To understand the difficulties and conflicts that arose during the negotiation process, it will be useful to examine the status of polar bear populations in each of the participating countries as well as the changes in national protection measures as pressure mounted for national and international action. In addition to state actors, the International Union for the Conservation of Nature and Natural Resources and the Polar Bear Specialist Group, as well as national and international advocacy organizations and the media, became players in the unfolding drama. Table 4.1 provides a chronology of some of the actions, both national and international, that were important to the achievement of the polar bear regime.

Table 4.1. Highlights in the history of the polar bear protection regime

1938	All-Russia Environmental Protection Society persuades the Northern Sea Route authority, Glavsevmorput, to prohibit hunting of polar bears from ships and at polar hydrometeorological stations.
1939	Norway establishes Kong Karls Land Polar Bear Reserve (Svalbard).
late 1940s–early 1950s	Glavsevmorput prohibits hunting of polar bears in additional areas of the Soviet Arctic.
1948	International Union for the Conservation of Nature and Natural Resources (IUCN) is created. It includes about 300 organizations (governmental and nongovernmental) from about 70 countries, plus 30 full government members.
1949	Government of Northwest Territories, Canada, restricts hunting of polar bears to holders of General Hunting License (most of these are Native people).
1950	Official regulations for Greenland prevent hunting from 1 June to 31 October throughout Greenland and completely protect females with cubs in Northeast and North Greenland.

Table 4.1.—continued

1954	Standing Committee on Arctic Animal Protection formed at General Assembly of IUCN.
21 November 1956	Russian Soviet Federated Socialist Republic (RSFSR) Council of Ministers adopts decree "On Protection of Arctic Animals," forbidding all hunting of polar bears in Arctic waters and on islands and shorelands bordering the Arctic Ocean (including by aboriginal people). Its effect is to reduce the take to about fifty bears annually.
January 1965	Officials from the United States Departments of State and the Interior suggest to a delegate of the Soviet Ministry of Foreign Trade the possibility of an international meeting on polar bears.
3 February 1965	Alaskan Senator E. L. Bartlett asks U.S. secretary of state to convene international meeting on polar bears, participants to be invited from all five circumpolar nations.
6–10 September 1965	First International Scientific Meeting on the Polar Bear held at University of Alaska, Fairbanks. Soviets propose that Arctic states initiate a five-year moratorium on polar bear taking.
29 January 1968	Establishment by IUCN of the Polar Bear Specialist Group (PBSG) composed of scientists from each of the five "polar bear" states, with first meeting in Morges, Switzerland.
July 1969	Federal-Provincial Administrative Committee for polar bear management established in Canada.
January 1970	Federal-Provincial Technical Committee for Polar Bear Research established in Canada.
1970	Authorization of Native-guided polar bear sport hunt in Canada and criticism of it by animal protection advocates.
February 1970	Second meeting of PBSG, beginning of negotiation of agreement. IUCN's Commission on Legislation prepares a draft "convention for research and/or conservation of the polar bear." Soviet scientists submit draft proposal recommending a five-year moratorium on all hunting of polar bears.
2 November 1971	Second draft convention is distributed to PBSG members.
late 1971–early 1972	IUCN prepares a draft protocol (Draft 1) that differs significantly from draft conventions.
January 1972	Soviets prepare a separate draft protocol, the result of discussions between Soviet Ministry of Agriculture and Soviet Foreign Ministry.
7–10 February 1972	Third meeting of PBSG in Morges. PBSG discusses IUCN draft documents—2 November 1971 convention and the draft protocol (Draft 1). PBSG agrees that a draft interim protocol should be presented to governments. PBSG also discusses the Soviet draft protocol, adopts seven resolutions incorporating some Soviet provisions, and calls on IUCN to prepare a protocol (Draft 2) and convention incorporating these provisions.

Table 4.1.—continued

August 1972	Special meeting of PBSG in Banff, British Columbia, to discuss second draft protocol (Draft 2).
October 1972	United States Congress passes the Marine Mammal Protection Act (MMPA) (Public Law 92-522), prohibiting all taking of marine mammals, including polar bears, but allowing exemption for Alaska Natives.
November 1972	IUCN prepares third draft protocol (Draft 3), called an interim agreement, and circulates it to five governments for comment. Work on the broader convention is set aside.
early 1973	Norway asked by IUCN to host final meeting on protocol.
March 1973	Four states (all except Soviet Union) agree to meet in Oslo 13–15 November 1973.
June 1973	Soviet Union sends comments and recommendations on Interim Agreement (Draft 3) to IUCN and proposes to make the draft interim agreement a permanent agreement.
June 1973	Norway establishes two nature reserves (including Kong Karls Land on Svalbard), three national parks, and fifteen bird sanctuaries, thereby protecting about half the area of Svalbard.
September 1973	IUCN prepares Draft 5 of agreement (Draft 3).
24 October 1973	Soviets finally receive explanations of changes incorporated in fourth draft (Draft 4) of agreement. These reflect Canadian, American, and Norwegian comments on the interim agreement (Draft 3).
August 1973	Norway places polar bears under total protection for a period of five years, banning all hunting except for scientific or other special purposes.
13–15 November 1973	Final negotiations on agreement (Oslo). Signing of Agreement on Conservation of Polar Bears by representatives of four polar bear nations (Soviet representatives at the meeting do not have authorization to sign).
1974	Greenland creates the world's largest national park— 270,271 square miles, or about one-third of Greenland's total area—where many species, including polar bears, are completely protected. Regulations concerning polar bear hunting elsewhere in Greenland are revised.
16 December 1974	Ratification of agreement by Canada.
23 January 1975	Ratification of agreement by Norway.
26 February 1976	Ratification of agreement by Soviet Union.
26 May 1976	Agreement on Conservation of Polar Bears enters into force (90 days after third ratification).
1 November 1976	Ratification of agreement by the United States.

Table 4.1.—continued

9 December 1977	Ratification of agreement by Denmark.
20–22 January 1981	Meeting at which five states agree to extend the agreement indefinitely.

Note: This chronology does not report all of the numerous changes in national laws and regulations pertaining to polar bears, either prior to or following the signing of the agreement.

Hunting practices in the United States and Norway first led to a call for international rules. In Alaska, aerial safaris caused a threefold increase in trophy harvesting of polar bears between 1945 and 1965. About thirty guide pairs, or sixty people, were involved in a half-million-dollar industry each spring. Lookouts in one plane would locate a bear by following its tracks on the ice and then slowly shepherd it to the place where a second plane, carrying the hunter, had landed. After the hunter shot the bear, the guides would skin it, and the hunter returned with his valuable trophy. This aerial trophy hunt, conducted largely in international waters, was responsible for 85 to 90 percent of the total take in Alaska.[6]

Although American scientists and game management authorities never regarded polar bears as "endangered," animal protection organizations argued that the species was threatened with extinction. These groups simultaneously pressured the United States Congress to stop the Alaskan trophy hunt, work toward an international polar bear agreement, and pass national legislation prohibiting the taking of any marine mammals, including polar bears.[7] In March 1972, hoping to avoid federal intervention, the Alaska Board of Game passed regulations halting the use of airplanes for hunting.[8] The regulations, which would have become effective in July 1972, never were put to the test.

---

6. Statement of Jack Lentfer, natural scientist, Alaska Department of Fish and Game, in "Moratorium on the Killing of Polar Bears," *Hearings before the Subcommittee on International Organizations and Movements of the Committee on Foreign Affairs, House of Representatives, on H.J. Res. 1179*, 92d Cong., 2d sess., 26 July 1972 (hereafter cited as *Hearings*); also Jack Lentfer, interview by Osherenko, Homer, Alaska, 18 February 1990; and Lentfer, "Polar Bear Management and Research in Alaska, 1962–72," in *Proceedings of the Fifth Working Meeting of the Polar Bear Specialist Group at Le Manoir, St-Prex, Switzerland*, supplemental paper no. 42 (Morges: IUCN Publications New Series, September 1976), 53. Proceedings of each of the PBSG's meetings were published by IUCN. They contain scientific papers presented at the meetings as well as brief status reports on polar bear populations and national conservation measures.

7. See *Hearings*, 45–69.

8. See Lentfer, "Polar Bear Management," in *Proceedings of the Fifth Working Meeting*, 53–55.

Congress terminated sport hunting of polar bears with passage of the Marine Mammal Protection Act (MMPA) (Public Law 92-522) in October 1972. This act placed a moratorium on hunting of all marine mammals by anyone except Alaska Natives, prohibited importation of polar bear hides, and made it illegal for persons under the jurisdiction of the United States to hunt on the high seas.

In Norway, extensive hunting by trappers, sealers, trophy hunters, and local Norwegians had by the end of the 1960s placed polar bears in danger of extinction in the Svalbard Archipelago, the only part of Norway in which polar bears are found.[9] In response, the Norwegian government banned the use of snowmobiles and airplanes for hunting polar bears in 1967 and in 1970 prohibited set-guns, banned hunting of cubs and sows with cubs, and introduced quotas.[10] In 1972 the Ministry for the Environment was established, which became the principal advocate for protection of polar bears on Svalbard and immediately achieved impressive results. During the first year of its existence, bears were placed under total protection for a period of five years, beginning with the 1973–1974 hunting season, banning all hunting except for scientific or other special purposes. Norwegians were also prohibited from trophy hunting in international waters. In June 1973, the government established three national parks, two nature reserves (including Kong Karls Land), and fifteen bird sanctuaries, protecting about half the archipelago.[11]

Canada is home to about half the polar bears in the world; this population has never been endangered. In some localities (such as Churchill, Manitoba), polar bears are so numerous that they have become a tourist attraction.[12] Canada has never permitted the use of air-

---

9. The major polar bear denning area, Kong Karls Land, has been protected as a polar bear reserve since 1939. In its act of 22 March 1957, the Norwegian Parliament passed a polar bear hunting law limiting the caliber of gun to be used, capture of live animals, and so on. No aboriginal people inhabit the Svalbard Archipelago. "Locals" in this connection means Norwegians living in settlements and at meteorological stations. The inhabitants of the Russian settlements of Pyramiden and Barentsburg were invited by the governor of Svalbard to take part in the quota allocation when this system was introduced in 1970 and were, upon application, given a quota of eighteen bears. This was not in accord with the existing Soviet law, however, which prohibited participation of Soviet nationals in the hunting of polar bears, and the procedure was not repeated.

10. *Kronprinsregentens resolusjon* of 26 June 1970. (In legal terms, this is the same as a royal decree, but made by the crown prince in the king's absence.)

11. *Kongelig resolusjon* (Royal Decree) of 1 June 1973. See also Ian Stirling, *Polar Bears* (Ann Arbor: University of Michigan Press, 1988), 191.

12. South of Churchill, in the Owl River denning area, about 100 to 150 cubs are born annually.

craft in polar bear hunting. By the late 1960s, provincial and territorial governments had primary responsibility for polar bear management, although the federal Canadian Wildlife Service played a significant role in research and management and provided a critical link with provincial and territorial agencies. The Canadian government was eager to protect the traditional right of Canada's indigenous people to hunt polar bears, and this was to become an important issue in regime negotiations.[13]

In 1968, the Northwest Territories game authorities set the first quotas on the number of bears that could be killed by each community in the Northwest Territories. The quotas were based on existing records of hides traded. Beginning in 1970 the Northwest Territories allowed part of the quota to be sold to sport hunters under conditions designed to benefit the local communities. Animal protection groups labeled this small and highly regulated Native-guided sport hunt "barbaric," "Canada's shame."[14] Despite the attention the issue received throughout the negotiations leading to the agreement, however, only a handful of settlements actually authorized such hunting at the time.[15] But because many of the skins taken by Natives had customarily been sold in the United States, Canada's efforts to protect traditional Native harvesting activities were dealt a blow in 1972 by the provision of the MMPA that prohibited the import of all polar bear products.

Denmark proper has no polar bears. The "Danish" polar bears are limited to Greenland, and some of them also inhabit adjacent areas in Canada. Although never endangered, the polar bear population in

---

13. In 1969 a Federal-Provincial Committee for polar bear research and management was established, followed shortly thereafter by creation of a Technical Committee comprised of biologists and researchers who study bears. See *Proceedings of the Second Working Meeting of Polar Bear Specialists, Morges, Switzerland, 2–4 February 1970*, supplementary paper no. 29 (Morges: IUCN Publication New Series, July 1970), 14; and George B. Kolenosky to Osherenko, 22 March 1991. See also Stirling, *Polar Bears*, 190–191.

14. Eric Dowd, " 'Sport' Hunting of Polar Bears in Canada Stirs Protests," *Christian Science Monitor*, 30 May 1973; Darryl Stewart, *Montreal Star*, 1 April 1971, p. Y. A few opponents of the Canadian sport hunt even went so far as to picket a gas station in Delaware whose owner had obtained a permit to hunt polar bears in Canada. See "Marchers Bear down on Arctic Gunner," *Wilmington Morning News*, 6 March 1972, p. 24.

15. In 1972–1973, five settlements allotted twenty-one tags to sport hunters; sixteen were purchased, and only nine hunters took polar bears. The following year, only three communities offered sport hunts (Ian Stirling and Pauline Smith, "Polar Bear Management Changes in Canada," in *Proceedings of Fifth Working Meeting*, 65). Smith and Jonkel attributed this drop to higher fur prices, which led Native hunters to prefer to hunt themselves and sell the skins. See P. A. Smith and C. J. Jonkel, Paper No. 6, "Resume of the Trade in Polar Bear Hides in Canada, 1973–74," in *Proceedings of the Fifth Working Meeting*, 72. The sport hunt has increased to about sixty licenses per year (Stirling to Osherenko in response to 5 March 1991 draft of this chapter, 30 April 1991).

Greenland was thought to have declined from 1920 until the 1960s, when it began to stabilize. As in Canada, the indigenous population of Greenland has traditionally harvested a sizable number of bears, but Greenland's approach to polar bear protection differs from Canada's insofar as Greenland has not created quotas. That the majority of polar bears in Greenland are taken by dog sleds, which are slow and generally have a short range, may prevent an uncontrolled increase in hunting pressure.[16] In addition, hunters are excluded from critical breeding areas, especially during the breeding season, and females and cubs are protected.

As early as 1937, the fur trade company Nanok established a closed season and prohibitions on killing females with cubs; these rules applied to the company's trappers operating in Northeast Greenland. Government regulations to control hunting in areas of northern and northeastern Greenland, although not for the more populated part of Greenland, were first put into effect in 1950. These regulations protected cubs and females with cubs throughout the year and all bears during the summer.[17] By 1956 regulations included restrictions on rifles and ammunition, prohibited hunting from aircraft, and forbade the use of poison, foot-traps, or spring guns.[18] By 1965, hunting was restricted to persons who had been resident for at least a year, and hunting from motorboats was prohibited in Melville Bay, one of three important breeding areas in Greenland.[19] In 1973, the Danish Parliament enacted legislation to prohibit hunting of polar bears from airplanes or snowmobiles throughout Greenland.[20]

In 1974, following the signing of the final international protection agreement, the Danish government, having consulted relevant Green-

16. Reported by Christian Vibe, Denmark's delegate to the PBSG, in *Proceedings of Second Working Meeting*, 15. Erik W. Born explains that there are no population studies (only harvest reports) for the period and therefore no data to document either decline or stabilization (Born to Osherenko, 9 April 1991).

17. Erik W. Born and A. Rosing-Asvid, "The Polar Bear (*Ursus maritimus*) in Greenland: A Review," *Technical Report, Greenland Home Rule Department for Wildlife Management*, no. 8 (1989): 126 [in Danish with English summary]. Sections on hunting regulations translated by Born, 9 April 1991, and appended to letter to Osherenko of the same date.

18. Regulations for Greenland (no. 218), 7 July 1956. Grønlands hjemmestyre, P.O. Box 2151, DK-1016, Copenhagen K, Denmark.

19. Christian Vibe, "The Polar Bear in Greenland," in *Proceedings of the First International Scientific Meeting on the Polar Bear, Fairbanks, 6–10 September 1965* (Washington, D.C.: U.S. Department of the Interior, Bureau of Sport Fisheries and Wildlife, and University of Alaska, 1966), 16–17.

20. Paragraph 4, Article 1, in Act no. 413 of 13 June 1973, "for Grønland om ervervsmæssigt fiskeri og fangst."

landic institutions, introduced even more stringent regulations restricting hunting to Greenland residents who had close social connections to a Greenland community and for whom hunting—as certified by their communities—was a main or secondary occupation.

In addition, also in 1974, the world's largest national park was created in Northeast Greenland—270,271 square miles, or about one-third of Greenland's total area—where many species, including polar bears, are completely protected. The only permitted hunting in the park is by members of local settlements within the area, using only dog sleds, kayaks, or skiffs.[21]

The Soviet Union made no scientific counts of the polar bear population, but there were numerous indications that in the Soviet Arctic the bear population had been declining since 1930, primarily because of ruthless hunting by non-Native residents as active development brought an increasing number of outsiders into the region. Between 1930 and the 1950s, man replaced the polar bear as the principal predator, hunting both the polar bear and its traditional prey, the seal. Furthermore, aboriginal hunters, who had formerly killed polar bears solely to meet the needs of their families and to feed their dogs, began to sell the increasingly valuable hides.[22]

In 1938, the All-Russia Environmental Protection Society persuaded the Northern Sea Route authority, Glavsevmorput, to prohibit hunting of polar bears from ships and, except in emergencies, at polar hydrometeorological stations. During the late 1940s and early 1950s, Glavsevmorput extended its prohibition of polar bear hunting to additional areas of the Soviet Arctic, and after 1956 all hunting of polar bears was prohibited in the Soviet Union.[23]

Before the polar bear regime was formed in 1973, no explicit regulations governed hunting of polar bears in international waters. Anyone with sufficient economic means and logistical support could hunt polar bears in waters outside the territorial limits of any state. Those advocating international agreement feared that the Japanese, who by 1972 were the major purchasers of polar bear hides offered at auction

---

21. Stirling, *Polar Bears*, 191; Born to Osherenko, 9 April, 1991.

22. There were no official statistics at that time covering the Soviet Arctic as a whole. Reports of bear sightings came from ice surveyors transiting between the Russian coast and the North Pole and from other eyewitnesses but not from scientific population surveys (Lentfer interview, 18 February 1990).

23. Savva M. Uspensky and L. K. Shaposhnikov, "Protection of Animal World of the Arctic," in *Priroda* (Nature), 21957, no. 6 [in Russian]; Savva M. Uspensky, *Polar Bear* (Moscow: Agropromizdat Publishers, 1989) [in Russian].

in Canada and Denmark, would mount their own ship-based hunting expeditions, as might some European companies.[24]

The IUCN, an international nongovernmental organization that has been called "the Red Cross of the conservation cause," played a significant role in furthering conservation measures among the polar bear states by providing a neutral base for scientist/managers (the Polar Bear Specialist Group) to meet to coordinate scientific research and discuss options for international protection measures.[25] The IUCN also played an active role as a third-party intermediary or facilitator: its Commission on Legislation prepared draft agreements, and its deputy director general acted as a go-between during the drafting and negotiation phases. The IUCN was not neutral, however. As the leading international conservation organization in the world, its representatives had an interest in promoting international cooperation as well as a continuing role for the IUCN. Also, the success or failure of its efforts to formalize an international regime would affect the organization's prestige and credibility.

The PBSG was created under the auspices of the IUCN's Survival Service Commission in January 1968. The group consisted of one or two polar bear scientists (many of whom also held positions as wildlife managers) from each of the five circumpolar states. The PBSG met at two-year intervals, primarily to report on progress of scientific research in the individual countries and to plan and coordinate future research. The group's work led to significant gains in the understanding of the population size, distribution, and migratory patterns of polar bears. The meetings were also partially devoted to developing recommendations to the IUCN and other agencies concerning national and international actions for the conservation of polar bears. As a result of increased research following an international meeting regarding polar bears in Fairbanks, Alaska, in 1965, and especially the coordination of scientific research provided through the PBSG, two crucial points became clear to the scientists and the public: first, that a significant number of polar bears cross international boundaries, and second, that sizable polar bear populations use areas outside the jurisdiction of any

---

24. In 1972, Japanese buyers purchased (at high prices) more than half the polar bear hides available at auctions in Canada and Denmark. See Smith and Jonkel, Paper No. 6, in *Proceedings of the Fifth Working Meeting*, 68–73.

25. The IUCN's members include both governmental and nongovernmental bodies. For a description of the IUCN, see *Hearings*, 53.

national government.[26] Individual nations had adopted significant conservation measures before November 1973, but it was these facts that underscored the need for an international regime and became a driving force toward its achievement.

"Are the days of the Arctic's king running out?" queried a March 1965 *New York Times Magazine* article.[27] This was one of the earliest examples of alarmist reporting of the polar bear situation in the American press. In late 1971 and 1972, a flurry of articles in the same vein by Lewis Regenstein, then national director of the Fund for Animals, appeared in important newspapers across the country, drawing congressional attention to the issue.[28] In 1972, and again in 1973, Congressman G. William Whitehurst of Virginia proposed a joint resolution calling for an international moratorium on the killing of polar bears.[29] At hearings on the resolution, Regenstein testified on the "desperate straits" and "grave danger of extinction" of the polar bear, and he continued to urge editorial writers to champion the cause.[30] On another front, in a 1971 lawsuit that went farther in the press than in the courts, Friends of Animals sued the secretary of the interior for failing to list the polar bear as an endangered species.[31]

Animal protectionists in the United States chose to highlight Russian

---

26. Thor Larsen, a member of the PBSG throughout the period leading to the formation of the regime, presents an account of the development of scientific knowledge throughout the same period in "Progress in Polar Bear Research and Conservation in the Arctic Nations," *Environmental Affairs* 4 (Spring 1975): 58–81.

27. Robert Murphy, "Are the Days of the Arctic's King Running Out?" *New York Times Magazine*, March 28, 1965.

28. The Fund for Animals, an animal protection organization headed by Cleveland Amory and based in New York, claimed thirty-five thousand members at the time. Regenstein is now director of the Interfaith Council for the Protection of Animals and Nature in Atlanta, Georgia, an affiliate of the Humane Society of the United States. For his articles see "The Polar Bear Nears Extinction," *Washington Post*, 21 October 1971, editorial page, reprinted as "Polar Bears in Peril," *Pacific Stars and Stripes*, 14 December 1971; "Polar Bear Is Threatened," *St. Paul Pioneer Press*, 31 October 1971, Focus section; "Is the Polar Bear Now Headed for Extinction," *San Francisco Chronicle and Examiner*, 31 October 1971, pp. 27–28; "Why the Polar Bear Faces Extinction," *New York Post*, 25 October 1971, p. 12. California congressman Jerome R. Waldie had Regenstein's *San Francisco Chronicle* article placed in the *Congressional Record*, 30 November 1971, pp. E 12730–12731.

29. H.J. Res. 1179. On 3 January 1973, Whitehurst introduced a similar resolution, H.J. Res. 118, and Senator Pell introduced a parallel but not identical resolution in the Senate, S. Res. 129, *Congressional Record*, 22 June 1973, p. S 11736.

30. Moratorium on the Killing of Polar Bears, *Hearings*, 24; Regenstein to Colman McCarthy, Editorial Department, *Washington Post*, 4 October 1971 (from Regenstein's files).

31. *Friends of Animals v. Morton* (Civil No. 1081-71, D.D.C.), filed on 2 June 1971, was on appeal in the D.C. Circuit (No. 72-1068) at the time of the congressional hearing in July 1972.

estimates that the population was as low as 5,000 and the designation as "endangered" in the IUCN's *Red Data Book of Rare and Endangered Species*. A frequently cited estimate set the worldwide population of polar bears at 10,000. Comparing these low population figures with the annual world harvest figure of 1,300 to 1,500 certainly suggested that the polar bear was severely threatened if not doomed.[32] The Soviet press made an important contribution as well when two Soviet scientists "portrayed the Soviet Union as the sole defender of the polar bear" in a letter published in *Selskaya Zhizn* (Rural life) that was summarized in the *New York Times*.[33]

The press in Norway also championed the polar bear. Coverage was generally balanced but sporadic and can be credited with bringing polar bear issues to the attention of the Norwegian public. On the archipelago of Svalbard, however, the situation was quite different. In the local newspaper *Svalbardposten*, hot conflicts surfaced repeatedly over a period of several years between the governor and hunters—as well as among miners in Longyearbyen, employees of the weather stations, trappers, and owners of safari vessels—concerning size and distribution of hunting quotas. Each of these groups, of course, wanted the others to reduce their hunting pressures in the face of declining bear populations.[34]

Concern for the polar bear coincided with other environmental causes. In the Arctic, public outcry arose over the possible environmental repercussion from oil discoveries at Prudhoe Bay and in Norway.[35] The campaigns against the harvest of baby seals off the coasts of Newfoundland and Labrador and use of the steel-jaw leghold trap drew thousands of new members to such organizations as Greenpeace and the International Fund for Animal Welfare. Environmental and animal protection groups were also successful in arousing worldwide opposi-

32. See Lewis Regenstein, "Why the Polar Bear Faces Extinction," *New York Post*, 25 October 1971, p. 12. Population estimates between 1959 and 1965 ranged from Savva Uspensky's low figure of 5,000–6,000 to 19,000 ("Notes: The Status of the Polar Bear," *Polar Record* 13 [September 1966]: 327).

33. The summary of the 18 March 1971 letter, which appeared in the *New York Times* on 21 March 1971, is reprinted in *Hearings*, 28-30. An abridged version appeared as Boris Bogdanov and Savva Uspensky, "The Russians Have Rescued Their Polar Bears from Extinction," *International Wildlife* (January–February 1972): 20.

34. The governor of Svalbard was the representative of the Norwegian authorities (*Sysselmannen*). See, for example, interview with Kjell Nygaard, *Svalbardposten*, 8 November 1969; also Governor Stephansen's reactions, ibid., 7 December 1969; and Stephansen further, ibid., 14 December 1969.

35. Olav Hjeljord, councillor for nature conservation at Svalbard, to *Svalbardposten*, 20 May 1972.

tion to commercial whaling. Although the polar bear campaign never drew as much attention as the other two, public concern for polar bears crescendoed as sentiment against killing of all wild animals mounted.[36]

Formation of the polar bear regime was not a linear process in which each step led to the next until the desired result was achieved. As is often true in the formation of international regimes, the process was considerably more complex. To facilitate understanding of the case, we have divided the history of this regime's creation into four phases (phases two and three overlap in time): (1) the initiative (1954–1968); (2) scientific coordination and drafting (1968–November 1973); (3) political preparations (October 1971–November 1973); and (4) final negotiations (13–15 November 1973). Table 4.2 provides an overview.

Table 4.2 Characteristics of the different phases of regime formation

Phases (duration)	Status	Level of actors	Progress toward regime
Initiative (14 years)	Discussions	Scientists/wildlife managers	Wish to cooperate
Scientific coordination and drafting (5 years)	Discussions	Scientists/managers Nongovernmental organizations	Draft convention/ draft protocol/ interim agreement
Political preparations (2 years)	Consultations	Diplomats Nongovernmental organizations	Draft agreement
Final negotiations (3 days)	Negotiations	Diplomats Nongovernmental organizations	Agreement

During the first phase (1954–1968), the IUCN urged protection and Russia led the response. The story began in 1948 with the creation of the IUCN, whose far-reaching membership included representatives from all five states with polar bear populations. At the IUCN General Assembly in Copenhagen in 1954, scientists from Denmark, Canada, Norway, Finland, and Sweden called attention to the decreases in Arctic animal populations. As a result, the General Assembly created a Standing Committee on Arctic Animal Protection. The assembly passed

---

36. For an account of the antisealing movement and the rise of Brian Davies's organization, the International Fund for Animal Welfare, see Alan Herscovici, *Second Nature: The Animal-Rights Controversy* (Montreal: CBC Enterprises, 1985), 74–78.

resolutions suggesting national action as well as international cooperation.[37]

The 1938 action of the All-Russia Environmental Protection Society
made the Soviet Union the first to institute measures for protection of
polar bears. The Commission on Environmental Protection[38] and the
Soviet Academy of Sciences Commission on the North, together with
experts from other institutions, prepared background documents in
support of a program for increased protection of animal populations in
the Soviet Arctic, which was approved at a session of the Council of
Ministers of the Russian Soviet Federated Socialist Republic (RSFSR).[39]

On 21 November 1956, the RSFSR Council of Ministers adopted a
decree "On Protection of Arctic Animals," protecting not only polar
bears but also walrus, reindeer, and birds in Arctic waters and on islands and shorelands bordering the Arctic Ocean. The decree also prohibited the aboriginal population from hunting polar bears, although it
did not ban aboriginal hunting of walrus or reindeer. The Main Hunting and Reserved Territories Authority (attached to the RSFSR Council
of Ministers) issued licenses for an annual catch of twelve to fifteen bear
cubs for zoos and circuses, the only permitted hunting. Poaching was
punishable by a fine ranging from two hundred to seven hundred ru-

---

37. The resolution creating the committee expressed hope that the countries involved
would cooperate in the preparation of an international convention for the protection of
Arctic marine mammals, specifically mentioning the walrus, hooded seal (*Cystophora cris-
tata*), and polar bear. For example, the assembly recommended that the Norwegian government limit hunting of polar bear cubs. See V. A. Chichvarin, "Fundamentals and
Character of International Law Concerning Protection of Arctic Nature," in *Problemy Sev-
era* (Problems of the North), vol. 2 (Moscow: Nauka, 1967) [in Russian]. In English, see
Kai Curry-Lindahl, "Conservation of Arctic Fauna and Its Habitats," *Polar Record* 17
(1975), 245.

38. Following the 1954 IUCN meeting, Soviet interest was heightened, in part because
the Chairman G. P. Dementiev and Learned Secretary L. K. Shaposhnikov of the Commission on Environmental Protection had participated in the 1954 meeting. Dementiev
headed the ornithology laboratory at Moscow State University, where he worked with
Savva M. Uspensky, who played a major role in polar bear protection in the USSR and in
creation of the international polar bear agreement. Shaposhnikov also was a colleague of
Uspensky's and coauthor with him of the *Priroda* article "Protection of Animal World of
the Arctic."

39. The entire Soviet Arctic zone was within the Russian Soviet Federated Socialist Republic. For Russian initiatives, see Alexander Arikainen, "Formation and Effectiveness of
International Polar Bear Agreement: A Soviet View" (unpublished paper prepared as
background for this chapter, 1990). The date of the approval by the Council of Ministers
is unknown.

bles.[40] The annual Soviet take was thus reduced to about fifty bears—the legal catch of cubs together with bears taken in self-defense and by poachers.[41]

Denmark, the only other state to take significant action following the IUCN resolutions, banned hunting of cubs and females with cubs in northern and northeastern Greenland and established a closed season throughout Greenland from the beginning of June to the end of August. In 1957 both Norway and Denmark (for Northeast Greenland) prohibited the use of traps and poison.[42] The IUCN resolutions had no effect on taking of polar bears in Alaska and Svalbard, in both of which the number of bears killed continued to increase.

Many Americans, however, found the Alaskan trophy hunting of polar bears to be unsportsmanlike and unethical. The absence of effective national rules to prohibit this hunting led to a demand for international cooperation. In 1961, the U.S. House of Representatives passed a resolution calling for a moratorium in the United States on the hunting of polar bears, but the Alaska delegation blocked its passage in the Senate. In 1965, as pressure continued to mount, U.S. senator E. L. Bartlett from Alaska asked Secretary of State Dean Rusk to convene "an international technical meeting concerning polar bears," with participants to be invited from all five circumpolar nations.[43] After informal inquiries suggested that there would be support among the ice states for such a meeting, formal invitations were extended to participate in the First International Meeting of Scientists on the Polar Bear, to be held at the University of Alaska in Fairbanks, 6–11 September 1965.[44]

Seventeen delegates representing the five polar bear states and two international nongovernmental organizations, IUCN and the Arc-

40. Uspensky and Shaposhnikov, "Protection of Animal World." Since 1974, the fine for poaching polar bears throughout the Soviet Union has been seven hundred rubles.

41. See Uspensky, *Polar Bears*, 139.

42. For Greenland, Regulations for Greenland (no. 218), 7 July 1956; for Norway, Act of 22 March 1957.

43. Senator E. L. Bartlett, letter to Secretary of State Dean Rusk of 3 February 1965, U.S. Department of State files. (The authors of this chapter obtained these files through a Freedom of Information Act request. The materials referred to here are unclassified and will be cited hereafter as USDOS files.) In January 1965, at a meeting with Soviet foreign trade and fisheries specialists, officials from the U.S. Department of State and the Department of the Interior had suggested the possibility of an international meeting on polar bears and had received an encouraging response.

44. USDOS files.

tic Institute of North America,[45] as well as twenty-seven observers, attended. This was the first opportunity scientists from the five polar bear countries had had to share information and identify needs for future research.[46] The delegates agreed to continue scientific cooperation through the exchange of data, and they accepted the IUCN as an appropriate forum for scientific cooperation.[47] They did not, however, set up an ongoing organization or agree to further meetings.

Following the 1965 meeting, Richard Cooley, a natural resource management expert from the University of Washington, obtained funding from the Conservation Foundation in the United States to try to organize another meeting.[48] His efforts resulted in the establishment and first meeting—in Morges, Switzerland, a neutral state—of the Polar Bear Specialist Group.[49]

One of the participants described that first meeting as "ticklish." Not all participants were persuaded that international action would be necessary, he explained, and everyone had tried to keep the meeting low key to ensure that the case for protection was well documented and the need for international cooperation substantiated before calling

---

45. The representative of the Arctic Institute of North America, a Canadian/American research and policy organization devoted to study of the Arctic, proposed that his institute perform the role of coordinator to arrange exchange of scientists and disseminate research and management findings to interested agencies, a role which IUCN eventually assumed. See "Unofficial Minutes of the First International Meeting on the Polar Bear," 17, University of Alaska Fairbanks Archives.

46. At the meeting, Jack Lentfer, who then worked for the Alaska Department of Fish and Game, posted a map showing where polar bears had been taken during American aerial hunts. The Soviets were particularly interested in this map, which confirmed that there had been hunting close to the Soviet coast (Lentfer interview, 18 February 1990).

47. "Statement of Accord," in *Proceedings of the First International Scientific Meeting*, 66.

48. See brief notice of grant to Cooley, who was then associate professor of geography and public affairs, University of Washington, Seattle, in *Alaska Sportsman* 32 (September 1966): 51. Russell Train, then president of the Conservation Foundation, continued to support international protection for polar bears as chairman of the (U.S.) President's Council on Environmental Quality.

49. Richard Cooley, telephone interview by Osherenko, 9 April 1989. Cooley traveled as a tourist to Moscow to arrange for the participation of Savva M. Uspensky in the PBSG and to confer with him about the creation of the group. He then served as the first technical secretary for the group. The Conservation Foundation, a nongovernmental organization based in Washington, D.C., also provided support for the first two meetings of the PBSG. Savva M. Uspensky was unanimously elected the first chairman of the PBSG. Cooley's account was corroborated by Lentfer interview, 18 February 1990, and by Savva M. Uspensky, interview by Osherenko, August 1989.

for action. Because discussion of possible protection measures occurred informally rather than during the actual meeting, no recommendations for protection resulted from this first PBSG meeting.[50]

The phase of scientific coordination and drafting lasted from 1968 to November 1973. The drafting of proposed agreements involved the IUCN and the PBSG. The IUCN, as an independent nongovernmental organization, was to prepare draft documents for discussion and act as a go-between for suggested changes in those documents. The PBSG, whose membership was made up of scientist/managers from the five polar bear countries, constituted the forum for discussion.

Before the second meeting of the Polar Bear Specialist Group in February 1970, the IUCN's Commission on Legislation prepared a draft of an "international convention for research and/or conservation of the polar bear." The members of the PBSG discussed the draft but decided to take no action on it beyond consultation with their national authorities before their third meeting, scheduled for February 1972.[51] They were also sensitive to the fact that states, provinces, and territories, not the federal governments of the United States and Canada, had jurisdiction to manage polar bears, and Denmark had to be sensitive to the role of Greenland.[52]

At the 1970 PBSG meeting, the Soviet scientists submitted their own draft proposal, in which they recommended a five-year moratorium on all hunting of polar bears. The Soviet document also raised the question of an international convention, although these words did not appear in the English version of the draft.[53] After a lengthy discussion of wording, the PBSG forwarded "An Appeal" to be sent by the IUCN to the governments of the four countries in which polar bear

---

50. Cooley interview, 9 April 1989.

51. *Polar Bears: Proceedings of the Third Working Meeting of the Polar Bear Specialist Group*, 7–10 February 1972, Morges, Switzerland, 7. We have been unable to find a copy of the first draft convention in any of the materials researched. Participants in the PBSG whom we interviewed disclosed, off the record, that the scientists were not very receptive to this first draft and focused later discussions on what they would like to see in an agreement rather than on the draft document. The formal report of the second working meeting notes that the PBSG considered "the possibility of an International Convention for Research and Management of the Polar Bear" and that the chairman of the IUCN's Commission on Legislation presented an outline of a framework for a convention (*Proceedings of the Second Working Meeting*, 7).

52. Andrew H. Macpherson to Osherenko, 15 March 1991, p. 2.

53. F. 54, op. 41, 393, d. 43, Archives of Russian Foreign Policy Documents, Moscow.

hunting continued, urging them to curtail harvests "drastically" for five years.[54]

The IUCN then prepared a revised draft convention, dated 2 November 1971, and distributed it to the members of the PBSG.[55] The key provisions called for management of polar bears by each national government so as not to exceed the maximum sustainable yield from each distinct population (Article I[3]), and required each state to control and regulate hunting, killing, and capture within its own territory and territorial waters as well as to extend regulation over its vessels and its nationals to the high seas (Article III[1 and 2]). The draft also proposed establishment of a Polar Bear Commission (Article V) that would be responsible for compliance with provisions of the convention and elaboration of recommendations for management (Article VI). Each of the participating states would have to submit to this commission an annual report detailing implementation measures taken that year (Article III[4]).

Within ten days of receiving this IUCN draft convention, the Soviet Ministry for Agriculture, the agency with jurisdiction to manage polar bears, sent the Soviet Foreign Ministry its own version of a convention. The two documents differed substantially. The Ministry for Agriculture proposed a ten-year moratorium on all commercial and sport hunting in regions where there is "single circulation of Arctic ice" (where transboundary movement of polar bears would be likely). Four exceptions were to be allowed, including one permitting hunting by Arctic aboriginal populations to satisfy their vital needs. Regulation by an international Polar Bear Conference would be instituted only after the ten-year moratorium period. The five ice states would be the sole parties to the proposed convention, and they would have the right, if they so chose, to extend the convention to include other Arctic animal species.[56]

54. The appeal appears in Appendix 9 of *Proceedings of the Second Working Meeting*, 85. A description of the discussion is found ibid., 7. Macpherson, a Canadian member of the PBSG at the time, recalled this second meeting as "quite difficult, with our Soviet colleagues proposing draconian measures which we saw in North America as quite unjustified, and we, in turn, asking for the evidence which would be necessary to support these, or alternatively the cooperation needed for us to visit their territories in search of the necessary evidence" (Macpherson, to Osherenko, 15 March, 1991; p. 2).

55. This draft was forwarded by the Soviet Ministry for Agriculture to the Legal Department of the Soviet Foreign Ministry early in December 1971. It is substantially the same as the draft "Convention on Conservation of Polar Bears," reprinted in *Hearings*, 20–22. Soviet scientists on the PBSG at the time were from the Ministry of Agriculture.

56. F. 54, op. 41, 393, d. 43, Archives of Russian Foreign Policy Documents.

The IUCN's next step was to prepare a "Polar Bear Protocol," apparently based, at least in part, on the Soviet draft convention. This draft protocol is also known as Draft One, the first in a series of five numbered drafts, together with their revisions, prepared by the IUCN in consultation with the PBSG and government officials before the final negotiating session in Oslo. It differs significantly from the IUCN's earlier draft conventions. Only the five states with polar bear stocks were to be parties to the protocol. Taking polar bears on the high seas would be prohibited (although with an exception for hunting "carried out as a continuation of the traditional rights of local people who depend on this resource"). The protocol would not create an international body for regulating or protecting the polar bear. Instead, each party would implement the ban on hunting on the high seas by regulating persons or vessels subject to its jurisdiction (Article I) and would "take appropriate action to protect polar bear denning and feeding areas within its own territory and to manage its own polar bear populations in consultation with other Contracting parties sharing these populations" (Article II).[57]

The IUCN apparently had in mind a two-tiered process. First, the five circumpolar states would sign a protocol to ban hunting on the high seas, including the polar ice pack. Each state, however, would continue to manage polar bear populations within its own territory and territorial waters. Later, a convention would be negotiated, open for signature by all states rather than just the five ice states, under which an international polar bear commission would be created to formulate and coordinate research, determine quotas and other regulations and restrictions, and recommend conservation measures to be implemented by the signatories.

The PBSG discussed both of the IUCN draft documents, the broader draft convention (2 November 1971) and the draft protocol, at its third meeting in Morges, 7–10 February 1972.[58] Participants agreed that a draft interim protocol should be presented to their governments for comment and possible signature, with the convention to follow later. The revised draft convention, however, was never formally submitted to the governments. PBSG members believed that five to ten years of additional re-

---

57. *Hearings*, 19.

58. The U.S. State Department had had no involvement in the drafting of these documents and was first informed of their existence in a message from the U.S. mission in Geneva. American members of the PBSG had provided copies to the Department of the Interior, and Lee Talbot, senior scientist with the (U.S.) President's Council on Environmental Quality, had received them as a member of the IUCN's Executive Board. See US-DOS files, 13 January 1972.

search would be needed to provide the scientific background for effective regulation of polar bear populations at the international level.[59]

A second draft of the protocol was discussed at a special meeting of the PBSG in Banff, Alberta, in September 1972. The IUCN circulated a third draft—called an interim agreement rather than a protocol—in early November 1972. Pending signature of this agreement, work on the draft convention was set aside. Before Christmas 1972, even though important issues remained unresolved, the deputy director of the IUCN asked Norway to host a "final meeting" on the proposed agreement.[60] By March all but the Soviets had agreed to a meeting in Oslo, 13–15 November 1973.

In late June 1973, the Soviets finally sent their comments on Draft Three, including eight specific recommendations, to both the IUCN and the Norwegian embassy in the Soviet Union. They received the next draft (Draft Four, dated July 1973), incorporating recommendations suggested by Canada, Norway, and the United States, in August 1973 but did not receive the specific comments explaining the suggested changes until 24 October, only three weeks before the Oslo meeting was scheduled to begin. Fearing that the Soviets might not agree to attend the meeting, Frank Nicholls, the IUCN deputy director, hastened to Moscow to talk with Soviet officials. The delegations from the other four states arrived in Oslo with the authority to sign an agreement, but the Soviet delegation, although it did attend, had not—understandably—had enough time to obtain such authorization. In any case, the Soviet Union was more cautious than the other states about indicating, in advance of the Oslo meeting, its readiness to sign an agreement.[61] This caution was natural, particularly with regard to the Arctic region, where politically sensitive issues had not yet been resolved.

During the third phase, political preparations (October 1971–November 1973), while the PBSG and IUCN were working on drafts of the agreement, diplomats in foreign ministries and environmental agencies were making political preparations, either on their own initiative or to prepare for the anticipated final agreement that would grow

---

59. *Proceedings of the Third Working Meeting*, 14. This PBSG meeting resulted in the adoption of seven resolutions. Significant among these were the first three, which dealt with plans for expanded and improved research activities, the fifth, which supported a ban on hunting polar bears on the high seas (with an exception for traditional subsistence hunting by local peoples), and the seventh, which recommended that the IUCN prepare the draft interim protocol for circulation and comment and asked for a new draft of the proposed convention. See *Hearings*, 4–6.

60. Reported in a telegram from American embassy in Oslo to secretary of state (and four other embassies), 14 February 1973, p. 2.

61. F. 54, op. 43, 415, d. 40, Archives of Russian Foreign Policy Documents.

out of the IUCN activities. Although in this case none of these diplomatic activities led to measurable results, they do indicate the importance of the polar bear issue on the national and international political agendas of the states involved.

In October 1971, the U.S. State Department prepared to initiate negotiation of an international convention for the conservation of polar bears, to be signed at the United Nations Conference on the Human Environment scheduled for Stockholm in June 1972.[62] This plan was dropped when the State Department learned of the work of the IUCN and PBSG already in progress. A second American initiative took place in September 1972, when Russell Train, chairman of the President's Council on Environmental Quality, proposed during a visit to Moscow that American and Soviet representatives sign the second draft protocol. Train was unable, however, to obtain permission from the U.S. State Department.[63] Finally, in January 1973, the United States proposed that final negotiation, including possible signing, of the interim agreement take place in February, when representatives of the five states would be in Washington, D.C., attending a conference to conclude an international Convention on Trade in Certain Species of Wild Fauna and Flora.[64] This suggestion did not appeal to the Soviets, however, who had not planned to send polar bear specialists to this meeting and

---

62. Telegram from the U.S. Department of State to its embassies in Copenhagen, Moscow, Oslo, and Ottawa, and to the U.S. missions in Geneva and the United Nations in New York, 28 October 1971; David Abshire, Assistant Secretary for Congressional Relations, to Hon. Thomas E. Morgan, Chairman, House Committee on Foreign Affairs, 26 July 1972, USDOS files.

63. Telegram from the U.S. Embassy in Moscow to the U.S. State Department and telegram in response, 19 September 1972, USDOS files. Train proposed signature of the IUCN protocol "or at a minimum announcement of intent to conclude [the] protocol" (p. 2 of telegram). The telegram announcing the State Department's refusal to permit signature of the protocol at that time offered three reasons: signature without consultation with the other three states would be seen as preemptive, especially in light of Canada's difficulties; broad U.S. clearance of certain language concerning jurisdiction would be necessary in light of Canada's jurisdictional claims; and principal State Department officials were not in Washington at the time (Telegram from Secretary of State to American Embassy in Moscow, 19 September 1972, ibid.).

64. Telegram from the U.S. State Department to its embassies in Copenhagen, Moscow, Oslo, and Ottawa, and to the U.S. mission in Geneva, 11 January 1973, ibid. The Washington conference led to the signing of the Convention on International Trade in Endangered Species of Flora and Fauna.

who were not yet prepared for final negotiations on the polar bear agreement.[65]

In November 1972, the Lands, Forest, and Wildlife Service within Environment Canada recommended to the Department of External Affairs that Canada likewise take the initiative and extend to the five polar bear states an invitation to a final negotiating session, including the signing of the as yet unconcluded agreement, to be held in Canada.[66] The suggestion was not followed up.

Following up on an initiative by Norwegian environment minister Olav Gjærevoll during the Stockholm Conference on the Human Environment, Norway was planning a general Arctic environment conference—of which the polar bear agreement should have been a part—for early spring 1973.[67] Although at the time there was some international political support for a broad agreement on protection of the Arctic environment, it did not prove to be enough to warrant expanding the talks, and the proposed conference did not take place.[68]

During the year preceding the final negotiations in Oslo in November 1973, the foreign ministries of the five ice states became more involved. Government policy makers consulted both bilaterally and multilaterally, particularly taking advantage of the chance to confer while in Washington in February 1973 for the conference on endangered species. In addition, Frank Nicholls consulted separately with the governments of each of the nations so as to incorporate their recommendations in the later drafts of the agreement. These consultations succeeded in resolving some of the outstanding differences and—more important—they made clear which conflicts remained and explored possible solutions.

Participants in the Oslo meeting confirm that the negotiations in the final phase (13–15 November 1973) were extremely difficult. Seven

---

65. Telegram from American Embassy Moscow to Secretary of State, 12 February 1973, ibid.

66. Files on Polar Bears, Department of External Affairs, Canada; Canadian Ministry of Environment to External Affairs, Ottawa, Ontario, 1 November 1972. Considerable prestige and publicity would accrue to the nation in which the signing ceremony was held, and Canadian officials probably thought they would also be better able to protect Canada's key interests if they were negotiating in their own country.

67. Environment Minister Olav Gjærevoll was a botanist with a special interest in Svalbard. The U.S. State Department's response to the Norwegian invitation to a Conference on Arctic Conservation was "forthcoming" but noncommittal. Telegram from the U.S. State Department to the Norwegian ministry of foreign affairs, USDOS, 13 February 1973.

68. Erik Lykke, interviews by Fikkan. Lykke headed the Norwegian delegation in Oslo.

members of the Polar Bear Specialist Group were present, not as a group but as scientific experts acting as members of their national delegations.[69] Representatives from the different foreign ministries were also present as members of the delegations. With the exception of Denmark, however, the delegations were not headed by foreign ministry representatives but by representatives of agencies with responsibility for managing polar bears, some of whom had met previously in connection with other environmental negotiations.[70] The atmosphere was both friendly and professional.[71]

What happened in Oslo is no less than astonishing. When the parties arrived, numerous issues remained unresolved, and some would be resolved in unanticipated ways. The agreement that emerged differed substantially from the five drafts that preceded it. The most prominent change was in the regime's geographic scope: coverage would include all areas frequented by polar bears, and the anticipated moratorium on hunting would apply within national territory as well as in international waters (with five exceptions). The parties also abandoned the idea of a later convention open to other nations, thus limiting the membership permanently to five. A less controversial but nonetheless substantial change introduced a management standard of "sound conservation practices based on the best available scientific data" (Article II).

The most difficult challenge for the negotiators, and the most time-consuming, was to define the geographical scope of the agreement. From the first draft documents, framed by the IUCN's Commission on Legislation, the parties became enmeshed in a jurisdictional mire.

The five drafts (including alterations) assumed that the five circumpolar states were working on an agreement to prohibit hunting of polar bears (with certain exceptions) in international waters but that management decisions within national jurisdictions would be left to the states. It was important from the outset, therefore, to define the boundary between national and international waters. By 1971, as nations were

---

69. This does not count John S. Tener of the Canadian Wildlife Service, who chaired PBSG meetings.

70. The heads of delegations were as follows: Canada, John S. Tener, Department of the Environment; Denmark, Jørgen Adamsen, Ministry of Foreign Affairs; Norway, Erik Lykke, Ministry of Environment (also elected chairman of the conference); Soviet Union, Ivan Anatoljevitsj Maksimov, Administration of Environment; United States, Curtis Bohlen, Department of the Interior. Each delegation had four to six members. Frank Nicholls (IUCN) participated and chaired the Working Committee.

71. Lykke, interviews by Fikkan, Oslo, Norway, 1 September 1989, and by Fikkan and Osherenko, Washington, D.C., April 1990; Curtis Bohlen, interview by Fikkan and Osherenko, Washington, D.C., April 1990; also, Thor Larsen, interview by Fikkan, 18 August 1989.

preparing for the Third Law of the Sea Conference (to be held in 1974 under the auspices of the United Nations) such jurisdictional lines had become controversial.[72] Even among the five ice states there were conflicting claims. Canada, in particular, had made claims to jurisdiction in Arctic waters that were disputed by the United States and others. No party was willing to risk establishing precedents in this agreement that might compromise its interests in the broader international negotiations. And some parties even hoped that language in the polar bear agreement would strengthen their position in the Law of the Sea negotiations. Thus the PBSG members found themselves embroiled in a debate over international legal questions that were part of a larger controversy. In the end, they did not succeed in agreeing on a definition.

When they arrived in Oslo, the negotiators were presented with a choice among the following descriptions of the area in which hunting, killing, and capture of polar bears would be prohibited: "on the high seas" (questioned by Canada); "beyond territorial waters" (Norway suggested this as an alternative; the United States and Denmark both preferred this alternative); "at sea beyond its territory" (also a Norwegian alternative); or "in the regions they [polar bears] inhabit" (Soviet proposal).[73] The first three choices did not have precise or agreed-upon definitions.

Additionally, the American delegation came to Oslo with the hope of delineating a large sanctuary in which polar bears would be protected, to include the most important polar bear denning areas as well as international waters. The sanctuary idea had been discussed among some of the negotiators as a possible solution during consultations preceding the final negotiations.[74] Delineating a sanctuary was acceptable to Canada and Norway but unacceptable to the Soviet Union.

---

72. Frank Nicholls confirms the importance of this issue at the Oslo meeting and notes that "it had bearing on the decision to limit agreement to the 'five' " (Nicholls, fax transmission to Osherenko, 17 March 1991). At the time, while the official state claims were by no means clear and consistent, various claims were being made based on the sector theory, historic claims, precedents for drawing baselines, the "sea-is-land" theory, and the archipelagic principle. See Kurt M. Shusterich, "International Jurisdictional Issues in the Arctic Ocean," in *United States Arctic Interests: The 1980s and 1990s*, ed. William E. Westermeyer and Kurt M. Shusterich (New York: Springer-Verlag, 1984), 240–267; E. J. Dosman, "The Northern Sovereignty Crisis, 1968–1970," in *The Arctic in Question*, ed. E. J. Dosman (Toronto: Oxford University Press, 1976), 34–57. Also see Donat Pharand, *Canada's Arctic Waters in International Law* (Cambridge: Cambridge University Press, 1988).

73. Draft Five, September 1973, of [Interim] Agreement on the Conservation of Polar Bears, 2 (Article I[1][a] and footnote to it listing alternatives), and Explanatory Note to Draft Five, point 16, 3.

74. Bohlen interview, April 1990; Lykke interviews, 1 September 1989 and April 1990.

After all the effort, however, the solution finally arrived at was as simple as it was ingenious: avoiding any definition of borders and protecting polar bears throughout their range, it allowed taking only "wherever polar bears have or might have been subject to taking by traditional means by [each country's] nationals" (Article III[1][e]). This solution satisfied the Soviet desire to extend the agreement to national territories and to avoid a later international convention open to other states. The Soviet proposal for the prohibition to apply "in the regions they inhabit" was the first suggestion to move away from a legalistic definition and to avoid the jurisdictional question.

All of the early drafts anticipated subsequent negotiation of an international convention, which would be open to accession by states other than the five. By limiting participation to the five polar bear states, the Soviets and Norwegians hoped to set an important precedent establishing a kind of club of five whose influence would dominate Arctic environmental and conservation affairs and possibly spill over in other issue areas. The Soviets made it clear that they did not support the idea of a later convention open to additional parties. The Soviets considered the agreement under negotiation, including only the five polar bear states, to be sufficient. At Oslo, this position was accepted by the other four states.[75]

The agreement contained no enforcement mechanisms should non-signatories violate the moratorium. The negotiators believed that as long as the regime included the two superpowers and applied to all the polar bear states, compliance in international waters would be universal.[76]

---

75. The Soviet definition of Arctic does not extend to subarctic areas. Government agencies and research institutes divide responsibility for the Arctic from the North, confining what is meant politically by Arctic to an area narrower than that encompassed by the definition of Arctic appearing in the U.S. Arctic Research and Policy Act of 1984, which encompasses the entire Bering Sea and the Aleutian chain and includes areas that are ecologically subarctic. The issue of membership in regimes dealing with the Arctic continues to be a contentious topic. The "Arctic club" has been expanded to eight, including Iceland, Sweden, and Finland, and it is these eight who, between 1989 and June 1991, participated in negotiations creating an Arctic environmental protection strategy. While Norway and the Soviet Union long argued that membership in regimes dealing with the Arctic should be limited to the five states with coastlines on the Arctic Ocean, the United States, in the context of negotiations to create an International Arctic Science Committee, successfully argued for membership to be open to all states with active interests or scientific programs in the Arctic region. See the Founding Articles for the International Arctic Science Committee, signed by representatives of national scientific organizations from each of the eight Arctic states, 28 August 1990, Resolute Bay, Canada, in *Arctic Research of the United States* 4 (Fall 1990): 67–69.

76. Lykke interviews, 1 September 1989 and April 1990; Bohlen interview, April 1990.

Although from the beginning the Soviet Union had wanted a total ban on the hunting of polar bears, all parties reached agreement at an early stage that indigenous people should be allowed to continue the hunting traditional to them.[77] The most serious conflict arose over whether Inuit and Indian settlements in Canada would be permitted to continue to use part of their quota for hunting by nonindigenous sportsmen with Native guides. Negotiators struggled over the language to use to describe the Native exemption from the ban on hunting. Before the Oslo meeting, the United States had proposed limiting its application to local people "who depend on this resource" and who "are not in the employment of other persons or under contract to deliver the skins or other parts of the animals to other persons."[78] Norway supported these proposals. Although the final compromise did not include these restrictions, neither did it explicitly permit Native-guided sport hunting. In the formal declaration accompanying its instrument of ratification, however, Canada indicated that its interpretation of the agreement term "traditional rights of local people" would permit the locally guided Canadian sport hunt to continue.[79]

All along, it had been the desire of the IUCN and the belief of the PBSG that the interim agreement would be succeeded by a convention that would be broader in scope (covering national territory as well as international waters) and open for all nations to sign. Accordingly, all of the drafts of the agreement had contained time-limit clauses in anticipation of negotiation of this convention. Just before the Oslo meeting, however, the Soviets indicated that they wanted a single, permanent agreement among only the five polar bear states, and the others agreed to this. Once ratified, the final agreement was to be in effect for five years; it would automatically become permanent after five years if none of the five states had requested termination (Article X[5]).[80]

What is most surprising about the Oslo meeting is that, although the

---

77. Objections to the terms "indigenous" or "aboriginal" people resulted in the use of the expression "local people" in even the earliest drafts, although everyone understood that this primarily referred to indigenous people.

78. Draft Five of [Interim] Agreement on the Conservation of Polar Bears, September 1973, together with Explanatory Notes 19 and 20 (IUCN). Transmitted with letter of Frank Nicholls (IUCN) to Henry Heymann (Department of State), 10 September 1973, USDOS files.

79. Paragraph 2 of Declaration, Canadian Minister of Foreign Affairs, ratification documents, deposited at Oslo, 16 December 1974, USDOS files, 20 December 1974.

80. By contrast, in Draft Five, the agreement would automatically terminate after five years unless the parties agreed to extend (or modify) it.

negotiators—with the exception of the Soviets—were authorized in advance to sign an agreement, they produced a document that differed substantially from the draft agreement brought to the meeting by the IUCN (Draft Five, dated September 1973). The reasons for the changes and an understanding of them form the basis of much of the analysis of regime formation that follows. The changes in participants from one phase to another (shown in Table 4.2) also contribute to an understanding of the formation of the polar bear regime. Details of the process of regime formation in this case will be elaborated further in the sections that follow as they help to support or refute the hypotheses being tested.

ANALYSIS AND HYPOTHESIS TESTING

In our search for an explanation for the formation of the polar bear regime, we turned to the theoretical literature and organized the analysis to follow the template of hypotheses (as summarized in Chapter 1). We found the theories based on power to be the least useful and the hypotheses stemming from interest-based theory to be the most useful. We view this case primarily as a result of bargaining among parties with different interests, but we could not dismiss the role of knowledge, consensus, and ideas in formation of the regime and particularly in determining much of its content. We also found contextual factors important, particularly in creating a "window of opportunity" in which the regime could emerge. Additionally, the case revealed useful information concerning the relative role of distinct groups of players and suggested additional hypotheses for future consideration that are neither covered in our template nor developed in the theoretical literature on regime formation.

Power-Based Hypotheses

In creating the polar bear regime, both of the superpowers, the Soviet Union and the United States, played active and important roles, but neither could be called a hegemon. Neither took advantage of its structural power to impose institutional arrangements favorable to itself on the others (coercive hegemony) or to supply institutional arrangements to others as public goods (benign hegemony). The United States played an active role at the bargaining table in Oslo, and the Soviet Union came to Oslo with explicit recommendations that drastically altered the final agreement. On balance, neither superpower was more influential than the other.

Although no party acted as a hegemon, various parties did exercise power in the negotiations. Canada, with the largest polar bear population and the largest polar bear territory, had a powerful position from which to assert its interests. Canada's power was based not on military might but primarily on the size of its polar bear population, its strong scientific program for the study of polar bears, and a good record of healthy polar bear populations. Canada's long history in Arctic affairs and its geographic dominance of the North American Arctic contribute to the self-confidence of Canadian representatives in Arctic affairs, if not to Canada's effective power in the Arctic. One member of the American delegation felt that the Canadians dominated the final negotiations.[81] The Canadians did succeed in satisfying their main concerns, to sanction a hunt by indigenous peoples and a Native-guided sport hunt (Article III) and to avoid language that could undermine Canada's position on jurisdictional questions in the forthcoming Law of the Sea negotiations.

Power and alliances also figured in formation of the regime. The discrepancy between the greater and lesser powers was an obstacle to bilateral agreements between nations with shared stocks of polar bears but encouraged multilateral agreements. For example, neither Denmark nor Norway, as small nations, felt comfortable entering into bilateral relations with the Soviet Union, and a basic concern for both of these lesser powers was that arrangements involving Greenland and Svalbard, respectively, be multilateral rather than bilateral. Thus for lesser powers, joining a multinational Arctic regime was possible whereas bilateral agreement with the Soviet Union was not.

The polar bear case—in which each of the five states had veto power—exemplifies the exact opposite of hegemony. Any state could have jettisoned an agreement, and each used this power (although not in the form of overt threats) to influence the outcome and to obtain provisions to promote its own interests. This mutual veto power,

---

81. Henry Heyman, telephone interview with Osherenko, Washington, D.C., December 1989. Heyman was one of two representatives of the U.S. State Department at the Oslo conference. He was largely responsible for dealing with the polar bear issue within the State Department. His sympathies lay more with the animal protection advocates than with the conservationist approach taken by the delegation head, Curtis Bohlen, who relied more on his own adviser within the Department of Interior, Richard Parsons, and on Frank Potter, a congressional assistant from the U.S. House of Representatives.

coupled with shared interests in protecting polar bears, combined to create ideal conditions for integrative bargaining. It is for this reason that interest-based theory offered a more accurate explanation for the formation of the polar bear regime. And we found that the role of power might be more fully explored under the interest-based hypothesis dealing with the role of individual leadership.

Interest-Based Hypotheses

The polar bear regime is a classic example of the proposition that regimes form when self-interested parties visualize a problem and its solution in contractarian terms and endeavor to coordinate to reap joint gains. The theory states that when a contract zone—or zone of agreement—exists or parties have reason to expect that one exists, the parties will bargain to reach a point of agreement within that contract zone so as to reap the available joint gains. Despite the presence of a contract zone, however, parties frequently fail to form international regimes: the presence of a contract zone is a necessary but not sufficient condition for reaching agreement. Therefore, we will examine several hypotheses from the interest-based theory section of our template in an attempt to identify some of the determinants of success (or failure) of institutional bargaining.

In this case, the five state actors expected to realize joint gains by coordinating their actions to conserve the polar bear population. The scientist/managers who formed the Polar Bear Specialist Group envisioned that this common goal would be likely to be facilitated first through coordination of their scientific work. Specifically, they would obtain better information on polar bear populations and population dynamics, knowledge they regarded as a necessary step toward improved management for conservation of polar bear stocks. Of course the interests of scientists differed somewhat from those of conservation organizations, sport hunting interests, government officials, and others involved in the process that led to formation of the regime. Nevertheless, the scientists and government agency representatives who served as delegates to the 1965 polar bear meeting in Fairbanks were able to agree to basic principles and goals: polar bears are an international circumpolar resource; until more precise management practices, based on research findings, can be applied, each of the nations with polar bear populations should take whatever steps it can to conserve its polar bears; cubs and females accompanied by cubs require protection throughout the year;[82] and international exchange of research and management information is essential.[83]

Despite a considerable base of agreement, parties differed on the scope, degree, duration, and timing of measures necessary for the conservation of polar bears, as well as on the specific issues identified earlier. One conservation group suggested an immediate 50 percent reduction in harvest for a five-year period beginning in 1965.[84] The Soviets were alone in seeking a complete moratorium on hunting. The Canadians—in part because estimates of their polar bear population were substantially higher than Soviet figures—actively opposed such drastic measures. Representatives of the Canadian government also opposed specific prohibitions sought by American delegates on hunting of females or cubs and on hunting in denning areas because in Canada such decisions are not within federal jurisdiction but rather under provincial authority. In addition, states had different views about the degree to which they were willing to turn over control of scientific research and management to an international decision-making process.

Having identified the availability of joint gains, but, at the same time, differing interests of the players, we turn next to an examination of ten of the twelve conditions set forth in Chapter 1 as necessary (or at least useful) for regime formation. As for the remaining two conditions, the case did not warrant lengthy discussion of the hypothesis that all key parties must be present at critical stages in the negotiations. The polar bear case supports this hypothesis because all of the key parties were present or participating during critical stages. The second condition,

---

82. Ironically, the final agreement did not include protection for cubs and females with cubs, which the American delegation wanted to include in the agreement. Instead, delegates to the Oslo conference adopted a separate Resolution on Special Protection Measures requesting the governments of the five states to ban completely the hunting of females with cubs and their cubs and to prohibit hunting of polar bears in denning areas during certain periods (Annex E of Summary Record of Conference to Prepare an Agreement on the Conservation of Polar Bears, Oslo, 13–15 November 1973).

Protection for female bears and cubs in Alaska has long been the subject of controversy. Protection in the Alaskan Beaufort Sea region was achieved only with the signing of an agreement between Canadian and Alaskan indigenous peoples of the Beaufort Sea in 1988 (Management Agreement for Polar Bears in the Southern Beaufort Sea, between Inuvialuit Game Council and North Slope Borough Fish and Game Management Committee, 28 January 1988). This agreement, however, does not cover the Chukchi polar bear population along the west coast of Alaska.

83. Statement of Accord approved by delegates to the 1965 Fairbanks meeting, in *Proceedings of the First International Scientific Meeting*, p. 66.

84. American Committee for International Wildlife Protection Submission, ibid., p. 64.

the relative roles of scientist/managers and diplomats, is considered in our discussion of knowledge-based theory.

The first hypothesis under interest-based theory asserts that institutional bargaining can succeed only when the prominence of integrative bargaining, the presence of a veil of uncertainty, or both make it easy for the parties to approach the problem under consideration in contractarian terms. In this case, the scope for integrative or productive bargaining as opposed to distributive bargaining was broad. A textual analysis of the draft documents leading to the final agreement reveals a gradual expansion of opportunities for mutual gains.[85] As issues arose, the parties found and explored new formulas leading to the creation of solutions not foreseen at the outset. In the process, they expanded both the geographic scope and the anticipated life of the agreement. An examination of Article III, especially, discloses a package of exemptions to the total ban on the taking of polar bears that demonstrates the pattern of adding specific provisions to meet particular interests of each state. The list includes, for example, an exemption permitting troublesome bears to be captured and transported away from Churchill (in Canada) and another allowing Norwegians to trap bears interfering with their seal harvest.[86] The major concerns of each of the five parties were addressed in the final agreement, resulting in each of the states' preferring creation of the regime to reaching no agreement.

We looked for attempts by the parties to broaden the range of issues in order to expand the pie (the possible range of distribution of gains and losses). There were two attempts to widen the scope of negotiations, the most notable being a Soviet initiative before the 1965 meeting in Fairbanks to include other Arctic species.[87] Similarly, shortly before invitations were extended to the 1973 meeting in Oslo, the Norwegian minister of environment proposed a broader agenda encompassing protection of Arctic ecosystems.[88]

The most significant change made in the agreement came during the final three days in Oslo. The parties deliberately moved away from any mention of jurisdiction—which would have entailed identifying the

---

85. See Jim Herbold, "The United States and the Polar Bear Agreement: The Representation of Interests in International Negotiations" (unpublished student paper, Dartmouth College, December 1989).

86. See Article III(1)(b) and (c), respectively.

87. See airgram from Department of State to American Embassy, Moscow, 12 April 1965, USDOS files.

88. This proposal by Environment Minister Gjærevoll was followed up later in 1973 by informal contacts to the respective embassies. The Soviets did not respond quickly, and when they finally did, they rejected broadening the scope of the negotiations.

boundaries between territorial seas and high seas—and intentionally increased the integrative nature of the bargaining process. Jurisdictional issues, on which costs and benefits can be readily calculated, are inherently distributional. Their removal from the negotiating table in Oslo was to prove crucial to formation of the regime.

Thus the case tends to confirm that the greater the opportunities for integrative (as opposed to distributive) bargaining, the greater the likelihood of success in regime formation.

The question of a veil of uncertainty concerns the degree to which the parties attempting to negotiate the terms of a regime were able to foresee the likely distribution of gains and losses that would result from alternative regime proposals or from the option of reaching no agreement. The hypothesis asserts that uncertainty or unpredictability increases the likelihood of reaching agreement on substantive provisions of international regimes because parties will tend to agree on "fair" formulations which all parties would find broadly acceptable regardless of the circumstances in which a particular party might find itself in the future.

Who would pay the costs and who would benefit from protecting polar bears? The answers to these questions are not obvious. Until 1972 (before restrictions on polar bear hunting were initiated for Svalbard and Alaska), participants might have thought that the Soviet Union—which had banned all hunting of polar bears since 1956—would be the biggest beneficiary of an international moratorium on the taking of bears, while Norway and the United States—because ending their sport hunting would involve the greatest policy changes—would pay the biggest costs. But there was always the possibility that the Soviets might want to resume hunting in the future,[89] in which case coordinated conservation would in the long term benefit the Americans and Norwegians as well. Toward the end of the negotiations the possibility of Japanese or Belgian entry into polar bear hunting also loomed on the horizon, increasing the uncertainty.

The degree of uncertainty in scientific knowledge about polar bear populations contributed substantially to the inability of negotiators to estimate the effects of various alternatives on their interests or even to be sure that reaching no agreement would seriously jeopardize the species or particular populations. By 1973, scientists believed that there were discrete populations of polar bears, but the theory of circumpolar migration of a single population had not been completely laid to rest,

---

89. Increased polar bear populations in the Russian Arctic have caused a renewed interest among Russians in reinstituting a limited hunt.

and the migration patterns and population dynamics had not been sufficiently studied to determine the degree of intermingling across national borders. The size of the total world polar bear population was
still undetermined as well. During the ten-year period preceding the
agreement, numbers ranged from the low Soviet estimate of five to ten
thousand bears to the high Canadian estimate of twenty thousand.[90]

Some delegates at the Oslo meeting expressed hope that this agreement would lead to further environmental cooperation, especially for
protection of Arctic ecosystems.[91] Although the hopes of many of the
signatories have undoubtedly been disappointed in this regard, that
they were only hopes, not fixed expectations, contributed to making
the bargaining process integrative rather than purely distributive.

In documenting the importance of a veil of uncertainty, we looked
for attempts to thicken the veil of uncertainty. In practice, in addition to
avoiding jurisdictional or distributional formulas, a negotiator wishing
to increase uncertainty might lengthen the time that the regime would
be expected to be in place and leave language resolving difficult issues
ambiguous or open to differing interpretations and later clarification.
Both of these devices were used in Oslo.

By making the agreement permanent and dropping language anticipating a later convention, the negotiators increased the length of time
this set of regime rules would operate. Moreover, the language of the
final agreement did not preclude future conflict. Considerable ambiguity remained for later interpretation. The most controversial section
(Article III[1][e]) could be interpreted to allow the parties almost free
reign over polar bear regulation within a wide area, subject of course to
the "sound conservation practices" principle stated in Article II. It
might also be interpreted as clearly defining a geographic area in which
states could allow only the four specific exemptions to the general prohibition on taking polar bears, the exceptions stated in subsections (a)
through (d). Curtis Bohlen, who headed the United States delegation in
Oslo, subscribes to the latter, more restrictive interpretation. Erik
Lykke, who headed the Norwegian delegation in Oslo, argues that the

90. See *Proceedings of the First, Second, and Third Working Meetings of the PBSG*, which record
the changing population estimates throughout the relevant period.

91. See, for example, statement of delegation leaders from the United States, the Soviet
Union, Norway, and Canada in documents from Oslo meeting. Bohlen explained (interview, April 1990) that shortly after the agreement, he was replaced in the Department of
the Interior and his successors had no interest in expanding Arctic environmental cooperation. Such hopes, in any case, were ongoing: in 1981, five years after ratification, the
Norwegians hosted a meeting to discuss continuation of the agreement as well as expansion of its scope.

broader interpretation is correct.[92] Leaving this ambiguity in the final agreement contributed significantly to uncertainty in an agreement intended to have long life.[93] The interpretation of Article III became important by 1990, when polar bear populations in Svalbard and Chukotka had recovered sufficiently that managers felt pressure to reinstitute hunting.[94]

Although the future brought more uncertainty than the negotiators of the regime anticipated, we still regard the formation of the polar bear regime as a classic case of integrative bargaining exhibiting characteristics typical of attempts to thicken the veil of uncertainty.

This case illustrates the proposition that negotiators are concerned not with the optimal allocation of scarce resources from an economic standpoint but with producing outcomes that all parties perceive as fair or as satisfying their key interests. Although the polar bear is a finite resource shared by several states, the negotiators in this case were able to avoid questions of allocation by applying a general (and therefore equitable) prohibition on hunting, with limited exceptions and restricted methods of harvest.

The parties subscribed to a strong prohibition regime to be applied equally to everyone, with exceptions to achieve fairness by accommodating each party's highest-priority concerns. These concerns included the Canadian and Danish need to protect subsistence hunting, the American interest in creating a large sanctuary in which no hunting would occur, Norway's need to be permitted to cull polar bear stocks as well as to protect seal rookeries, sealers, and scientists from polar bears, and the Soviet Union's desire for a broad prohibition on hunting with narrow exemptions applicable to national territory as well as international waters.[95]

---

92. Discussions among Lykke, Bohlen, Fikkan, and Osherenko, Washington, D.C., April 1990.

93. Michael J. Bean, a leading authority on wildlife law, highlighted this and other ambiguities in his discussion of the polar bear agreement in his book *The Evolution of National Wildlife Law* (New York: Praeger, 1983), 267, 268.

94. For Svalbard, Pål Prestrud, head of the Polar Division, Norwegian Ministry of Environment, interview by Fikkan, 25 May 1989. For Chukotka, Arikainen suggests that the polar bear is a natural resource that could be used to benefit the socioeconomic condition of the aboriginal population of the Soviet Arctic. See "Formation and Effectiveness of International Polar Bear Agreement," 22.

95. The number and percentage of polar bears taken by Norwegian sealers declined dramatically between 1955–1956, when sealers took 240 bears (68 percent of the Norwegian take) and 1965–1966, when sealers took only 3 bears (1 percent) (Proposal No. 6 (1974–75) to the Norwegian Parliament), available at Universitetsbiblioteket, Oslo.

By the time the negotiators arrived in Oslo, the most serious conflict remaining to be resolved was the question of jurisdiction, or definition of the geographical scope of the agreement. According to our hypothesis, "the existence of salient solutions (or focal points describable in simple terms) increases the probability of success in institutional bargaining." But was there a salient solution to the jurisdiction question?

Just before the Oslo meeting, the Soviets indicated that they wished the agreement under negotiation to be the final or permanent one. They suggested deletion of the word "interim" in the title and the omission of Article V (in Draft Five), which called for continued consultation for the purpose of concluding a broader convention. If there were to be no later convention, all polar bear habitat, within as well as beyond national borders, would have to be included in the agreement. The Soviet call for a permanent agreement opened the way for an ingenious and simple solution that made definition of jurisdictional boundaries unnecessary. The Soviets had proposed that the ban apply simply "to the area [polar bears] inhabit," a solution that avoided the jurisdictional problem but one that others must have found too intrusive on national sovereignty. The final solution, suggested by Curtis Bohlen, the head of the American delegation, first prohibits all taking of polar bears anywhere (without reference to geographic limits) but then allows for exceptions to apply "wherever polar bears have or might have been subject to taking by traditional means by [each country's] nationals" (Article III[1][e]). In this way, the solution draws the boundary between areas where polar bears may be hunted and where they may not be hunted by historical precedent rather than legalistic delimitation criteria. Until this simple solution was proposed, eliminating the need to use complicated legal terminology, the parties had struggled through the numerous drafts without real progress on the issue. Although there had been any number of possible jurisdictional solutions, four of which had been presented in the Nicholls drafts, all parties were able to accept the new and distinctive formula that suggested the parties not think in jurisdictional terms while at the same time preserving the national sovereignty of each party.

Bohlen remembers his proposal, which occurred to him after the first full day of negotiations in Oslo, as a way of circumventing the jurisdictional problem and at the same time satisfying the Americans' main concern to define a large polar bear sanctuary within which no hunting would occur.[96] Furthermore, the solution simultaneously extended the prohibition on hunting, killing, and capturing to the entire polar bear habitat, not only the high seas or international waters, while maintaining the authority of the five states to manage polar bears in the coastal waters and on land. It should have also seemed desirable to the Soviets, who had hoped for a complete moratorium on taking.

Canadians participating in the Oslo meeting were pleased with the new language, which, in their view, recognized Canada's right to manage the polar bear resource "in the waters between the arctic islands and in certain areas seaward of the perimeter of the Arctic Archipelago." They regarded this arrangement as "a form of recognition of Canada's sovereignty in and around the islands on a historical basis."[97] Canadian delegate Charles Jonkel wrote, "It sets a new precedent for national management of renewable (and other) resources in areas 'traditionally managed (or utilized)' by Canada. It will strongly support

---

96. Bohlen's understanding was that this would result in the limitation of hunting to an area roughly three miles from shore. He believed hunting by dog sled had been limited to that range. Hunting by snowmobile might (in his view) be even more circumscribed because hunters are less able to venture far onto the sea ice by snowmobile (Bohlen, interview April 1989, Washington, D.C.). Canadian negotiators believed that the traditional hunting area was much larger, extending from a few miles to many tens of miles seaward (External Affairs, File 67-10-5-4). In limited areas of the Arctic, hunting by dog sled traditionally extended up to seventy-five miles from shore, as was documented in *Inupiat Community of the Arctic Slope v. United States (ICAS II)*, 548 F. Supp. 182 (D. Ak. 1982), affirmed 746 F. 2d 570 (9th Cir. 1984).

Interestingly, there is no mention of a sanctuary in the agreement, and Norwegian delegates remember no further discussion of a sanctuary after the first day in Oslo. The American delegation, however, continued to describe the agreement as creating a polar bear sanctuary: "The agreement binds the Contracting Parties to the present minimal levels and methods of taking (virtually providing a sanctuary for polar bears, wherever they exist)." None of the other delegations viewed the agreement in this way, nor have any of the non-Americans we interviewed described the agreement as creating a sanctuary. Rather, delegates from other states remember the discussion of sanctuaries (opposed by the Soviets) as having been dropped.

Sanctuary to the Soviets and others suggested specific national designation of defined areas (such as preserves or reserves), which would receive special ecological protection. This of course might have required intrusion on the authority of national governments to manage such areas. In the fall of 1973, the Canadians, after having spoken to the Americans, proposed organizing working groups during the Oslo meeting, one purpose of which was to define the boundaries for polar bear sanctuaries. See Report of the United States Delegation, 16, 9, USDOS files; further information from Lykke interview, 1 September 1989.

97. Report of the Canadian Delegation to the Conference to Conclude an International Agreement on the Conservation of Polar Bears, Oslo, Norway, 13–15 November 1973, 4, Files of Department of External Affairs, Ottawa, Canada.

Canada's position in the Arctic Waters Pollution Prevention Act, and at the Law of the Sea Conference."[98]

The idea of devising a geographical limit based on historical practice rather than a legalistic description dramatically increased the probability of successful achievement of the agreement. But although it was a salient solution, it was neither clear nor unambiguous, and the possibility of later disputes over application and interpretation remained.

This case offers extensive data demonstrating that the perception of a crisis increases the probability of success in efforts to negotiate an international regime. It is more difficult, however, to see any link between this public perception of crisis and the specific content of the regime that was formed.

In the late 1960s and early 1970s, scientific and other conferences called attention to growing threats to the Arctic ecosystem.[99] These resulted in two moderate resolutions concerning polar bears[100] and material for articles in the popular press but generated no immediate impression of crisis. Animal protection organizations actively sought an international moratorium on polar bear taking and attracted considerable attention in the media. It was these groups, together with the media, that created a sense of crisis to which politicians and policy makers had to respond.

Scientists only belatedly contributed to the sense of urgency about the need for international action to protect the polar bear, basing their recommendations on newly acquired knowledge that separate stocks of polar bears cross national boundaries and that some of these stocks had

98. Charles J. Jonkel, "An Analysis of the Agreement on the Conservation of Polar Bears," 9, file 67-10-5-4, polar bears, dated 15 November 1973, Department of External Affairs, Canada. In addition, the solution opened the door for the Canadian interpretation that it could allow a sport hunt guided by local people using traditional methods in accord with Canadian law, thus satisfying one of the main obstacles to Canadian concurrence. For the future, this exemption appears to allow the parties to reinstitute sport hunting within the historically defined area so long as such hunting is "in accordance with sound conservation practices based on the best available scientific data" (Article II).

99. These included "Change in the North: People, Petroleum and Environment," held 24–27 August 1969 at the University of Alaska; an Arctic International Wildlife Conference held in Whitehorse, Yukon Territory, 21–22 October 1970; and an International Conference on Bear Research and Management in Calgary, Alberta, 6–9 November 1970, at which scientists from four of the five polar bear states presented research papers on polar bears.

100. The 1965 Conference on Polar Bears in Fairbanks had produced a detailed resolution. At the IUCN Conference on Productivity and Conservation in Northern Circumpolar Lands, 15–17 October 1969, participants included brief mention of polar bears in Resolution Three, concerned with threatened species.

declined dramatically.[101] Although summary reports of the first two PBSG meetings had appeared in the IUCN *Bulletin* and certain other journals with limited circulation, it was not until the 1972 meeting in Morges that the Polar Bear Specialist Group made a concerted effort to alert the public, issuing a detailed resolution recommending strong action and asking the IUCN to draft both a "protocol" and a permanent treaty.[102]

Neither the PBSG nor the key delegates to the Oslo meeting believed that the polar bear was in danger of extinction.[103] Stimulated by media attention, however, public and congressional support for international action acted as a continuous goad to the U.S. State Department and contributed to a favorable political environment in which to negotiate the terms of an international regime. Public pressure both in Canada and in the United States probably influenced Canada's willingness to participate in the negotiations, even though it did not alter the opposition of Canadian negotiators to any measures that would restrict Canada's right to continue to permit and manage limited hunting by sportsmen as well as by aboriginal peoples. On balance, we believe that a sense of crisis, or at least a sense of urgency, at once reported in and generated by the media, created an environment conducive to regime formation and increased the probability of success in the negotiations, although it did not greatly influence the content of the regime.

In Denmark and Canada, the need for polar bear protection was a nonissue because most polar bear populations there were not threatened. Furthermore, the formal relationship of federal government to local administrations and indigenous people was such that interference by federal authorities was not welcome. Once the issue was on the international agenda for consideration, however, Canada's strong interest

---

101. Thor Larsen reported in a scientific paper, "Progress in Polar Bear Research and Conservation," that the take of polar bears on Svalbard in a single year approached 20 percent of the population.

102. The PBSG recommended that the IUCN "strongly urge all nations concerned: (i) . . . to prohibit hunting of polar bears on the high seas including the area of the circumpolar pack ice, except where such hunting is carried out as a continuation of the traditional rights of local people who depend on this resource; and (ii) To protect, within their own territories, polar bear denning and feeding areas and to manage their own separate polar bear populations in consultation with other nations sharing these populations" (reprinted in *Hearings*, 6).

103. See Regenstein to Curtis Bohlen, 14 April 1972; and Nathaniel Reed, assistant secretary of the interior, to Regenstein, 5 December 1972, regarding the issue of whether polar bears were biologically an "endangered" species. Both letters are from Regenstein's files.

in protecting its autonomy in managing the largest polar bear populations gave the issue a higher profile, as did the Canadian interest in
halting Alaskan aerial hunts. Some Canadian scientists believed that an
international agreement "would add to the country's prestige in the international conservation community and make it easier to obtain fi-
nances for research purposes."[104] The long lag between Denmark's
signing and ratification of the agreement appears to indicate that the
issue was not a high-priority matter there.

In the Soviet Union, protection was largely provided by national measures enacted in 1956. But because some Soviet polar bear stocks are
part of populations shared by at least two other nations, international
protection became important. This issue was certainly on the national
agenda, although it was not a high priority.

Both Norway and the United States enacted strict protection measures
before the final negotiating meeting in Oslo. When Norway introduced
quotas in 1970, polar bears became a hot topic and eventually occupied
the attention of international policy makers. Norway instituted a five-year
moratorium in 1973 but viewed an international agreement as important
to make national protection measures permanent.[105] Although the Marine Mammal Protection Act guaranteed protection in the United States,
an international agreement provided the necessary constitutional authority for intervention by the federal government on states' rights in this area
of wildlife management (and further, it guaranteed protection in international waters).[106] Politically, the issue had become prominent in Norway
and the United States by 1972 but could hardly be characterized as a high
priority on their international agendas.

Table 4.3 shows how imperative formation of a treaty was for each of
the five countries at various stages in formation of the regime.

We attempted to determine the views of each state actor in Table 4.3,
but our efforts to do so highlighted a fundamental misconception embodied in the hypothesis—that a state actor is a single entity with a single viewpoint. The truth is that some of the domestic actors in each state
(with the exception of Denmark) viewed international protection of polar bears as a high priority, while others hardly noticed ongoing efforts

---

104. Kolenosky to Osherenko, 22 March 1991. See also Macpherson to Osherenko, 15
March 1991, 2–3.

105. Erik Lykke interview by Fikkan, 26 March 1990.

106. For a brief discussion of federal treaty-making power as a basis of federal intervention into an area of law left to the states in the U.S. Constitution, see Bean, *Evolution of
National Wildlife Law*, 19–20.

Table 4.3 Relative importance of issue to each state at different stages of regime formation

Phases	United States	Soviet Union	Canada	Denmark	Norway
Initiative	urgent	extremely urgent	not urgent	indifferent	somewhat urgent
Drafting	urgent	urgent	not urgent	not urgent	urgent
Political preparations	somewhat urgent	less urgent	somewhat urgent	not urgent	urgent
Final negotiations	somewhat urgent	less urgent	somewhat urgent	not urgent	urgent

to form a regime. Certain agencies, both governmental and nongovernmental, as well as individuals within them, saw the issue as a high priority, and their initiative and energy helped to push the policy makers. For example, individuals in the United States Council on Environmental Quality (CEQ)[107] appeared to place the polar bear agreement relatively high on their agendas but had to work through the State Department, to which the issue was not a high priority.

In summary, high priority on the national agendas of all of the parties was not a necessary factor in establishment of the polar bear regime. In some states, keeping an issue out of the limelight may enhance prospects for regime formation, but there is no basis for arguing that a low profile in all countries is necessary.

Those who shaped the polar bear regime dealt with the question of compliance by leaving implementation and enforcement to the individual states that were parties to the regime. As we have shown, the players in the formation of this regime placed a high premium on not intruding into the management systems of each state. This decentralized form of compliance appears to be the only mechanism ever seriously considered by the PBSG or the negotiators in Oslo. Reluctance of the parties to commit to ongoing expenses contributed to the decision not to create a secretariat or commission within the terms of the agreement.[108] The decentralized compliance mechanism was simple and probably effective because the negotiators (who were the leading spokesmen for stronger regulations to protect the species they studied or managed) welcomed

---

107. This council, created in 1970, advises the president and executive branch of the federal government on environmental issues and oversees implementation of the National Environmental Policy Act.

108. Frank Nicholls, fax letter to Osherenko, 22 March 1991, p. 2.

the added impetus of an international agreement to implement and maintain the regime rules.

The question of compliance in international waters by nonmember states remains. The decision to transform the interim agreement into a permanent treaty among the five circumpolar states, covering both international waters and national territory, raised a question of the international application of this treaty to nations other than the five signatories. Erik Lykke explained that the negotiators believed that other nations would not dare to violate an agreement entered into by the two superpowers.[109] In short, the five signatories made rules for the entire area—territory clearly beyond their own national sovereignty—and expected nonsignatories to comply. (This is not an uncommon practice in international relations. The fur seal regime's prohibition on pelagic sealing was intended to apply to all nations and in international waters, although only four nations were parties to it; see Chapter 2.) This assertion of the preeminence of the five polar bear states in the Arctic was very much in accord with the expressed interests of Norway,[110] Canada, and the Soviet Union.

Compliance is monitored in part through continuing scientific exchanges. Any significant drop in polar bear populations would be reported and discussed in the PBSG. The parties regarded the decentralized approach coupled with scientific exchanges to be an effective compliance mechanism. The lack of controversy over the question of compliance tends to confirm the hypothesis that the availability of compliance mechanisms which the parties regard as clear-cut and effective increases the probability of success in institutional bargaining. Although commentators have criticized the regime for its lack of enforcement mechanisms,[111] the parties have had strong incentives to implement and enforce the agreement, and compliance with it has been high.

In the polar bear case, we would have expected leadership to be most critical when negotiations had reached a dead end or stalemate, when existing ideas for resolution had been exhausted, and when energy was required to implement some emerging consensus. We particularly looked for leaders to appear following the 1954 IUCN meeting, following the 1965 Fairbanks meeting, when the parties engaged in discussions at the political level, and in Oslo when resolution of jurisdictional problems remaining in the draft agreement became imperative.

---

109. Lykke interview by Fikkan, 26 March 1990.

110. In Norway, "Arctic" is normally defined as the area north of the + 10° C average July isotherm. This excludes Iceland, Finland, and Sweden.

111. See Lyster, *International Wildlife Law*, 61; and Stirling, *Polar Bears*, 192.

No international activity followed the 1954 IUCN meeting. The first international action occurred when the United States, at the behest of Alaskan senator E. L. Bartlett, convened the Fairbanks meeting eleven years later. In the intervening years, despite the Soviet ban on polar bear hunting, the plight of polar bear populations only worsened as hunting increased dramatically both from the United States and in Norway. The failure to initiate international cooperation can be explained, at least in part, by a lack of leadership in that period.

At the other points, individual leaders did emerge, and they proved important to the forward movement of the regime formation process. The 1965 conference in Fairbanks adjourned without establishing mechanisms for following up on the consensus that had developed during the meeting. After that meeting, however, Richard Cooley—who had been in Fairbanks only as an observer—stepped into a leadership role. Cooley obtained funds from the Conservation Foundation and went to Moscow to secure the participation in future polar bear meetings of a prominent Soviet polar bear scientist who had not come to Fairbanks, Savva M. Uspensky. Uspensky advised Cooley to arrange a meeting of polar bear scientists in a neutral country under IUCN auspices and to invite him personally rather than inviting the Soviet government to send a delegation. A typical example of what Young terms an "entrepreneurial" leader, Cooley was further instrumental in arranging the first meeting of the PBSG and served as technical secretary at several of the early meetings.[112]

Despite extensive coordination on scientific matters, the PBSG was unable to find solutions to several of the critical conflicts impeding progress toward a polar bear agreement. Frank Nicholls, deputy director general of the IUCN from May 1970 through April 1976,[113] played a key role as a go-between, working to negotiate changes in the five successive drafts of the agreement. He also arranged to bring political leaders and scientific advisers together in Oslo in November 1973 for the meeting that resulted in the final resolution of outstanding issues, and he traveled to Moscow to ensure Soviet participation at that meeting. Normally, a third-party intermediary is not a stakeholder in the conflict and would not fit the definition of an entrepreneurial leader. Because of the peculiar character of the IUCN, however, Frank Nicholls engaged in a difficult balancing act, filling the role of facilita-

---

112. Cooley interview, 9 April 1989; Uspensky interview, August 1989. See also Stirling, *Polar Bears*, 189.

113. Nicholls is an Australian with a background in science (physics and chemistry). He had worked in research management before his affiliation with the IUCN.

tor (and occasionally mediator) while at the same time behaving like an entrepreneurial leader representing an organization with a strong interest in building a body of international law relating to conservation. Although his role approximated that of Mostafa Tolba in the ozone case (see Chapter 5), he did not advocate preferences of his own organization but adopted a role more fitting for a third-party intermediary. Nicholls reports that close links between the IUCN and several influential senior Soviet scientists who shared an interest in conservation (including an IUCN vice-president and the chairman of one of the IUCN commissions) facilitated the IUCN's role.[114]

In November 1973 in Oslo, Norwegian delegate Erik Lykke organized and chaired the final three-day session. He was able to steer the meeting to a successful conclusion despite the lack of agreement beforehand either on procedures or on certain substantive issues. And during the Oslo meeting, Curtis Bohlen, head of the U.S. delegation, found the solution to the jurisdictional problem and achieved its acceptance.

Judging from interviews, the observations of other participants, and our personal knowledge, Cooley, Uspensky, Nicholls, Lykke, and Bohlen all fit the description of an entrepreneurial leader, exercising entrepreneurial skills at different times. None can be characterized as an intellectual leader in the context of this case. We have highlighted the role of certain individuals here only to illustrate and examine the hypothesis at hand; we do not mean by singling out these few to leave the impression that they were the only people to exercise leadership throughout the long period of regime formation. Much of the written record is too scanty to determine when credit should be accorded to particular individuals.

Only Bohlen performed a leadership function as an official representative of a powerful nation. Although others at the negotiating table may have deferred to him because of the structural power of the United States, he also had to exercise caution so as not to appear to abuse that power. Lykke, by contrast, could use his role as the representative of a less powerful nation to guide the Oslo meeting to closure. Nicholls probably chose Norway to host this final meeting anticipating that Lykke would play this role. Thus a combination of structural and entrepreneurial leadership activities facilitated formation of the polar bear regime.

Although Young confines his discussion of leadership to individuals, the Polar Bear Specialist Group—by providing ideas to define the

---

114. Nicholls, fax letter to Osherenko, 17 March 1991.

agenda and the issues to be included in the agreement—played a role resembling Young's description of an intellectual leader. This international regime was one of the first to adopt an ecological approach, and the members of the PBSG individually and as a group developed the scientific knowledge underlying it. The group's role, however, is better described as knowledge-based influence (which will be dealt with in the next section) than as leadership.

Efforts to form a polar bear regime would probably have failed in the absence of individual leaders at critical junctures in the four-step process of regime formation. This case tends to confirm that leadership is a necessary, though not sufficient, condition for regime formation. Furthermore, this case demonstrates that more than one leader can function at the same time or as part of the same process. A condition for success in this context may be that the goals of the different leaders must be compatible.

Does regime formation require that the parties share some concept of the common good and elevate this over national interests or current national policies? To explore this question, it is useful to examine the interests and values of individuals as well as states. In this case, most of the players involved in negotiation of the regime had both personal and national interests at stake. Some derived a significant portion of their income from scientific research on polar bears and thus would benefit from enhanced cooperation, particularly in research. Some were managers or policy makers whose reputations and incomes would be affected by their success in forming a regime. We found, however, that most—perhaps all—of them cared deeply about the welfare of both polar bears and the Arctic environment. Members of the Polar Bear Specialist Group appear to have been motivated first and foremost by their strong desire to protect the polar bears.[115] Likewise, those more directly involved in the policy making, such as Lykke and Bohlen, were motivated in their career choices not purely by money or prestige but by deeply held values regarding the importance of particular environmental issues, in this case their shared interest in the common good of protecting the polar bears. They were anything but neutral, personally, about the outcome of the conflicts in which they were professionally engaged. We would not say that they set aside national interests, but rather that they found ways to accommodate the most important national interests to ensure

---

115. See, for example, Kolenosky, comments to 5 March 1991 draft of this chapter, 75, attached to his letter of 22 March 1991.

that their shared value-oriented goal of polar bear protection could be achieved.

Regime formation appears in this case to have been facilitated because the key players had a shared conception of the common good, but though these values to some extent transcended or shaped national interests and government policies, success still depended upon satisfying national interests to make the regime salable to politicians at home.

Knowledge-Based Hypotheses

We turn now to the work of theorists who have argued that ideas, knowledge, scientific consensus, and norms—beyond shaping interests of the parties and affecting structural power—have a dynamic of their own.[116] Theorists debate whether shared perceptions, beliefs, learning, and causal understandings that arise among the relevant parties to propagate this knowledge are important, or even necessary, conditions for regime formation.

This poses the question in our case study of whether the new views of human/environment relationships embodied in the science of ecology, which is based on the interconnectedness of organisms and the environment and was the driving force of an emerging environmental movement at the time, played a direct role in creation of the polar bear regime. Could the regime have come into being without the emergence of this set of ideas and values in the early 1970s? Certainly the number of multilateral environmental regimes formed in the 1970s suggests that this set of ideas was significant in the development of a stream of international institutional arrangements to cope with transboundary pollution and promote environmental protection.[117] This question parallels, to a considerable degree, the thinking underlying our section on contextual factors, in which new trends or changes in human perception or cognition are viewed as important along with geopolitical events.

---

116. For a capsule summary and critique of cognitive theory see Stephan Haggard and Beth A. Simmons, "Theories of International Regimes," *International Organization* 41 (Summer 1987): 509–513.

117. From 1969 to 1979 more than fourteen international agreements dealing with conservation and environment were signed. The steep rise in new conservation agreements is shown on Figure 2 in Gail Osherenko, "Environmental Cooperation in the Arctic: Will the Soviets Participate," *Current Research on Peace and Violence* 12 (1989): 147.

The polar bear convention lies at the cusp between two branches of thought about nature. It follows a long line of early agreements focused on specific species (migratory birds, fur seals, whales, and fish) rather than on ecosystem protection. At the same time, it departs from the conservation values of this earlier era, which focused on protecting species predominantly for consumptive use. The polar bear agreement incorporates recreational and aesthetic values as well and goes so far as to ban commercial harvesting. Unlike earlier conventions, the agreement first prohibits all taking and later lists the few exceptions. And rather than using a standard of management such as maximum sustainable yield, the agreement calls upon the parties "to protect the ecosystems of which polar bears are a part, with special attention to habitat components such as denning and feeding sites and migration patterns" (Article II).

Therefore, we tend to agree with the most general view of the cognitive theorists that knowledge and values are of direct importance to regime formation and do not merely contribute indirectly either to structural power or to determination of the interests of state actors.

It is difficult in this case to confirm the more specific hypothesis that agreement regarding causal relations and appropriate responses is a prerequisite for regime formation. The scientist/managers of the Polar Bear Specialist Group shared some basic common values regarding the importance of protecting polar bears, but they did not completely agree on either the cause of decline of polar bear populations evident in some areas or the appropriate international response.

The members of the PBSG developed, over time, a base of scientific knowledge that led to some agreement on the status of the species. They agreed, at least by 1972, that there were several different highly mobile populations of polar bears (separate stocks), each with a vast range. They determined that some of these stocks were severely depleted or rapidly declining as a result of overhunting, although they disagreed on whether the stocks were threatened with extinction. They shared a common set of values with respect to the importance of protecting healthy stocks of bears. They agreed on the need for international cooperation to remedy the situation and specifically on the desirability of at least banning the abhorrent practices of aerial and ship-based safari hunting.

Goodwill and consensus on some issues, however, should not be mistaken for consensus on every point. There was considerable disagreement on questions ranging from total polar bear population figures to the design of the regime and the degree to which states should relinquish their sovereign authority to international regulation.[118] The lack of consensus on such key points makes it difficult to confirm the hypotheses of the knowledge theorists regarding the necessity for consensus on cause-and-effect relationships and appropriate solutions.

Was there an epistemic community[119] operating as a midwife in the polar bear case, bringing a new set of commonly shared values and knowledge to bear on the problem, pressing its case at every turn? We concluded that in this case no epistemic community developed a common view of the problem and an appropriate solution that it succeeded in pushing on policy makers in the relevant countries. In trying to determine the membership in a potential epistemic community and to verify the degree of consensus necessary to conform to the theory, we found ourselves engaged in a post hoc reconstruction of reality. Close analysis of the players in this case revealed disparate views and values (even among those who would be excellent candidates for inclusion in an epistemic community). Instead of a group of influential individuals able to push policy makers to accept their shared perception of the problem and solution, we found a few entrepreneurial leaders—such as Bohlen and Lykke—behaving not as members of an epistemic community but as autonomous individuals, using the ideas of the PBSG when the ideas were useful but devising their own solutions when necessary to satisfy disparate interests.

On balance, we see the regime as resulting from bargaining among different interests. The interests of various actors were not reconciled by coming to a common understanding of causes and agreeing to consensus solutions; rather, their interests were sufficiently accommodated in a final package of provisions so that each signatory found the agreement preferable to no agreement at all.

The relative importance of scientist/managers, diplomats, and those holding political appointments is addressed by two related interest-based hypotheses in our template (see hypotheses 7a and b in the Appendix). These assert that there is a greater likelihood of regime formation when (a) negotiators "concentrate on scientific or technical

118. Frank Nicholls, for example, may have favored a broader international treaty covering national territory as well as international waters and open to other states as regime members. But because he played the role of a neutral facilitator and was not a member of the PBSG, one could argue that he was not a member of the epistemic community. It would be hard to argue, however, that he was not an influential player in the process of regime formation.

119. Emanuel Adler and Peter M. Haas, "Conclusion: Epistemic Communities, World Order, and the Creation of a Reflective Research Program," *International Organization* 46 (Winter 1992): 367–390.

considerations as opposed to political issues," and (b) negotiators with scientific or technical competence play a greater role than those with political credentials. This case tends to disconfirm both of these hypotheses.

Members of the PBSG were influential scientists and wildlife managers within their governments.[120] For example, Savva Uspensky in the Soviet Union, Thor Larsen in Norway, and Christian Vibe in Denmark were influential both because of their reputations as polar bear scientists and their positions in or connections to their governments. Uspensky, the Soviet representative, is a good example of the generally narrow gap in the Soviet Union between scientist and policy maker—he was a highly respected polar bear scientist who held key positions in government agencies.[121] Jack Lentfer, the leading American polar bear scientist, had worked for both the federal and the Alaska state governments. He participated in the Oslo meeting as a representative for the state of Alaska although he was an employee of the U.S. Department of the Interior at the time.[122] These scientist/managers shaped the early drafts of the agreement, formulated the issues, and contributed substantially to the content of the regime. But other actors were important in bringing the issue to the attention of policy makers and in negotiating the final agreement.

Players in the policy arena, such as Senator Bartlett (referred to by one informant as "initiator" and "godfather" to the agreement[123]), Russell Train and Lee Talbot (Council on Environmental Quality), Curtis Bohlen and Richard Parsons (Department of the Interior), played active roles in the United States. In all likelihood, Train, Bohlen, and other Americans favored a stronger regime than was created, but they were also pragmatists, skilled in the art of deal making and willing to compromise to reach a balance between their ideological and political goals. Without this group of policy makers, we suspect that the PBSG would not have had the political muscle or know-how to reach agreement on the regime's structure and rules. The entry of policy experts with diplomatic skills in the United States and in Norway (Lykke espe-

---

120. Thor Larsen, a member of the PBSG, wrote: "Many [Polar Bear Specialist] group members had close contact with legislators and politicians in their respective countries, which permitted effective and realistic approaches" ("Progress in Polar Bear Research and Conservation," 306).

121. He is still an outspoken advocate of environmental protection.

122. In some instances, scientists appear to have more influence on politics when they stick to their metier but cooperate closely with the administrators than when they take administrative positions.

123. Harington to Osherenko, 6 May 1991, 4.

cially) appears from the record to have been crucial to formation of this regime.

Train testified that CEQ had "sounded out" the other four polar bear states in the fall of 1971 regarding "the possibility of negotiating an international convention on the conservation of polar bears."[124] Finding that the other nations preferred to wait for the recommendations of the Polar Bear Specialist Group, the CEQ requested the IUCN (probably through Talbot, senior scientist at the CEQ and a representative to the IUCN at the time) to ask the PBSG to address the issue of international action to protect the polar bears. This tends to substantiate the idea that the PBSG carried considerable weight in the policy arenas of all five states. At the same time, the record indicates that, beginning in about 1971, the interest of the CEQ, along with congressional pressure, reopened the issue of polar bear protection at the U.S. State Department. This issue had been dormant since the 1965 meeting in Fairbanks, which had been arranged by the State Department.[125]

We concluded that both scientists and diplomats played a crucial role in formation of the polar bear regime. The scientist/managers contributed substantially to the content of the regime but might have continued talking and coordinating scientific research indefinitely without reaching closure on regime rules. It took continued pressure by animal protection advocates pushing for an international agreement plus the efforts of skilled diplomats who acted as entrepreneurial leaders to reach closure.

Contextual Factors

Having examined the three major theoretical frameworks, we were left with a nagging sense that our explanation of regime formation was incomplete. We then turned to what we termed in the template of hypotheses "contextual factors" and found that these had importance in explaining the timing of the emergence of the polar bear regime. We came to realize the critical role of larger world and national events in creating a window of opportunity within which a regime might form.

The protection of polar bears became an attractive issue at a time when both East and West were looking for areas in which they could

---

124. *Hearings*, 7.

125. There is a significant gap in the State Department records between 1966 and 1971 when the State Department, trying to respond to a request from Congress, discovered that the PBSG had a draft interim agreement that the IUCN advised them could be obtained from Lee Talbot at the CEQ.

build cooperation. Politically, they sought issues not closely linked to military or security concerns, discrete or safe issues with which to symbolize detente.[126] At the same time, in the wake of the 1972 Stockholm Conference on the Human Environment, leaders were striving for concrete examples of environmental cooperation. The signing of the 1972 U.S.-USSR Agreement on Cooperation in Environmental Protection set in motion an array of cooperative East-West efforts on environmental issues. Although concern for the polar bear's well-being had arisen much earlier, the regime could not have come into being at the height of the Cold War and probably not before the first Earth Day in 1970 activated a generation of Americans who had been warned in 1962, by Rachel Carson's *Silent Spring*, of the fragility of our environment.[127]

Other economic and political conditions were also right for agreement. In Japan, polar bear skins were increasing in value, suggesting that there was some reason to fear a non-Arctic state's initiation of a hunt. In Norway, the economic importance of sealing was declining, which, in turn, reduced pressure to trap polar bears seen both as competition and danger for seal hunters. And in Alaska, the economic importance of a continued sport hunt, even though polar bear hunting was still a $450,000 a year business, was no longer a major obstacle in the face of increased opposition to the "unsportsmanlike" aerial hunt.

The rising interest in animal protection and growing awareness of the value of nonconsumptive uses of wild animals—for tourism or wilderness values—also contributed to a mood conducive to cooperation. Passage of the Marine Mammal Protection Act in the United States in 1972 marked a historical departure in the management of commercially valuable wildlife.[128] That act declared marine mammals "to be re-

126. The polar bear convention was by no means the only symbol of detente during this particular period of warming of the Cold War. The Treaty on the Limitation of Anti-Ballistic Missile Systems (SALT I) was signed on 26 May 1972, during President Richard Nixon's visit to Moscow. This treaty had been under negotiation for more than two years and was considered a major breakthrough in East-West relations. While in Moscow, Nixon also signed an interim agreement on certain measures with respect to the limitation of strategic offensive arms and six other cooperation agreements.

127. Rachel Carson, *Silent Spring* (Boston: Houghton Mifflin, 1962). This book, published in fifteen languages by 1963, is widely credited as marking the beginning of the environmental revolution. The first Earth Day was celebrated in the United States on 22 April 1970. It was one among a number of turning points in environmental awareness. For a useful discussion of the period 1962–1972, with which we are particularly concerned, see John McCormick, *Reclaiming Paradise: The Global Environmental Movement* (Indiana: Indiana University Press, 1989), chaps. 3 and 4. He also discusses the Stockholm Conference in chap. 6.

128. Bean, *Evolution of Wildlife Law*, 291.

sources of great international significance, esthetic and recreational as well as economic." The act's primary management objective is "to maintain the health and stability of marine habitat"; its secondary objective is the attainment of optimum sustainable populations.[129] These dual goals shifted management strategies from the traditional objective of maximum sustainable yield for commercial purposes to noncommercial use.

Had the parties not been able to reach agreement in November 1973, national protection measures for Alaska and Svalbard that were already in place would have begun to stabilize these threatened polar bear populations and thus reduce public concern. Then the polar bear issue might have been rapidly overtaken by larger environmental issues on policy makers' agendas. Three to five years later, the polar bear agreement would not have seemed so much on the cutting edge of environmental agreements as the environmental movement shifted from species-specific approaches to negotiation of agreements embracing protection of entire ecosystems.[130]

The polar bear case does give credence to the hypothesis that regime formation is significantly affected by contextual factors that help to explain why a particular regime emerges within a specific time frame. In national legislative arenas, passage of a law is dependent not solely on bargaining but also on having the right set of circumstances and the right combination of individuals in key positions to press that measure ahead of hundreds of others waiting for hearings or a vote. Likewise, in the international arena, contextual factors (including broad political and social trends), although not sufficient to explain regime formation, are nevertheless an indispensable part of the explanation.

CONCLUSIONS

No hegemonic state, benign or coercive, used its superior structural power or preponderant material resources to impose an international regime for the protection of the polar bear or to induce others to form one. Nor did we find that any other configuration of power provided an explanation for the formation of this regime. Although power did not

---

129. Public Law 92-522, section 2(6), passed 21 October 1972, codified as 16 U.S.C. section 1361(6) (Supp. V 1981).

130. Notable examples are the 1980 Convention on the Conservation of Antarctic Marine Living Resources and the 1979 Convention on the Conservation of Migratory Species of Wild Animals (Bonn Convention).

play a dominant role in bringing the regime into being, considerations of structural power were important in understanding the role of the states and, to an extent, individual leaders during the process of negotiation.

We regarded hypotheses under the category of interest-based theory as most applicable to this case. The parties conceptualized the question of polar bear protection in terms of endeavoring to reap joint gains (the maximizing of protection) by bargaining to form a contract (specifically, the international agreement). They reached agreement through a lengthy process of consultation (with the aid of the deputy director general of the IUCN acting, in part, as a third-party intermediary) and direct negotiation to resolve their differences.

We examined eight of the ten interest-based hypotheses and found some support for seven of them. The most significant finding to emerge from our study of the history of the polar bear regime's formation was the resolution of the conflict over jurisdiction by a simple and salient solution which avoided the question of national jurisdiction in Arctic waters.

This case also illustrates well the role that individual leaders exercising entrepreneurial skills play in regime formation. It demonstrates that more than one leader can function at the same time or in the same case. A condition for success, however, may be that the various leaders assert compatible goals.

This was a classic case of integrative bargaining exhibiting characteristics typical of attempts to thicken the veil of uncertainty. During the final negotiating meeting, the parties moved away from the inherently distributional issues of jurisdiction, agreed to ambiguous provisions, and lengthened the time period (shifting from creation of an interim agreement to a permanent regime). These changed provisions made it more difficult for parties to calculate their long-term costs and benefits and were important in reaching closure.

Less strong evidence emerges from this case regarding the parties' concern for equity over efficiency and the importance of devising clear-cut and effective compliance mechanisms. But we could not dismiss equity as a potentially important factor in formation of the polar bear regime. The underlying structure of the agreement—a general ban on hunting—is equitable. It applies to everyone, and the exemptions allowed were created for reasons of fairness rather than efficiency. On the question of compliance, although commentators have criticized the regime's lack of explicit enforcement mechanisms, the parties regarded reliance on national programs as an effective and clear-cut way to implement and enforce the regime rules.

The case offered a rich record of efforts on the part of conservation and animal protection advocates to portray the polar bear as an endangered or threatened species and to convey a sense of crisis and urgency. We found that the success of these interest groups and individuals in capturing media attention contributed significantly to bringing a regime into existence but had less influence on the substantive terms of the regime.

Both scientists and diplomats played a crucial role, the former contributing substantially to framing the issues and determining the content of the agreement, the latter finding a salient solution, providing entrepreneurial leadership, and proving essential in reaching closure.

We concluded that knowledge and values are important to regime formation and are not merely factors contributing either to structural power or to determination of the interests of state actors. The pivotal ideas and values of the time, which redefined human/environment relationships (and which were shared by many of the key negotiators), played a direct role in creation of the polar bear regime. But the case did not confirm the more specific hypotheses with regard to the need for consensus on cause-and-effect relationships and appropriate solutions and the need for an epistemic community actively promoting a common set of causal views and political values.

Contextual factors—larger world and national events—contributed substantially to the formation of the international polar bear regime. And contextual concerns provided a necessary window of opportunity within which the regime could form when other conditions for regime formation were also met.

Finally, the case suggested an additional hypothesis not included in our template, namely, that states will give up the least amount of autonomy necessary to achieve the goals of the regime.[131] The specific exemptions provided in Article III of the final agreement indicate great solicitousness for the autonomy of scientific and management authorities in each state. Except in waters outside the area where local people had traditionally hunted, national control was preserved in each case. Although the IUCN originally drafted a treaty that would have created an international commission to recommend management practices that parties would have been obliged to consider, the final agreement created a coordination regime in which implementation and compliance are left to each member.

---

131. C. R. Harington, a participant in the process from 1965 through the Oslo meeting, confirms this point in his letter to Osherenko, 6 May 1991.

The important role of scientist/managers in formulating the issues and setting the agenda for negotiation may have been a key reason for the emphasis on preservation of national autonomy. The ethics of the scientific community allow for vigorous debate but require respect for the views of other scientists. This attitude contributed to the reluctance of PBSG members to dictate specific management standards or rules to be applied within national territory or to create a supranational policing mechanism[132] and was further bolstered by the strong conservative tendency in international law to maintain the status quo.

Throughout the negotiations, the parties debated the degree to which they should engage in joint management, whether they would agree to "cooperate" or only to "coordinate," but in the end negotiations produced no supranational legislative (rule-making), executive (implementation), or judicial (dispute resolution) structures. This should not be regarded as an impediment to the creation of an effective regime. One of the beauties of a prohibition arrangement such as the polar bear regime (first prohibiting all taking, then spelling out exceptions) is that there is less need for administrative apparatus than would be necessary for a regime such as the international whaling regime, which calls for regular collective decision making. This case illustrates that those who have a role in shaping new regimes should seek solutions that minimize limitations on autonomy and require the least possible supranational administrative apparatus necessary to achieve their goals.

---

132. When asked about discussions concerning the issue of compliance or enforcement of the regime, John S. Tener emphatically responded that to question the honesty or good intentions of professional colleagues would have been insulting. Tener, who was director of the Canadian Wildlife Service in the early 1970s and later became assistant deputy minister of Environment Canada, chaired PBSG meetings and headed the Canadian delegation to the Oslo meeting.

CHAPTER FIVE

Stratospheric Ozone: Regime Formation in Stages

PETER M. HAAS

Analyzing collective efforts to protect stratospheric ozone from depletion by man-made chemicals yields a Rashomon-type view of multiple realities revealed from different perspectives. A satisfying analytic explanation of the origin of multilateral environmental cooperation requires the use of several different social science theories of cooperation and regime creation. Although each theory satisfactorily explains a part of the broader story, all need to be invoked to explain the full range of outcomes.

This chapter analyzes the evolution of arrangements to protect stratospheric ozone. Although these arrangements do not specifically deal with the Arctic, they are appropriate as part of a study of international regime formation in the Arctic. The still evolving global regime governing stratospheric ozone depletion has developed through three stages: the adoption of the 1985 Vienna Convention, the 1987 Montreal Protocol, and the 1990 London Amendments. Ozone depletion in the Arctic was discovered by scientists in early 1989.[1] But by the time scientists had recognized this localized problem, its full collective treatment was already well under way through the international regime analyzed in this chapter. Analytically, the ozone case is revealing because international cooperation on a highly technical issue was reached before complete scientific consensus emerged. Studying the negotiation

---

1. Richard A. Kerr, "Arctic Ozone Is Poised for a Fall," *Science* (24 February 1989): 1007–1008.

and implementation of the three stages for ozone protection also allows the analyst to counterpose competing explanations of regime creation, each based on a study of different recurrent international practices. States typically seek to pursue power, to insulate their domestic economies from foreign threats, yet also to improve their technical understanding of problems that may affect them. In light of these interactions, the analyst may identify the potential for collective learning about more environmentally effective ways of managing shared international resources.

Unlike many recent environmental cases, the ozone case is one in which the United States played an active and constructive role. It provides useful comparisons when studying other environmental and resource issues in which the United States also took an active role, including multilateral Arctic regimes. A focus on power aids in understanding the resources available to the United States which allowed it to pressure others to accept its preferred view. Yet power alone does not explain the source of the hegemon's interests or the array of substantive policy alternatives among which delegates chose. An epistemic view is necessary to supplement the hegemonic view to explain the way the issues were posed in international negotiations and the origins and shifts of interests in such key countries as the United States, Germany, and the United Kingdom. Bargaining theory, in turn, helps us to understand the specific trade-offs that occurred during negotiations to protect the ozone layer. Whereas most of the major parties' interests may be relatively easily identified by their economic positions, an epistemic lens is needed to identify the original American interests that played such a key role in the entire process of regime creation. Contextual factors were surprisingly unimportant. Collective action was possible only when international environmental concern placed ozone protection on the international agenda, but domestic public opinion and technological capabilities had little influence on regime creation. Thus none of these three bodies of theory is adequate on its own, although each contributes to an understanding of regime formation in this case.

The story of the negotiations associated with developing a regime to regulate chlorofluorocarbons (CFCs) is fairly straightforward. It progresses from a shock of concern in the early 1970s which generated national regulations, to the signing of the broad 1985 Vienna Convention, the signing of the 1987 Montreal Protocol, and the June 1990 revision of the protocol to reflect evolving scientific understanding about stratospheric ozone depletion.

In 1985 twenty states and the European Community signed a weak treaty calling for further research on depletion of stratospheric ozone.

In September 1987 twenty-four states and the EC signed a treaty calling for a staggered reduction in the production and consumption of five chemical compounds (CFCs 11, 12, 113, 114, 115) that threatened the ozone layer and froze production and consumption of three other related compounds (halons 1211, 1301 and 2402). In June 1990 the signatories accelerated the control of ozone-depleting substances by calling for total elimination by the year 2000 of the previously regulated substances, while also controlling two additional substances (carbon tetrachloride and methyl chloroform) and creating an international fund to subsidize the transition to alternative chemicals. Whereas current arrangements call for the elimination of CFCs by the year 2000, Germany has already imposed outright bans on the production and consumption of CFCs by 1995, and the Netherlands will eliminate them by 1997.

Chlorofluorocarbons are a family of chemical compounds containing chlorine, fluorine, and carbon. They were discovered by General Motors in 1931 and became widely used because of their highly desirable industrial properties. They are inert, nontoxic, noncarcinogenic, and nonflammable. Widespread commercial applications were found: as a coolant in commercial and residential refrigeration and air conditioning (CFC-11 and CFC-12) as well as mobile air conditioning (CFC-12); as a blowing agent in the production of plastic foam and foam insulation (CFC-11 and CFC-12); in solvents for cleaning metal and electronic parts (CFC-113); as aerosol propellants (CFC-11 and CFC-12); and for fire extinguishing (halons). Global production quadrupled during the 1960s, peaking in 1974 at 812 million pounds.[2]

Concern about the depletion of the ozone layer first emerged in the United States in 1970, when scientists on the President's Science Advisory Council voiced fears that supersonic transports could destroy up to 50 percent of the earth's ozone layer. Although widespread supersonic transport use never occurred, in 1974 F. Sherwood Rowland and Mario Molina, chemists at the University of California at Irvine, revived concern about the ozone layer. They calculated that chlorine rising into the stratosphere in CFC emissions could upset the natural ozone balance by reacting with and breaking down ozone molecules, hence depleting the thin layer of stratospheric ozone that filters ultraviolet rays from reach-

---

2. Cynthia Pollock Shea, *Protecting Life on Earth: Steps to Save the Ozone Layer*, Worldwatch Paper 87 (Washington, D.C.: Worldwatch Institute, 1988); James K. Hammitt, Kathleen A. Wolf, Frank Camm, William E. Mooz, Timothy H. Quinn, and Anil Bamezal, *Product Uses and Market Trends for Potential Ozone-Depleting Substances, 1985–2000* (Rand Corporation, R-3386-EPA: Santa Monica, California, 1986).

ing the earth.[3] Earlier publications had related chlorine to ozone depletion but had not investigated the origins of stratospheric chlorine. Because CFCs have long residency times in the stratosphere, ozone
depletion would be largely irreversible. Scientists later determined that
to freeze current levels of ozone depletion, an immediate cut of 85 percent in use would be necessary. Such studies were possible because of
the invention in the late 1960s of sensitive equipment capable of monitoring slight amounts of CFCs in the stratosphere.

Most policy makers in industrialized countries soon came to regard
ozone depletion as a global problem: they believed that most of the global population would suffer from ozone depletion and that most also
contributed to it by using CFCs. The major threats, it eventually developed, would come from increased ultraviolet radiation reaching the
earth's surface, which would result in public health problems (cataracts
and skin cancer), possible loss of agricultural productivity, and a loss of
fisheries yields.[4] Although statements about ozone loss resonated with
references to collective goods from which everyone could benefit and
which required coordinated action, informed observers note that negotiations remained a question of economics and opportunity costs of regulation. Subsequent international negotiations hinged on efforts by
governments to protect the markets of their CFC producers.

The scientific community was split with respect to acceptance of the
Rowland-Molina hypothesis. Modeling efforts became more sophisticated over the next ten years, but the hypothesis was not confirmed until 1988. The more refined models also yielded more conservative estimates of ozone depletion, reducing public concern.

Much of the scientific community disputed the Rowland-Molina hypothesis. Without actual observations, they doubted the existence of
ozone depletion, questioned the computer models that related CFCs to
possible ozone depletion, and suggested alternative hypotheses for
ozone depletion. The Chemical Manufacturers Association, an industry
trade group, funded $18.9 million of research from 1972 to 1985 to
evaluate the Rowland-Molina hypothesis.[5] This hypothesis was the only
scientific explanation that ascribed environmental degradation to hu-

---

3. Mario Molina and F. Sherwood Rowland, "Stratospheric Sink for Chlorfluo-
romethanes: Chlorine Atom Catalyzed Destruction of Nature," *Nature* 249 (1974):
810–812.

4. Shea, *Protecting Life*, 14–17; U.S. Government Accounting Office, *Stratospheric Ozone*,
GAO/RCED-89-49 (February 1989), 11–12.

5. Chemical Manufacturers Association, *Fluorocarbon Research Program Revision No. 21*,
June 1985, p. 24.

man intervention through the interjection of CFCs into the environment. Three other widely considered hypotheses explained ozone depletion as the result of naturally occurring atmospheric dynamics, independent of human interference.[6]

Although the Rowland-Molina hypothesis remained unconfirmed until 1988, it immediately captured popular attention. Media reporting and activity of nongovernmental organizations (NGOs) focused short-term public attention on CFC uses, in particular the most common (and easiest to substitute for) use as an aerosol propellant. Between 1975 and 1980 the United States and eight other countries banned the use of CFCs as aerosol propellants.[7] Many European governments passed nonbinding voluntary limits on aerosols, and the European Community placed a cap on production capacity in 1982. With the existing voluntary bans on aerosols, this cap effectively built in a surplus capacity of 30 percent for European CFC producers. The United Nations Environment Programme began a series of assessments of the science of the problem.

Subsequent international negotiations reflected the prior domestic arrangements of the states. The wide variety in national approaches greatly inhibited international agreement. States attempted to ensure that they would not have to adopt more stringent regulations than they already had and tried to project their existing regulations into international law to obtain a comparative advantage for their CFC producers. The European Community pushed for global production cuts, which would allow European producers to expand their production to fit the new niches, while the United States and the Nordics pushed for consumption cuts consistent with their national efforts.

Following this initial spate of legislation, total CFC production fell in 1977 and leveled off until 1983. In the interim, industry developed additional applications for CFCs, in particular the use of CFC-113 as a solvent for computer chip manufacture. The share of total CFC production held by CFC-113 more than doubled between 1975 and 1982. With a resurgence in total CFC production in 1983 and 1984, led by the spectacular leaps in 113 production, concern about ozone depletion was renewed.

In May 1981, UNEP's Governing Council authorized it to initiate discussions for a global convention on CFCs. Reflecting their prior domestic regulatory experiences, Europe and the United States could not agree on the appropriate way to regulate CFCs—whether by produc-

---

6. Richard Stolarski, "The Antarctic Ozone Hole," *Scientific American* 258 (January 1988): 30–36.

7. Thomas B. Stoel, Alan S. Miller, and Breck Milroy, *Fluorocarbon Regulation: An International Comparison* (Lexington, Mass.: Lexington Books, 1980).

tion or consumption, all uses or selected applications, reductions or merely a freeze in usage.

The Toronto Group, consisting of the United States and several consumer countries without production facilities (Canada and the Nordic countries), wanted deep cuts applied to different forms of CFC use, while the European Community wanted a production freeze on all CFCs. For instance, the Toronto Group would discriminate between CFCs used for aerosols, air conditioning, and other purposes. The Toronto Group believed that the Europeans' approach would still permit unacceptable amounts of ozone depletion, but European Community countries refused to adopt additional cuts that would entail costs for their CFC producers. The possibility of mutual interests was further dissipated by the developing countries. Although fairly muted at most of the talks, they were suspicious of the entire affair because it might inhibit their domestic economic growth efforts.

After several years of deadlock, countries were barely able to adopt a weak framework treaty.[8] In March 1985, twenty states and the European Community finally adopted the Vienna Convention for the Protection of the Ozone Layer, which called for continued research but did not specify collective regulatory measures. It encouraged the control of substances that might deplete stratospheric ozone but did not specify any particular substances. Although with hindsight the Vienna Convention may be seen as a crude first step in a decade-long international effort to develop an ozone regime, in 1985 it was seen as a very weak instrument and a sign of the absence of international consensus on protecting stratospheric ozone. Without compelling evidence for the need for collective action, countries simply argued for international action consistent with their domestic status quo.

No sooner was the Vienna Convention concluded than new scientific findings regenerated collective concern. In mid-1985 the director of the Atmospheric Physics Department of the British Antarctic Survey, Joseph Farman, published an article describing a rapid and unexpected thinning of the ozone layer over Antarctica during the Antarctic springtime, based on a recalculation of existing satellite data. The United States and the United Kingdom launched a joint effort in 1986 to investigate the hole and determine its cause by providing actual ground-level and stratospheric measurements to supplement ongoing modeling exercises.

---

8. Peter H. Sand, "Protecting the Environment," *Environment* 27 (June 1985:18–20); Jutta Brunnee, *Acid Rain and Ozone Layer Depletion: International Law and Regulation* (Dobbs Ferry, N.Y.: Transnational Publishers, 1988), 228–236.

American scientists offered several competing hypotheses to explain the thinning, only one of which blamed chlorine from CFCs. Compelling evidence that correlated chlorine with the thinning of the layer (a "smoking gun") did not emerge until late 1987, after the conclusion of global negotiations. The Antarctic hole mobilized concern about the problem of ozone depletion, yet it could not be explained or predicted by using existing global atmospheric models. In the absence of a strong explanation for the causes of the Antarctic ozone hole, CFC manufacturers and the European Community contended that additional CFC controls were unnecessary and unjustified.

Collective understanding about the causes of ozone depletion and the costs of protective measures improved during 1986. In May and September, UNEP sponsored workshops on economic issues related to CFC control. In February and July, the U.S. Environmental Protection Agency (EPA) convened symposia on risk assessment and health effects from ozone depletion. In June, UNEP and the EPA cosponsored an international conference on ozone depletion and climate change, which generated a rough consensus on the urgency of the problem and the range of remedial costs.[9] In July, the National Aeronautics and Space Administration (NASA) released a three-volume study summarizing the results of a multinational research effort on stratospheric ozone which further attracted the attention of policy makers.

In September 1986 the scientific uncertainties were abruptly dismissed from policy discussions. Du Pont, the world's largest CFC producer and leader from 1980 to 1986 of industry opposition to controls, announced that it regarded CFCs as the likely cause of ozone depletion and accepted the need for some form of global regulation. Although the company certainly hoped to gain an edge in the market for CFC alternatives, the Du Pont decision was made by scientists working in the research wing of the Freon (CFC) products division. They had developed and run their own models, become convinced of the scientific legitimacy of the Rowland-Molina hypothesis, and drafted the 1986 statement. Later, they encouraged top-level management to accept and act on subsequent scientific findings.[10] The statement by Du Pont undermined opposition to a treaty.

---

9. James G. Titus, ed., *Effects of Changes in Stratospheric Ozone and Global Climate* (Washington, D.C.: USEPA and UNEP, 1986).

10. Joseph P. Glas, "Protecting the Ozone Layer: A Perspective from Industry," in *Technology and Environment*, ed. Jesse H. Ausubel and Hedy E. Sladovich (Washington, D.C.: National Academy Press, 1989); William Glaberson, "Science at Center Stage in Du Pont Ozone Shift," *New York Times*, 26 March 1988, pp. 41, 43; interviews with Du Pont officials, Wilmington, Delaware, 1988.

In the fall of 1986 the United States formulated a new and more stringent position through interagency discussions between the EPA's Office of International Activities and the State Department's Bureau of Oceans, Environment, and International Science, calling for 95 percent cuts in the production of a wide variety of CFCs and, ultimately, their elimination. But the choice to support such a strong environmental regime remained under domestic consideration during much of the period of the international negotiations in Montreal, and the final U.S. position remained in doubt until late in the talks. After an administrative policy review battle in the early months of 1987, the new American policy finally received the endorsement of President Ronald Reagan in June. Until then, however, the U.S. position was without administration approval and the diplomats were acting on their own.[11]

International negotiations on a new ozone protocol had resumed in Montreal in December 1986. After five contentious bargaining sessions and seven drafts, the Montreal Protocol on Substances That Deplete the Ozone Layer was finally adopted by twenty-four states and the European Community in September 1987.

Political cleavages appeared early in the negotiations as states expressed incompatible interests. The CFC producers—particularly Japan, France, Germany, Italy, the United Kingdom, and the Soviet Union—were concerned about the trade implications of CFC regulation.[12] Although these countries were also consumers of CFCs, their policy processes and delegations were dominated by those sympathetic to the concerns of the companies that produced CFCs. Du Pont had indicated support only for a treaty, not for a strong treaty. Other companies feared loss of markets from the regulation of CFCs. States producing CFCs generally opposed stringent controls, wished coverage to apply to a limited list of substances, advocated a slower schedule for implementing controls, and demanded more scientific support than did consuming countries. By encouraging consistency with the prior European Community regulations, EC members could find legal justification and precedent for their position. The CFC consumers, led by the Nordic countries and the Netherlands, pushed for more stringent con-

---

11. David Doniger, "Politics of the Ozone Layer," *Issues in Science and Technology* 4 (Spring 1988):86–92; Mark Crawford, "Ozone Plan: Tough Bargaining Ahead," *Science*, 4 September 1987, p. 1099.

12. For a listing of global CFC-producing companies and their locations, see U.S. House of Representatives Subcommittee on Health and the Environment of the Committee on Energy and Commerce, *Ozone Layer Depletion*, Serial No. 100-7 (Washington, D.C.: Government Printing Office, 1987), 419–420; also Mostafa K. Tolba interview by author, Nairobi, Kenya, 29 March 1990.

trols for a broader list of substances, with a more rapid schedule and less scientific support.

For the most part, developing countries had little interest in the treaty. Egypt and Venezuela were modest supporters of a treaty, but most other states were fairly quiet. Not being producers, they were largely concerned about loss of access to CFCs. As major future consumers, India and China feared that their own ambitious modernization and refrigeration plans could be impeded by a strong treaty and argued for concessions to developing countries. India and China together account for only about 2 percent of world CFC consumption yet aspire to provide refrigerators to most households. Because they have virtually 40 percent of world population, such changes would enormously increase their consumption of CFCs. They expected that social disruption from denying their populations refrigerators and air conditioners would be greater than the social costs resulting from ozone depletion. China plans to have refrigerators for 15 percent of its population by the end of century, with an increase in CFC production from the present 10 to 15 million kilograms per year to as much as 131 million kilograms per year.[13] The provision of alternative technologies would undoubtedly meet with a stiff response from the few northern CFC manufacturers, who would try to keep tight hold on the patents from which they were gaining high early profits.

Several points of disagreement persisted throughout the talks but were ultimately resolved in the final hours at Montreal. Consuming countries wanted coverage of all five major CFCs, while producing countries wanted fewer to be covered. Consuming countries wanted sharp reductions in usage, while producers merely wanted a freeze at current levels. Consuming countries advocated a more rapid schedule of controls than did producing countries. Developing countries wanted exclusions so they could pursue development plans which required CFC usage, as well as assistance in developing alternative chemicals. Many countries were split about whether CFCs should be regulated through the control of consumption or production. Countries were also split about compliance measures. They were easily able to agree that banning imports of bulk CFCs from nonparties would not violate General Agreement on Tariffs and Trade rules, but they had difficulty determining whether nontreaty violators would be faced with embargoes of bulk CFCs or products made with or containing CFCs. Producers

---

13. Maria Elena Hurtado, "Into the Deep Freeze," *South* 103 (May 1989): 76; Diane Brady, "Developing Countries Seek Support in Ozone Effort," *Our Planet* 1 (1989): 23.

and consumers disagreed on whether a schedule of phased reductions in CFCs should require periodic scientific justification at each step (the producers), or whether each step should occur automatically unless there was strong countervailing scientific evidence available at the time. This final disagreement was resolved by compromise: subsequent cuts would be automatic unless overruled by countries responsible for two-thirds of the world CFC consumption.

The rapid adoption of the Montreal Protocol was the consequence of growing scientific consensus, creative bargaining, and pressure applied by the United States at international negotiations. In February, the head of the U.S. delegation, Richard Benedick, announced that unless cuts in CFC use were approved, Congress would unilaterally introduce legislation to close American markets to products that use CFCs.[14] Although the U.S. ambassador did not consider this threat very important, it seriously rearranged the range of alternatives available to other producers, particularly Japan, who dreaded possible interference with trade in CFCs.[15] Unilateral action by the United States in response to congressional initiatives and lawsuits introduced by environmental groups could have curtailed access to the world's largest market for CFCs. This move led to a counteroffer by the European Community of a short-term freeze followed by 20 percent cuts and on a wider variety of CFCs than had initially been tolerated. Later, as scientific consensus grew, movements for control accelerated, fueled by such scientific findings.

The European Community's reluctance to adopt stringent cuts on CFC consumption persisted. It supported only a cap on the production of a small number of CFCs, with a gradual, phased introduction of such measures. Changing domestic conditions within major European Community countries, however, facilitated the transformation of this position. West Germany became much more interested in controlling CFCs following the increased influence of the Green party in December 1986 elections. In March 1987 the German chancellor expressed concern about the stratospheric ozone layer and insisted on a ban on CFC use as an aerosol propellant. In May the Bundesrat (the German upper house

---

14. Richard E. Benedick, "International Efforts to Protect the Stratospheric Ozone Layer," *Current Policy* no. 931, 2. At a congressional hearing in May 1987, Senator John Chafee asked Benedick whether such bills would help him negotiate a strong treaty.

15. Richard Elliot Benedick, "Ozone Diplomacy," *Issues in Science and Technology* 6 (Fall 1989): 43-50; Benedick, "The Ozone Protocol: A New Global Diplomacy," *Conservation Foundation Letter*, no. 4 (1989): 1–4; Benedick, *Ozone Diplomacy: New Directions in Safeguarding the Planet* (Cambridge, Mass.: Harvard University Press, 1991).

of parliament) called for the elimination of CFCs.[16] Still, the United Kingdom and France, major CFC producers, remained opposed to the more stringent positions of the United States and UNEP. Institutional change within the European Community removed the blocking power of these states. By natural rotation in January 1987, Britain's chairmanship of the European Community Council of Ministers ended, thereby eliminating British ability to delay discussions and block compromises.

A final shift occurred in May 1987, following the introduction of new scientific information. UNEP's executive director, Egyptian microbiologist Mostafa Tolba, convened a group of modelers in Würzburg, West Germany, and they determined that their models agreed on key predictions. In turn, they offered compelling support for the range of CFCs that should be controlled and the need for fairly rapid entry into force. Moreover, they realized that the developing countries could be offered a ten-year exclusion from compliance because of their relatively small contribution to overall stratospheric chlorine loading and thus could increase their consumption by expanding refrigeration and similar programs.

Deft bargaining in Montreal yielded a final set of compromises acceptable to all the parties. Mostafa Tolba choreographed negotiations closely throughout the conference, and Lee Thomas of the United States and Laurens Brinkhorst of the European Community bargained through the early hours of the final day. The Montreal Protocol finally called for a 50 percent reduction in consumption of five major CFCs (11, 12, 113, 114, 115) by 1998 and a consumption freeze on halons in 1992. Production was allowed to continue at 10 percent more than the consumption controls to guarantee future provision of CFCs to developing countries. The developing countries also received a ten-year postponement on enforcement, an accommodation designed to assure their support for the treaty.

The United States was flexible, making some final concessions to conclude the deal while prevailing in its areas of key concern—the variety of CFCs to control and at least a 50 percent cut. Other countries also made concessions in areas of importance to them. A complicated formula was adopted which combined consumption and production controls to satisfy both the United States and the European Community: the cuts were to be staggered; the Soviet Union would be allowed to complete construction of a CFC plant; shifts in use between CFCs would be allowed (to buy out Japan, which was primarily concerned about CFCs used in computer manufacture); and the developing countries were to be given a ten-year exemption from compliance. Although

---

16. German Bundestag, ed., *Protecting the Earth's Atmosphere: An International Challenge* (Bonn: German Bundestag, 1989), 202–204.

covering only bulk chemicals, the treaty provides for future annexes for products made with, and containing, CFCs. The treaty also calls for ongoing scientific reassessment to determine whether stratospheric changes require modifications in the treaty's arrangements.

The Montreal Protocol entered into force on 1 January 1989, but it was shortly overtaken by accelerating scientific consensus. Ozone depletion reached a historic high in 1987, and in March 1988 a new multinational Ozone Trends Panel Report was released in the United States. The report, which finally presented findings from Antarctica that related CFCs to ozone depletion, triggered extensive alarm and calls for more stringent additions to the protocol. Du Pont responded within a week by announcing its intention to discontinue CFC production by the end of the century. In September, EPA administrator Lee Thomas called for absolute elimination of CFCs. In November, the United Kingdom called for 85 percent cuts. In February 1989, evidence from the recent Antarctic expedition demonstrated that the ozone was being depleted more rapidly than originally predicted. Scientific consensus now existed that earlier measures were too moderate to yield the desired effects. Moreover, by late 1989 the ozone crisis had soared on domestic political agendas, and European politics were taking a distinctly green hue.[17]

In early March 1989, environment ministers of the European Community called for full elimination as soon as possible, and in the following week 123 countries called for absolute elimination by the end of the century. At the first governmental review meeting of the Montreal Protocol in May 1989, 81 countries adopted a resolution agreeing to phase out all production and consumption of CFCs by the year 2000, as well as to establish a fund to ameliorate the costs of adjustment for developing states.

Scientific consensus had its full impact in June 1990 at the second annual review conference. The Montreal signatory parties amended the Montreal Protocol in light of emerging scientific consensus, in particular in reaction to the Ozone Trends Panel Report. The parties agreed to eliminate production of the five CFCs and three halons regulated by the Montreal Protocol by the year 2000. New substances believed to threaten the ozone layer were controlled as well. Carbon tetrachloride, a substance dismissed at earlier talks because of its relatively weaker impact on ozone depletion, is to be eliminated by 2000, and methyl chloroform will be phased out by 2005.

---

17. Michael Renner, "A Green Tide Sweeps Europe," *Worldwatch* 3 (January–February 1990): 23–27; Sara Parkin, *Green Parties: An International Guide* (London: Heretic Books, 1989); "The Greening of British Politics," *Economist*, 3 March 1990, pp. 49–50; Tom Burke, "The Year of the Greens," *Environment* 31 (November 1989): 18–20, 42–45.

Yet the real debate in London concerned who should pay. Until the last minute, the United States opposed the creation of any funding arrangements. Finally a $160 million fund was established to provide and subsidize purchase of CFC substitutes by developing countries. The fund will be increased by $40 million each when India and China ratify the updated protocol because those two countries were the main beneficiaries of the fund.[18] Although it is a political concession that reflected northern willingness to tolerate short-term free riding by developing countries other than China and India, the fund is inadequate to compensate India fully for its costs to replace CFCs, which are estimated to be more than $560 million through 2010.[19] The Indian delegate at the 1990 London talks spoke forcefully of ecological imperialism, of the unfair financial burden which the North was placing on the South to counteract a problem that was felt predominantly in the North.

In sum, a fairly coherent regime for stratospheric ozone protection emerged through these three rounds of negotiations. The status of the Montreal Protocol in 1991 is presented in Table 5.1.

Table 5.1 Status of the Montreal Ozone Protocol

	Number of countries[a]	Developed countries[b]	Less developed countries
Signed	46	26	20
Ratified	70	26	44

Source: Data provided by United Nations Treaty Office, 4 February 1991.

[a]Includes the European Economic Community, Ukraine, both East and West Germany, Byelorussia

[b]Includes South Africa, Israel, Spain, Portugal, Byelorussia, Ukraine.

Note: Many countries that later acceded to and ratified the Montreal Protocol were not present at Montreal and did not sign the treaty.

ANALYSIS AND HYPOTHESIS TESTING

Power-based, interest-based, and cognitive theories each seek to explain the formation of the ozone regime. None of these theories by itself, is fully sustained throughout the history of the regime's creation although each captures and explains part of the story. Some key propositions are underdeveloped in most theoretical formulations and hence are difficult to evaluate fully.

---

18. Shane Cave, "Wealthy Nations Pay Up on Ozone," *Our Planet* 2 (1990): 15.

19. Sue Montgomery, "Fund to Combat Ozone Depletion," *Development Forum* (September–October 1990): 9.

Power-Based Hypotheses

In the ozone case, a hegemonic power was necessary but insufficient to explain creation of the regime. The United States was an issue-specific hegemon, even if it had already lost its previous global hegemony. It possessed sufficient resources to sway other parties and the will to do so. It was the only party with global resources that could sway negotiations. Other influential parties, including Germany, were able to influence regional groupings of which they were members, but they could not directly influence the outcome of international talks.

The issue-specific hegemony of the United States was based on its dominance in science, its diplomatic competence, and its market dominance—80 to 90 percent of the world's atmospheric science is done in the United States. The Americans sent large and well-prepared delegations to all of the bargaining sessions. The United States sufficiently controlled world production of CFCs so that unilateral action could effectively transform relative prices for consumers elsewhere in the world. CFCs are produced by twenty-one companies, with operations in sixteen countries. Du Pont, with 50 percent of the U.S. market and subsidiaries and joint ventures in Canada, Japan, the Netherlands, Argentina, Brazil, and Mexico, is responsible for more than 25 percent of global production and is the only company to produce CFCs for the three major world markets: North America, Europe, and Japan.[20] Moreover, the United States possessed the will to use the power it had. Congress could deny foreign producers of CFCs and products containing CFCs access to the U.S. market, as Senators John Chafee and Max Baucus threatened in 1986, although the bills never came to a vote.[21] Although Ambassador Benedick disputes the role of power, the Japanese feared that American regulations would make Japanese electronics exports incompatible with the standards in the largest market.[22]

The evidence in this case presents a strong argument for hegemony as a necessary precondition for regime creation. The United States actively promoted agreement. By credibly threatening an outcome that

---

20. U.S. House of Representatives Subcommittee on Health and the Environment of the Committee on Energy and Commerce, *Ozone Layer Depletion*, 100th Cong., 1st sess., serial no. 100-7, 9 March 1987, pp. 419–420; John H. Cumberland, James R. Hibbs, and Irving Hoch, eds., *The Economics of Managing Chlorofluorocarbons* (Washington, D.C.: Resources for the Future, 1982).

21. Draft Senate Bills S. 570 and S. 571, 100th Congress, 1st Session, 1987.

22. Karen Litfin, "Ozone Politics: Power and Knowledge in the Montreal Protocol" (paper presented at the Annual Meeting of the International Studies Association, Vancouver, British Columbia, March 1991), 39.

was least desirable to any other party, the United States encouraged other parties to reconsider their options and thus made compromise and agreement possible. The concentration of power correlated with diplomatic leadership, collective action was facilitated by the exercise of leadership, and the hegemon's interests were clearly reflected in the collective outcome. Before early 1987 most of the CFC-producing firms and the European Community preferred little action to collective action, but they least desired unilateral action by the United States that would require awkward short-term market adjustments for them. Because all preferred a homogeneous world market, the U.S. delegation was able to force other governments to discuss means of regulation on American terms by threatening to take unilateral action through congressional legislation. A managed market would result, but at least it would have roughly comparable national measures. Institutional bargaining had been impossible before the U.S. delegation exercised this power because there was no area of joint gains mutually recognized by the various parties.

Theorists of hegemonic stability disagree on whether a hegemon deploys its power for the collective benefit (benignly) or solely for its own benefit (coercively). It is difficult to evaluate such contending hypotheses because of the lack of clarity associated with these terms. They have two meanings. Benign can either mean that the hegemon used benign techniques to obtain its objectives or that its objectives also satisfied the interests of other parties.

According to the first criterion, the United States was coercive by threatening to close access to U.S. markets. Yet benign effects may accrue regardless of the motivation of the hegemon if the effects are associated with collective goods which all enjoy but which would be unavailable without the hegemon's actions.[23]

Applying the second criterion yields ambiguous results. The United States does not benefit disproportionately from the institutional out-

---

23. Robert O. Keohane, *After Hegemony: Cooperation and Discord in the World Political Economy* (Princeton: Princeton University Press, 1984); Charles P. Kindleberger, "Dominance and Leadership in the International Economy: Exploitation, Public Goods, and Free Rides," *International Studies Quarterly* 25 (June 1981): 242–254; Kindleberger, *The World in Depression, 1929–1939* (Berkeley: University of California Press, 1986); Duncan Snidal, "The Limits of Hegemonic Stability Theory," *International Organization* 39 (Autumn 1985): 579–614. Other authors focus on the distribution of institutional gains from specific arrangements, arguing that a coercive hegemon will gain materially from the institutional arrangements it helps to establish. See Robert Gilpin, *War and Change in World Politics* (Cambridge: Cambridge University Press, 1981); Stephen D. Krasner, "State Power and the Structure of International Trade," *World Politics* 28 (April 1976): 317-347; and Joseph Grieco, *Cooperation among Nations* (Ithaca: Cornell University Press, 1990).

comes, but it is less clear whether the United States was truly providing a collective good or acting to promote others' interests. The United States had to introduce domestic controls over CFCs as a consequence of a lawsuit brought by the Natural Resources Defense Council. But not all countries believe the regime provides a collective good. An intact ozone layer is a collective good for the industrialized northern countries, which will suffer most acutely the public health effects of depleted ozone. But many developing countries question whether they benefit equally from the regime. Most were obsessed by the costs rather than the gains from the regime.[24] By December 1989 very few had ratified or even signed the Montreal Protocol and by spring 1992 the major CFC consumers among the developing nations had not yet acceded to the regime, indications that many developing countries do not view the Montreal Protocol as conferring mutual benefits.

The power-based explanation is insufficient on several counts. The regime may have been the best the United States could get, but it is not entirely isomorphic with U.S. interests. The differential controls between consumption and production in the Montreal Protocol, the exemptions for developing countries, and the concessions to India and China at London are all outside the objectives of the United States. Thus hegemonic interests do not map perfectly onto the substantive form of the regime because the United States—unable to impose in full its preferred outcome—was forced to make concessions to other parties.

The hypothesis pays insufficient attention to the power of other parties that enabled them to press successfully for bargaining concessions from the United States. Although the United States could threaten unilateral actions, it needed support and reciprocity from other countries to establish the legitimacy of its actions. Entirely unilateral action was out of the question. Thus developing countries could still demand some concessions to provide the necessary legitimacy for the American package. The European Community was able to extract concessions on control measures, Japan obtained shifting between individual CFCs, and the Soviet Union was allowed to complete construction of a new CFC plant.

Curiously, preponderant research activity and consequent control over knowledge—a key structural resource, according to Susan Strange—operated against the interests of strong domestic economic

---

24. Peter Usher, "Climate Change and the Developing World," *Southern Illinois University Law Journal* 14 (1990): 257–264.

actors within the United States.[25] Scientists generally pressed for strong and rapid CFC regulations despite the objections of the powerful CFC manufacturers' trade organization. The Alliance for Responsible CFC Policy, an industry trade group representing more than five hundred American CFC producers and consumers, continued to urge cautious and conservative measures (largely conservation and research) long after Du Pont and much of the scientific community had accepted the Rowland-Molina hypothesis and accepted the Antarctic ozone hole as real.[26]

The hypothesis is also weak on timing and motivations. Whereas the United States possessed roughly the same hegemonic resources throughout the 1980s, it chose to exercise leadership only in 1986. These points are explained in greater detail below. The U.S. interests were not a priori evident from a review of its position. The decision for vigorous regulation of CFCs ran counter both to the interests of such strongly entrenched domestic interest groups as the alliance and to the doctrinaire opposition to regulation that characterized the Reagan administration.[27]

In studying the ozone regime, international power arguments require assistance from domestic-level analyses to specify the ends to which power will be deployed. Robert Putnam's theory of two-level games suggests some additional necessary conditions for U.S. leadership in this case.[28] He argues that international negotiations occur in a national and an international setting. The range of options open to negotiators is determined to a large extent by domestic coalitions that have formed around different policy options. In the ozone case, the 1986 breakdown of the industry coalition in the United States—precipitated by Du Pont's public acknowledgment of the need for an international treaty—gave the U.S. delegation leeway to promote other

---

25. Susan Strange, *States and Markets* (London: Pinter Publishers, 1988).

26. See statements reprinted in Alliance for a Responsible CFC Policy, *The Montreal Protocol: A Briefing Book* (Rosslyn, Va.: Alliance for a Responsible CFC Policy, 1987).

27. See Doniger, "Politics of the Ozone Layer"; Crawford, "Ozone Plan"; Lynton K. Caldwell, "The World Environment: Reversing U.S. Policy Commitments," in *Environmental Policy in the 1980s*, ed. Norman J. Vig and Michael E. Kraft (Washington, D.C.: CQ Press, 1984), 320. Caldwell identifies the major themes in U.S. foreign environmental policy during the 1980s: "Three considerations, essentially domestic in origin, appear to have influenced Reagan's environmental policies abroad . . . desire to obtain advantage wherever possible for American economic interests . . . ideological bias against any increases in U.S. financial contributions to intergovernmental agencies . . . preference for reliance upon market forces as a corrective to environmentally harmful practices."

28. Robert Putnam, "Diplomacy and Domestic Politics: The Logic of Two-Level Games," *International Organization* 42 (Summer 1988): 427–460.

objectives. The decision of the United States in 1986 to exercise its he-gemonic resources was possible only after the domestic breakup of the logjam created by industry opposition to a treaty.

Interest-Based Hypotheses

Richard Benedick, primary negotiator for the United States, places heavy reliance on many interest-based factors to explain the success of the Montreal Protocol. He attributes its success largely to creative and integrative bargaining, stressing the constructive effort to forge politi-cal arrangements satisfactory to all parties while also constantly apply-ing the most current scientific understanding of the problem to the ne-gotiations. The following review of interest-based hypotheses suggests that many of them apply to the actual negotiation stage of the Montreal Protocol, although they do not shed light on the origins of state inter-ests or the dynamics by which interests may change. Benedick does not adequately account for the extensive political pressure on the U.S. po-sition. Because many of these hypotheses are confirmed concurrently, it is impossible to allocate causal weighting to each one individually. Al-though the utility of the interest-based research program is upheld, the relative sufficiency and applicability of individual hypotheses within that program cannot be adequately investigated in this case.

A contract zone did not emerge until midway through the negotia-tions on the Montreal Protocol, fairly late in the process of international regulatory efforts, which began in the mid-1970s. The Vienna Conven-tion was weak because of the absence of a clear-cut contract zone in which the parties could realize mutually beneficial outcomes. Interest-based explanations correctly predict the failure of efforts to create a re-gime without the existence of a contract zone.

Distributive bargaining prevailed at Vienna, as the various blocs were locked into their preferred approaches to CFC regulation and were un-willing and unable to reach a meaningful compromise. Bargaining at Montreal and London had both integrative and distributive elements. Integrative bargaining was present when scientific uncertainty ob-tained and nations could agree on the desirability of generating addi-tional scientific understanding which would shed light on the costs and benefits of cooperation. Integrative bargaining in this sense prevailed during the period between the Vienna Convention and the beginning of talks on the Montreal Protocol, as all parties were trying to amass bet-ter information about the costs to their populations from ozone deple-tion and the economic costs of controlling CFCs. Integrative elements were apparent as well through most of the Montreal and London talks, as parties used new information and side payments to expand the win-set sufficiently broadly to include the desires of all parties. The CFC producers were able to establish control arrangements that satisfied all their needs by establishing differential schedules for CFC production and consumption, shifting between CFCs, and tolerating exclusions for low-consuming developing countries. The London phase was marked by a rise in distributive concerns, leading the developed countries to create a new fund to facilitate compliance with the regime by develop-ing countries.

At Vienna the veil of uncertainty was thick, but countries were unable to overcome their different approaches to the problem sufficiently to engage in serious discussion of their obligations under an international regime. By the time negotiations for the Montreal Protocol resumed in late 1986, the veil of uncertainty had been greatly thinned. Intervening studies on atmospheric chemistry, the health and environmental effects of ozone depletion, and economic estimates of the costs and benefits of controls allowed actors to be relatively confident of the ways in which a stratospheric ozone regime would affect their interests. Industrial countries would encounter public health problems—eye ailments and skin cancer, for example—from ozone depletion, whereas developing countries would face increased costs for coolants and refrigerants as a result of the measures to control CFCs. The amount of money ap-proved in London was too low to offset what would certainly be higher prices in the future for CFC alternatives. The effects from ozone de-pletion on crop and fishery yields might have altered assessments by the various countries of their costs and benefits, but these effects remain poorly understood and were never widely publicized.

A simple fact of politics is that countries generally pursue outcomes they regard as equitable (for them) rather than outcomes that are effi-cient. Identifying arrangements that actors perceived as equitable proved important for the successful creation of the ozone regime. At Montreal and London the developed countries granted numerous con-cessions to the less developed countries (LDCs) to assure their support, including a grace period for compliance and financial assistance. Yet the success of these equity considerations in persuading LDCs that their interests were fully met is suspect: they have not yet been suffi-cient to attract India and China to ratify the Montreal Protocol or adopt the London Amendments; and the anticipated costs of compliance ex-ceed the benefits, even when health and environmental costs to be averted by the major LDCs are included among the benefits.

No salient solutions existed during most of the ozone talks. No salient solution helped the negotiators at Vienna or Montreal to reach agreement. Scientific discussions in 1986 offered a salient solution of 85 percent reductions in CFC use, which would be necessary to stabilize ozone depletion at current rates, but the political climate was still too contentious for such a solution to attract agreement. In fact, leading up to Montreal, the complexity of the contract zone, given the multiple dimensions about which parties disagreed, precluded the emergence of a simple salient solution for the parties. They were not able even to apply the same standard to consumption and production. The final compromises were so complicated and delicate that at Montreal the final draft of control measures was not submitted to UNEP's legal office for checking. By the time of the London meeting, however, a salient solution did exist. Because various control measures had been introduced, the final move to eliminate CFCs entirely—the salient solution—had an inherent appeal.

Two weak models, which might be construed as salient solutions, existed for the negotiations, although they had little relation to the broader array of agreements that the regime embodies. The equal treatment of parties, whereby all countries limit CFC usage equally, may be considered a very modest salient solution. This solution was violated in actual practice by extending exemptions to countries with low CFC consumption.

UNEP's prior experience with the Mediterranean Action Plan also supplied a crude template for the organizational design of the stratospheric ozone negotiations. Following the Mediterranean experience, UNEP, in the late 1970s and early 1980s, supported concurrent efforts to regulate CFCs while also continuing to study and assess their threat to the stratospheric ozone layer. Although UNEP's formula was borrowed from prior experience, the processes did not contribute to broader agreement on the draft protocol.

Exogenous shocks or surprises may generate or renew attention to a particular problem, thus precipitating a political crisis and focusing political pressure on parties responsible for creating a regime. Exogenous shocks did help drive the talks in this case. Scientific alarms about ozone depletion from CFCs in 1973, 1985, and 1988 all jump-started international action, which had been stalled.

Shocks were necessary conditions for creation of the ozone regime but were insufficient alone to explain new outcomes. Although exogenous shocks stirred public opinion and encouraged leaders to seek an international treaty, different actors drew differing inferences from them. Those committed to a strong treaty interpreted them to justify the need for accelerated action, whereas those opposed stressed the enduring scientific uncertainty in interpreting the shocks and questioned the ability of existing scientific consensus to show a causal relationship between ozone depletion and CFCs. It is this difference in inference that makes the epistemic community explanation presented below more compelling.

Issues that are high on the political agendas of states may be easier to resolve because of the potential political leverage that may be brought to bear on their resolution. Ozone depletion as an issue generally had far from high-profile status on the policy agendas of the participating governments. In the United States it reached the top level of the administration's agenda only in May 1987, when President Reagan approved the U.S. bargaining position after several sessions of the cabinet-level Domestic Policy Council and a three-month internal review of the U.S. position. By this time, American delegations at international negotiations had already pressed for a strong treaty. For the United States, reaching the top level of the policy agenda and being accepted by the chief executive helped to confirm and establish the policy initiatives already formulated by the epistemic community and EPA and State Department officials. As illustrated in Table 5.2, the issue remained far from the top of the agenda for most other parties until after the conclusion of the Montreal Protocol, when public concern mounted and leaders were pressured to adopt the more stringent London Amendments.

Table 5.2 Prominence on national political agendas

	Year when issue first became a concern	Extent of influence		
		Vienna	Montreal	London
U.S.A.	1987	none	none	moderate
U.K.	1987	none	none	strong
France	not yet	none	none	none
Germany	1985	none	strong	strong
Japan	not yet	none	none	none
China	not yet	none	none	none
India	not yet	none	none	none
Sweden	1970s	strong	strong	strong

In several countries—the United States, Germany, and the United Kingdom, for example—the publicity that the Montreal Protocol received, combined with new scientific evidence on the serious threats to the ozone layer and campaigns by major NGOs, increased public concern with ozone depletion after the regime was created. British Friends of the Earth launched a crusade for environmentally friendly products, including a campaign against products containing and made with CFCs. The United States was still willing to act in the face of emerging public environmental concerns in 1990 and oppose the establishment of an ozone fund at London.

At Vienna and Montreal many of the Nordic countries that participated in the Toronto Group expressed a conception of the common good. Yet few other countries shared this conception. Consensus at Montreal was forged through clever and hard bargaining. The outcome was in doubt up through the final day of the conference. It was not until London that most northern countries expressed cosmopolitan views, and they easily accepted accelerated controls on CFCs. Yet many developing countries, in particular India and China, lack such a conception of the common environmental good. More profoundly, the identification of a particular good as "public" or "common" is itself contested. Luther Gerlach, a cultural anthropologist, claims that a definition of "commons" is culturally determined and subject to political manipulation.[29]

The functionalist and neofunctionalist traditions of international relations theory suggest that issues (or elements of issues) that are regarded as technical are easier to resolve than issues relating to high politics and national security. This is because the former will be relegated to midlevel bureaucrats and technocrats who will be able to forge consensus free of broader foreign policy visions and concerns about preserving national sovereignty. Although the ozone issue was generally viewed as a highly technical scientific problem, most officials were keenly aware of the economic consequences of scientific and technical decisions. American, British, and French officials were aware from the outset of the potential costs to American CFC producers and loss of international trade for the United States as a whole. The U.S. delegation, though led by individuals sensitive to the technical dimensions of the problem, always had industry representatives as observers, as well as delegates responsible for articulating broader foreign policy concerns. Finally, though many technical decisions had to be made during the negotiations, negotiators were always conscious of the broader political and economic implications, and the final decisions still required the approval of political leaders in each country who were responsible for the broader national policy positions.

---

29. Luther P. Gerlach, "Cultural Construction of the Global Commons," in *Culture and the Anthropological Tradition*, ed. Robert H. Winthrop (Lanham, Md.: University Press of America, 1990), 319–420.

Widespread representation of relevant parties is necessary for negotiations to be regarded as legitimate and for countries to be willing to
comply with the ensuing regime. The Vienna failure occurred without
active participation from many of the major parties. Developing countries did not become concerned and energetic participants in negotiations until 1987, and even then only Argentina, Brazil, Egypt, Kenya,
Mexico, and Venezuela were actively involved. There was broader representation at the Montreal conference, but India did not attend. The
regime was successfully adopted without the involvement of such major
CFC-consuming LDCs as India and China, although it remains to be
seen how effective and stable it can be without their active involvement.
By London full participation had been achieved.

The availability of compliance mechanisms that allowed parties to determine whether cuts in CFC production and consumption were truly
occurring increased support for the regime. The primary compliance
mechanisms in this regime involved the distribution of data about CFC
production by UNEP and an industry group, the Chemical Manufacturers Association. Circulation of such data—sanitized by the CFC
firms to be sure that no proprietary market information would be
revealed—persuaded policy makers of the need to control growing production. These data also provided information on other countries' production levels and compliance with the treaty, thus helping to overcome
temptations to ride freely. The need for information-based compliance
mechanisms limited the scope of the regime, however, because it is
much easier to monitor trade in bulk chemicals, about which companies
report to the Chemical Manufacturers Association, than in products
made with or containing CFCs, which pose much greater problems of
verification and measurement.

Leadership, primarily entrepreneurial, played an important role in
regime creation in this case. Several individuals took leadership roles,
all pressing for similar ends. In particular, Mostafa Tolba played an active part from 1983, when, he said, the "science became clear to me."[30]
He was convinced that chlorine was responsible for ozone depletion. In
late 1986 he proposed a total phaseout of CFCs by the end of the century. He chaired meetings and pressed his own preferences for a treaty
that would require at least 30 to 40 percent cuts in CFC use. More
broadly, he was responsible for generating and speedily presenting new
scientific information to the political debates. In doing so, he acted also
as an intellectual and charismatic leader. Tolba's guidance was based on

---

30. Tolba interview, 29 March 1990.

his reputation as a scientist and on his own energy, as well as on UNEP's administrative resources, which were necessary for running meetings. The role of UNEP—and Tolba—has been to educate countries about the possibility of mutual gains and to elaborate particular outcomes that might provide mutual benefit. Not only did leadership help overcome the collective reluctance to cooperate, it also served to identify points for mutual gain.

Other leaders existed as well. Winfried Lang, head of the Austrian delegation, constructively led many bargaining sessions. His leadership was entrepreneurial, based on his diplomatic skills, because the country he represented had little leverage. Richard Benedick, head of the U.S. delegation up until the Montreal conference, likewise served as a leader at many sessions, persuasively bargaining while pushing other countries closer to his preferred position.[31] Benedick was both an entrepreneurial and a structural leader: his personal influence and diplomatic skill were backed by the hegemonic reputation of the United States, which he invoked when necessary to support his objectives.

Leadership may be a necessary condition for regime creation, but it is not a sufficient one. Without domestic allies to diffuse, interpret, and promote UNEP's information, Tolba's leadership and UNEP's broader support for conferences and diffusion of research findings would have been ineffectual.

Applying a pure interest-based explanation to the ozone case does not explain motivations of individual leaders. They were probably motivated by an entrepreneurial instinct together with a desire simply to do their jobs, but they were also motivated by scientific knowledge. Following his certainty about the science, Mostafa Tolba became much more actively involved in the talks. State interests are generally underspecified as well. Theorists typically treat interests by assumption, taking them as given or manifestly clear. Yet the state interests of such important parties as the United States and Germany changed during the course of the ozone talks. Correlation of the successful conclusion of the ozone talks with the presence of interest-based variables misses the importance of the change in a different variable—national interests—at an earlier stage in the process. A study of domestic politics is necessary to identify the origins of many state interests. Putnam's two-level game analysis helps to explain how the logjam was broken, as does the epistemic community analysis presented below.

---

31. See the history of the negotiations recounted by a principal U.S. negotiator, Benedick, *Ozone Diplomacy*.

Knowledge-Based Hypotheses

The ozone case does not confirm Cooper's hypothesis that consensual knowledge is necessary for regime creation.[32] Agreement on the Montreal Protocol preceded complete consensual knowledge. It was not until nine months after the treaty was signed that incommensurate hypotheses about the causes of the Antarctic ozone hole were resolved, and consensual knowledge was fully established only by the time of the London meetings.

A focus on epistemic communities does better in explaining the background for regime creation. Epistemic communities also help to explain the origins of major party interests. In turn, because major parties were able to exercise sufficient power to frame or bound the debate, these beliefs served to frame the issue. Institutional bargaining occurred within parameters established by the epistemic community.

In this case, a small transnational group of scientists and policy makers constituted an epistemic community. Its members accepted the Rowland-Molina hypothesis and developed models to elaborate it. They also began monitoring for actual ozone depletion, as well as publicly supporting policies that would ban CFCs. This group shared causal beliefs that related stratospheric ozone depletion to the infusion of chlorine from CFC use, as well as a strong normative desire to protect the environment. In the presence of scientific uncertainty in an area in which the consequences of action or inaction could be vast and irreversible, they believed it would be better to be safe than sorry, even at great cost. Because of their environmental values, the members of the group advocated anticipatory action despite the range of uncertainties.

The epistemic community was composed principally of atmospheric physicists and chemists. It extended worldwide, although it was most heavily represented in the United States. Members included the staff of the United Nations Environment Programme, especially Executive Director Mostafa Tolba, such distinguished scientists working in the United Kingdom as Joe Farman and Martin Holdgate, and from Europe, among others, Paul Crutzen, who worked at laboratories in the Netherlands, Sweden, and West Germany. Although high-level officials in the United States government (the Department of State and the EPA)

---

32. Richard N. Cooper, "International Cooperation in Public Health as Prologue to Macroeconomic Cooperation," in Cooper et al., *Can Nations Agree? Issues in International Economic Cooperation* (Washington, D.C.: Brookings Institution, 1989), 178–234.

lacked the scientific training, they shared many interests with this group.[33]

Ultimately, as these individuals and their allies gained influence in their various countries, they shifted the behavior of these countries. To a great extent they exercised influence through a combination of persuasion and usurpation of bureaucratic decision making. Argumentation also was used to sway some policy makers. The epistemic community appropriated other policy decisions by virtue of its newfound political power and national bureaucratic leverage. In the United States the epistemic community exercised its influence through a combination of both of these processes. Some officials, sympathetic to the modeling mode of understanding, were convinced by arguments. Others were bureaucratically outmaneuvered. Officials in the United Kingdom were more impervious to scientific arguments until it was clear that these must be heeded for reasons of domestic political convenience. Thus an analysis of epistemic communities requires attention to the domestic factors that shape a government's willingness to heed new advice and to hire new personnel. In the United States and Britain, for instance, the media and NGOs did much to heighten public concern about ozone depletion, which in turn led to pressure on their governments to take new actions.

The epistemic community assumed a dominant position in UNEP by the early 1980s. Tolba, a highly regarded microbiologist, became convinced early through his contacts in the scientific community of the need for strong anticipatory action to protect the ozone layer. His scientifically trained staff was similarly convinced by associates. In addition, some of the midlevel bureaucrats became disillusioned with their role as objective purveyors of science. Lawyers and policy makers ignored them during the early years of negotiations for the Vienna Convention. They assumed a new activist role by which they deliberately sought to extend their networks of influence and connections throughout the transnational scientific community, thus indirectly gaining entry to and influence over the political decision makers who were obstructing their position at international meetings.

Shocks precipitated the involvement of the epistemic community in decision making. Confronted with pressure to do something about an

---

33. The beliefs of the individuals in this group can be gleaned from discussion and anecdotes presented in Lydia Dotto and Harold Schiff, *The Ozone War* (Garden City, N.Y.: Doubleday, 1978); also Sharon Roan, *Ozone Crisis* (New York: Wiley, 1989). A fuller description and analysis of the ecological epistemic community is found in Peter M. Haas, "Banning Chlorofluorocarbons: Epistemic Community Efforts to Protect Stratospheric Ozone," *International Organization* 46 (Winter 1992): 187–224.

endangered ozone layer, government officials in Washington looked to the scientific community for advice on the nature and extent of the threat with which they were unfamiliar. In turn, they received technical advice that was strongly informed by the epistemic community's environmentalist disposition to protect nature from human encroachment. The Rowland-Molina hypothesis and the 1985 Antarctic ozone hole led governments to solicit new advice. The advice was not uncritically adopted, however, because many U.S. government officials considered the question of the economic impact of proposed measures to be equally important. Thus the scientific information did not carry the day solely because of the power of its inherent argument but also because of the bureaucratic power exercised by individuals within and close to the administration who were pushing such information. In conjunction with the public uproar, the epistemic community helped transform debate from "Should we protect the ozone layer?" to "*How* should we protect the ozone layer?"

Yet an epistemic community analysis extends well beyond the realm of bureaucratic politics. Members of the epistemic community in the United States prevailed over such strong adversaries as the Departments of Commerce and Defense, as well as overcoming the profound ideological resistance to environmental regulation that typified the Reagan administration. The major policy makers pushing for a strong regime were members of the epistemic community, and their actions reflected their causal and normative beliefs. They endorsed positions not only well beyond the traditional policies of their departments but also beyond what would gain them individual advancement in the administration.

Epistemic analyses best explain the variation in different countries' support for the regime as well as the timing of such support. Countries responded to the ozone threat at different rates. The first actively to encourage global controls were those in which the epistemic community was strongest: the United States, Canada, Sweden, Finland, and Norway. American support for ozone protection was strongest when the epistemic community had access to U.S. decision making. The epistemic community did not assume influence until late 1984, when the Reagan administration backed down following the excesses of the James Watt and Anne Gorsuch era. As heads of the Interior Department and Environmental Protection Agency, respectively, these officials drew widespread public ire for their outspoken commitment to development and unfettered economic growth and were ultimately forced to resign. New officials more sympathetic to the environmental arguments were involved at high levels—Lee Thomas at the Environmental Protection Agency, for example, and Richard Benedick in the State Department. Consequently, the United States pushed for a strong treaty during the period of the epistemic community's influence, from 1985 until 1989. Benedick and Thomas helped in the fall of 1986 to draft the American bargaining position, which called for CFC cuts up to 95 percent. When John Sununu came to control the White House and international environmental policy after 1988, much of the epistemic community's access and influence was lost, resulting in a shift in the United States away from an environmentalist attitude and a diminishing U.S. role in London.

Other countries came to support more stringent efforts as the members of the epistemic community gained influence in them. The epistemic community had great difficulty in gaining access and influence in state bureaucracies in developing countries, in part because of a general lack of interest in those countries as well as greater institutional impediments to entry for new actors.

In the United Kingdom, one of the last countries to support the Montreal Protocol, the transnational epistemic community's advice did not receive a hearing until domestic political obstructions were overcome. Scientific consensus did not emerge in the United Kingdom until the summer of 1988. Prime Minister Margaret Thatcher had distrusted the findings of the Ozone Trends Panel, suspecting that they were biased toward American interests because of NASA's strong role in the panel's formulation and that they exaggerated the rate of depletion and risks. She demanded rigorous proof of the existence of the ozone hole and its cause from British scientists whom she respected. She then reconvened her own Stratospheric Ozone Review Group (SORG). SORG's first report, in August 1987, had downplayed the extent of the ozone threat and the role of CFCs. By and large, SORG members had few connections with U.S. scientists. SORG member Joe Farman, however, "discoverer" of the Antarctic ozone hole in 1985 and also a member of the epistemic community, had publicly dismissed the findings of the earlier panel as based on out-of-date science. Thatcher delayed any domestic action while awaiting the findings of the reconvened group. SORG published its executive summary in June 1988 and its final report in October 1988, supporting and confirming the findings of the 1987 Ozone Trends Panel. The House of Lords Select Committee on the European Communities, responding to a preliminary version of the report, announced in July that it accepted that CFCs were responsible for the ozone hole and proposed an extension of the Montreal Protocol to cut CFC use by 85 percent. The real turnaround came at the end of September 1988, when Thatcher, in a speech to the Royal Society, called for immediate emergency action to safeguard the ozone layer, fight acid rain, and delay global warming, stating that "protecting the balance of nature [was] one of the great challenges of the late twentieth century."[34] Shortly thereafter, she invited countries to attend an ozone conference in London in early March 1989, called for the 85 percent cut in CFCs, and restored funding, along with a slight increase, to the Antarctic Survey.

Epistemic arguments must also take into account bureaucratic and domestic politics. The sudden British shift to support of CFC controls may have been the result of several converging factors. Domestic advice from Thatcher's own scientists, whom she trusted, may well have been a strong step. The timing is certainly suggestive. Before the SORG's second findings, the British position had essentially been driven by the Department of Trade and Industry, which was oriented toward protecting ICI, England's sole CFC producer. Additional factors reinforced the pressure from British scientists. Just before her speech to the Royal Society, Thatcher had received papers warning of global warming (not ozone depletion) provided by British ambassador to the United Nations Sir Crispin Tickell, a long-standing Thatcher confidant interested in climatic issues.[35] Domestic politics may have played a role as well. Thatcher's speech came a week before the Labour party congress. Domestically, the environment had suddenly become a hot topic that summer because of the widely publicized deaths of North Sea seals (from unclear causes) and the refusal of British authorities to allow the toxic-waste-loaded cargo ship *Karin B* entry into the United Kingdom. Thatcher's personality may have made a difference too. She had university chemistry training and was singularly responsive to advice couched in such terms as "as a scientist, Prime Minister, you will appreciate. . . . " The British story illustrates one country's response to the regime for ozone which was brought about in part by the epistemic community. It identifies as well some of the political forces with which the epistemic community interacted.

France is still fairly inactive in the ozone sphere. Very little ozone research has been conducted domestically, and the French Ministries for the Environment and Industry have paid little attention to the findings. Moreover, the policy-making process has been successfully dominated by the Ministry for Industry, which has an innate bias toward the interests of the French CFC producer, ATOCHEM.[36]

---

34. Geoffrey Lean, "Tories Plan 'Green Bill,' " *London Observer*, 2 October 1988, p. 1.

35. "The Greening of Margaret Thatcher," *Economist*, 11 March 1989, pp. 55–56; Geoffrey Lean, "Ozone: UN Acts to Tighten Controls," *London Observer*, 5 March 1989, p. 2.

36. For a list of French research see *La protection de la couche d'Ozone* (packet) (Paris: Secretariat d'Etat à l'Environnement, 1989).

The overall lag between European and American responses may be caused by differences in political, cultural, and social relations between the scientific community and government on the two continents. The highly fragmented nature of American government and society facilitates access by a strongly motivated group of technical experts. The more confrontational atmosphere in the United States also facilitates early entry of epistemic communities into the policy-making process. In European countries, where there are fewer entry points, smaller scientific communities, a less accepted role for policy service, and a less antagonistic, contentious, and controversial set of relations, it takes much longer for scientists to be heard.[37] Better relations between science and government, a less autonomous role for public science, and more bureaucratically secure policy makers work against ready access by such nonstate actors. Furthermore, unlike their European counterparts, whose predispositions are less strictly methodological, American regulators often have a "preference for rigorous quantitative analysis"[38] similar to the approach with which many scientists are comfortable. In the United Kingdom, with its traditional mode of negotiated solutions, the style of scientists has to be much more moderate. Overall, the size and mobility of such groups of specialists is much weaker in Europe than in the United States.

Differences in domestic structure, however, merely mean that to have an influence, epistemic communities were forced to operate through different channels and with different styles in different countries. Despite the differences in process in different countries, the outcomes proved similar and occurred following the mobilization of the epistemic community.

Contextual Factors

Decisions are not made in a vacuum. Regime creation may be the result of such broad international forces as the climate of public opinion or technological change as well as the narrower factors already discussed.[39]

---

37. For comparative studies of science policy and patterns of technical advice to policy makers, see Ronald Brickman, Sheila Jasanoff, and Thomas Ilgen, *Controlling Chemicals* (Ithaca: Cornell University Press, 1985); David Vogel, *National Styles of Regulation* (Ithaca: Cornell University Press, 1986); Sheila Jasanoff, *Risk Management and Political Culture* (New York: Russell Sage Foundation, 1986); and Thomas M. Dietz and Robert W. Rycroft, *The Risk Professionals* (New York: Russell Sage Foundation, 1987).

38. Jasanoff, *Risk Management*, 30.

39. See, for instance, Robert Cox, *Production, Power, and World Order* (New York: Columbia University Press, 1987). The Russian participants in this volume's preparation at the April 1990 workshop on Arctic regime formation in Washington, D.C., suggested similar propositions.

The regulation of CFCs would have been impossible without a prior shift in international consciousness. It was not until Rachel Carson's publication of *Silent Spring* that the public in industrialized countries, as well as governments, came to appreciate that threats to public health could be the result of willful human intervention in the natural environment, and that collective measures were necessary to protect the environment. Such an environmental consciousness remained diffuse throughout the 1980s in the industrialized countries and is still incipient in the developing world. Table 5.3 presents public opinion data from the Organization for Economic Cooperation and Development (OECD) showing level of concern with broad issues of air pollution, including ozone depletion, in different countries at different times.

Table 5.3 Percent in each country "very concerned" about air pollution problems

Country	1982	1988
United States	46 (1984)	58 (1990)
Japan	43 (1981)	41 (1990)
Finland	21 (1983)	61 (1989)
Norway		39 (1990)
Belgium	25	34
Denmark	34	45
France	28	36
West Germany	36	45
Greece	52	53
Ireland	24	30
Italy	43	62
Luxembourg	37	40
The Netherlands	38	54
Portugal		41
Spain		52
United Kingdom	24	32

Sources: OECD, *OECD Environmental Data—Compendium 1985* (1985), 266. OECD, *The State of the Environment* (Paris: OECD, 1991), 281.

It is striking that in many cases opinion changed little during the 1980s, suggesting that public environmental consciousness may be a background condition for creation of international environmental regimes but is not directly involved with the creation of specific regimes. Moreover, public opinion studies have increasingly shown that although people may express concern about global problems, they are politically mobilized to act only on local problems.

Technological change is a common background condition that generates technical solutions to environmental problems and hence greatly facilitates the creation of regimes for such issues. Indeed, many important features of the dynamics of the ozone regime are technological. Ozone depletion was caused by unanticipated consequences of a new industrial substance, the problem was identified by highly sophisticated new monitoring equipment, and solutions ultimately rest on the development of alternative substances. The cost of implementing the Montreal Protocol in the United States alone is estimated at $2.7 billion, and producers still lack clear-cut commercial alternatives through which to claim the economic rents created by the elimination of CFCs and halons.[40]

The ozone regime is in part the triumph of subjective forces over objective forces. Minerva's owl flew well before dusk. The Montreal Protocol and London Amendments banned CFCs before it was clear that commercial alternatives were available. Contextual factors fail to contribute to the explanation of formation of the ozone regime.

Conclusions

A dynamic analysis of the creation of the ozone regime is also possible. National behavior contributing to regime creation is a result of prior choices as well as a response to systemic circumstances and conditions. In this view, knowledge-based variables helped to explain the setting in which negotiations were conducted and power was exercised.

Once the actors understood the domain for which they were trying to conclude a regime, bargaining progressed. The Montreal Protocol and London Amendments occurred in large part because of the identification and application of relevant knowledge by the epistemic community. The Würzburg meetings and the Ozone Trends Panel both established incontrovertible scientific facts to which the negotiators responded: rapid, strong cuts of a wide variety of CFCs were necessary to prevent depletion of stratospheric ozone. Bargaining occurred in light of such conclusions. The interest-based hypotheses identify some conditions that contributed to regime creation. The power hypotheses further identify resources that allowed the United States to drive negotiations so that the final regime more closely approximated U.S. interests than those of the other parties. In summary, regime creation occurred through institutional bargaining within a contract zone delimited by an epistemic community. Within the contract zone, the final agreement was closer to the interests of the issue-

40. *Economic Report of the President* (Washington, D.C.: U.S. Government Printing Office, 1990), 210.

hegemonic United States by virtue of the leverage the United States was able to exercise from its power resources.

Counterfactual thought experiments help shed light on the interplay of these forces. The United States, pursuing its self-identified interest, exercised power over other countries. But its interest came from the epistemic community. Without American power there would have been no incentive for other countries to defer to American interests, and collective outcomes would probably have never been any stronger than the Vienna Convention. Without the epistemic community, American interests would have been different, yielding a correspondingly weaker treaty, and the Montreal Protocol would surely have been delayed awaiting broader technical consensus. Without environmental interests, other parties would have been driven purely by technological concerns, which at the very least would not have yielded commitments to eliminate products before commercial alternatives were available. The final regime would have been little different from the hodgepodge of national strategies developed in the late 1970s.

The ozone regime emerged out of a process of negotiation. Different stages are best explained by different hypotheses. The evaluation of the explanatory adequacy of these hypotheses is summarized in Table 5.4.

The absence of necessary conditions identified by interest-based and knowledge-based hypotheses correctly predicts the relative weakness of the Vienna Convention. The Montreal Protocol and the London Amendments are correctly predicted by a combination of all three sets of explanations. But many of the interest-based conditions were present without successful regime creation as well. None of the sets of hypotheses, taken alone, was adequate to explain this process. Taken together, each offers insights into part of the process. Knowledge-based hypotheses help in understanding the timing of negotiations and the array of interests different actors were seeking to satisfy. Interest-based bargaining helps to explain the selection of specific outcomes, once the existence of mutual gains had been made apparent by an epistemic community. Power-based explanations provide further insight into the pressures that drove parties to agree on specific alternatives within the contract zone available for agreement.

Each of the groups of theory provides a necessary but insufficient explanation of the formation of the stratospheric ozone protection regime. In decreasing order of abstraction, knowledge-based theories helped in locating the discussions, interest-based theories helped in understanding the range of options, and power-based theories helped in understanding which of the knowledge- and interest-selected outcomes resulted. The parameters of the bargaining space were defined by the epistemic community as well as by the specific interests of the dominant national actor, the

Table 5.4 Evaluation of explanatory adequacy of different hypotheses at different stages in the process of negotiation

Hypotheses	Vienna	Montreal	London
Power-based			
Hegemony	no	yes	no
Interest-based			
Integrative or distributive	distributive	both	integrative
Veil of uncertainty	thick	medium	thinner
Equitable solution	no	yes	unclear
Salient solution	no	no	yes
Shocks	no	yes	yes
National priority	no	no	maybe
Common good perceived	Nordics—yes others—no	USA/UNEP/ Nordics—yes others—no	yes LDCs—no
Role of science and technology	yes	yes	yes
Relevant parties	no	yes	yes
Effective compliance mechanisms	irrelevant	yes	yes
Leadership	yes	yes	yes
Knowledge-based			
Consensual knowledge	no	no	yes
Technical uncertainty	high	high, declining	low
Shocks	no	yes	yes
Epistemic community mobilized	no	yes	yes

United States. Although the epistemic community framed the discussions around the need for rapid establishment of stringent controls over a wide range of chemicals, it had little impact on specific provisions of the regime. The location within the bargaining space in which precise compromises occurred was a consequence of the exercise of power combined with adroit bargaining and the willingness of the United States to make timely concessions.

CHAPTER SIX

Arctic Haze and Transboundary Air Pollution: Conditions Governing Success and Failure

MARVIN S. SOROOS

Transboundary atmospheric pollution rose to prominence on the global agenda of environmental problems during the 1980s. International concern over atmospheric pollution grew as scientific evidence mounted on the scope and consequences of acid rain, the depletion of the stratospheric ozone layer, and an apparent trend toward global warming. International regimes exist to address acid rain in Europe and North America and ozone depletion globally, and a framework convention on climate limit change was adopted at the United Nations Conference on Environment and Development in June 1992.

By contrast, an atmospheric phenomenon known as Arctic haze—a specific type of transboundary air pollution prevalent over the north polar region during the winter months—has received little attention outside of the scientific community. Research carried out since 1976 reveals that the haze consists of anthropogenic pollutants that originate in the heavily industrialized, midlatitude regions of Eurasia and are transported to the Arctic region by prevailing weather patterns during the winter season. Scientists continue to study the environmental consequences of Arctic haze, in particular its possible impact on fragile Arctic ecosystems and the global climate.

This case study differs from others in this volume in two respects. First, no international regime has been created specifically to address the problems posed by Arctic haze. A diplomatic initiative among the eight Arctic rim states that began at a conference in Rovaniemi in 1989 did lead to signing in June 1991 of the Declaration on the Protection of the Arctic Environment, including adoption of the Arctic Environmental Protection Strategy. This general-purpose environmental agreement does not address Arctic haze specifically, but its priorities include some aspects of the haze problem such as air pollutants and acidification. At this nascent stage, however, the strategy hardly constitutes a regime, either for preserving the Arctic environment generally or for lessening the specific problem of Arctic haze. Studying a case in which no regime has been established, however, can be of significant assistance in distinguishing the factors that have favored the creation of other regimes.

The Arctic haze problem is also distinctive in view of the possibility that the condition will be ameliorated by a broader regime dealing with long-range transboundary air pollution (LRTAP) among the industrialized countries of the Northern Hemisphere. The LRTAP or acid rain regime, created in the late 1970s through negotiations conducted under the auspices of the United Nations Economic Commission for Europe (ECE), was an outgrowth of the Helsinki Accord of the ongoing Conference on Security and Cooperation in Europe (CSCE). It addresses problems associated with acid precipitation that have become increasingly apparent in the non-Arctic regions of Europe and North America. Thus, though Arctic haze was not a significant consideration in the creation of the LRTAP regime, the regime may accomplish reductions of emissions of air pollutants in the industrialized regions where the haze-causing pollutants originate, thereby reducing the need for a more narrowly focused Arctic haze regime.

The regime's foundation agreement is the Convention on Long-Range Transboundary Air Pollution adopted in 1979. This framework treaty has been augmented by several protocols, the first being a 1984 agreement on the long-term funding of an existing monitoring network. A 1985 protocol mandates a reduction in national sulfur emissions or their transboundary fluxes of at least 30 percent (from 1980 levels) as soon as possible but no later than 1993. A 1988 protocol requires that nitrogen oxide emissions or transboundary fluxes not exceed 1987 levels after 1994. A 1991 protocol specifies a 30 percent reduction by 1999 in emissions of volatile organic compounds, using 1988 as a base year.

All of the Eurasian states that are significant sources of haze-causing pollution, including the former Soviet Union, have ratified the 1979 framework treaty. Most of these states have ratified the 1985 sulfur protocol, but three major sulfur emitters—Poland, the United Kingdom, and the United States—have not become parties. The Sofia protocol on nitrogen oxides came into effect in February 1991 upon the ratification of the sixteenth state. In the case of the United States, the 1990 amendments to the 1970 Clean Air Act are projected to accomplish a 50 percent reduction in emissions of sulfur dioxide and nitrogen oxides.[1]

Any impact the LRTAP regime has in reducing emissions of transboundary air pollutants such as sulfur and nitrogen oxides and volatile organic compounds in the heavily industrialized regions of Eurasia may partly ameliorate the Arctic haze phenomenon. Sulfur emissions declined by 25 percent in the OECD countries during the 1980s, but it is unclear how much of the reduction can be attributed to the LRTAP regime.[2] Nor is it possible to quantify the impact of these reductions on the haze phenomenon.

It is apparent, however, that the LRTAP regime is not an adequate international response to the Arctic haze problem. The Arctic Environmental Protection Strategy adopted at the 1991 ministerial meeting in Rovaniemi notes both a need to supplement the ECE's air-monitoring network with programs that measure air quality and deposition in Arctic areas and to study the impacts of these pollutants in the distinctive and fragile environment of the Arctic.[3] Moreover, the LRTAP regulations do not apply to emissions of many of the aerosol-forming pollutants that contribute to the haze phenomenon such as graphitic carbon and traces of heavy metals. Finally, although the LRTAP regime applies to air pollutants from the area of the former Soviet Union west of the Ural Mountains that drift across its western boundaries into the European and Nordic countries, it does not limit the pollutants that flow out over the Arctic Sea, which are major contributors to Arctic haze.

Nearly a century ago, Norwegian explorer Fridtjof Nansen noted dark stains on polar ice and hypothesized that they were caused by airborne pollutants.[4] Nevertheless, it was generally assumed that the natural environment of the Arctic was pristine. The presumption did not seriously come into question until the 1950s, when J. Murray Mitchell,

---

1. William K. Reilly, "The New Clean Air Act: An Environmental Milestone," *EPA Journal* 17 (January–February 1991): 4.

2. Organization for Economic Cooperation and Development (OECD), *Environmental Indicators* (Paris: OECD, 1991), 21.

3. Arctic Environmental Protection Strategy, adopted at Rovaniemi, Finland, 14 June 1991. For the official text see *Arctic Research of the United States* 5 (Fall 1991): 29–35.

4. B. Ottar, "Arctic Air Pollution: A Norwegian Perspective," *Atmospheric Environment* 23 (1989): 2349.

Jr., a climatologist taking part in the Ptarmigan weather reconnaissance flights, observed puzzling patches of haze that obscured visibility over the region.[5] Even then, however, this atmospheric phenomenon was not attributed to anthropogenic pollutants, and it was not investigated further.[6]

Glenn E. Shaw, a scientist from the University of Alaska in Fairbanks, "rediscovered" Arctic haze in 1972, when he went to Point Barrow, Alaska, to take what he thought would be unremarkable measurements of the Arctic atmosphere to serve as a reference point for the composition of unpolluted air. On arrival, Shaw was immediately struck by the whitish rather than blue color of the air. When his measurements indicated a significant volume of aerosols in the air, he speculated that this was not a naturally occurring phenomenon but rather the result of pollutants that did not appear to originate locally.[7]

In 1975, with support from the U.S. Office of Naval Research, Shaw teamed up with Kenneth Rahn of the University of Rhode Island to take systematic measurements of the haze in an effort to identify its origins. They analyzed samples of air taken from light aircraft above Point Barrow during the spring of 1976 and concluded that the haze consisted primarily of dust carried by wind currents from the great deserts of China and Mongolia.[8] Returning in November 1976, however, the team observed a different type of haze, which contained such elements as vanadium, manganese, and aluminum along with high levels of sulfate—telltale signs that the condition was caused by pollutants from industrialized regions.[9]

The dust observed in the spring of 1976 turned out to be attributable to unusual atmospheric circumstances occurring after the seasonal pollution had dissipated. Subsequent ground-level readings taken each

5. Reported in J. Mitchell, Jr., "Visual Range in the Polar Regions with Particular Reference to the Alaskan Arctic," *Journal of Atmospheric and Terrestrial Physics*, Special Supplement (1957): 195–211; also Ottar, "Arctic Air Pollution," 2349.

6. For overviews of scientific knowledge on Arctic haze, see Kenneth A. Rahn and N. J. Heidam, "Progress on Arctic Air Chemistry, 1977–1980: A Comparison of the First and Second Symposia," *Atmospheric Environment* 15 (1981): 1345–1348; also Leonard A. Barrie, "Arctic Air Pollution: An Overview of Current Knowledge," *Atmospheric Environment* 20 (1986): 643–663; and Leonard A. Barrie et al., "Arctic Contaminants: Sources, Occurrence and Pathways," *Science of the Total Environment* 122 (1992): 1–74.

7. Kenneth A. Rahn and Glenn E. Shaw, "Sources and Transport of Arctic Pollution Aerosols: A Chronicle of Six Years of ONR Research," *Naval Research Reviews* 24 (1982): 5; John Carey, "Peering into the Mystery of Arctic Haze," *International Wildlife* 18 (March–April 1988): 27.

8. Rahn and Shaw, "Sources and Transport," 5–7.

9. Kenneth A. Rahn, "Who's Polluting the Arctic," *Natural History* 93 (1984): 30–31.

year at Point Barrow revealed that pollution-caused haze was the norm.[10] The thickest haze of the Arctic winter has been observed over Alaska's North Slope. Although the haze over Point Barrow is significantly less dense than the smog occurring over such major cities as New York or Los Angeles, it is comparable to pollution levels recorded above midsized, midlatitude cities in the United States and is much greater than the contaminants over remote areas of the continent. Moreover, air samples taken elsewhere in the Arctic indicated the presence of haze during the winter months from Alaska eastward to Scandinavia and as far north as the pole, a region that covers approximately 9 percent of the Earth's surface.

Haze consists of a mixture of gases and particles that are suspended in air. Scientists refer to these as aerosols. Some of the components of the aerosols observed over the Arctic region are naturally occurring substances: for example, soil dust and sea salt particles are present in the haze over Point Barrow.[11] Of more concern are the concentrations of particles in the Arctic haze having a chemical composition attributable only to human activities and bearing a distinct similarity to aerosols in the air above heavily polluted industrial areas far to the south. The winter haze includes significant concentrations of sulfate, twenty times as great as the levels observed during summer in the Arctic.[12] Another of the principal components of the haze is graphitic carbon, otherwise known as soot, which is a catalytically active carrier for reactive or toxic trace substances.[13] Organic compounds originating in pesticides and fungicides have also been detected in Arctic haze,[14] as have traces of almost every pollution element found at midlatitudes.[15]

Soon after scientists became aware of the magnitude of the problem of Arctic haze, they began seeking ways to trace sources of the pollutants. Because of the complexity of air flows, it has been impractical, if not impossible, to calculate back-trajectories for pollutants over thou-

10. Bette Hileman, "Arctic Haze," *Environmental Science and Technology* 17 (1983): 233a.

11. Richard A. Kerr, "Pollution in the Atmosphere Confirmed," *Science* 212 (29 May 1981): 1013.

12. Kenneth A. Rahn, "Arctic Haze Provides a Clue to Polar Circulation," *Maritimes* 23 (February 1979): 9.

13. H. Rosen and T. Novakov, "Combustion-Generated Carbon Particles in the Arctic Atmosphere," *Nature* 36 (1983): 769.

14. Jozef M. Pacyna and Michael Oehme, "Long-Range Transport of Some Organic Compounds to the Norwegian Arctic," *Atmospheric Environment* 22 (1988): 243–257.

15. Rahn, "Who's Polluting the Arctic," 32–33, 87.

sands of kilometers from the Arctic to their origins. With the help of Leonard Barrie of the Canadian Atmospheric Environment Service, more practical techniques have been developed that identify the chemical "signature" of air found in a given geographical region.[16] Scientists have been able to draw conclusions about the pathways of the pollutants by combining data on the chemical signatures of haze aerosols with knowledge of the normal seasonal patterns of high- and low-pressure systems in the Arctic region during the winter months. Pollutants over the Scandinavian Arctic for the most part have been carried northward from Europe and the British Isles. The haze evident in Alaska during the early part of the winter season appears to originate primarily in the heavily industrialized areas of the Volga-Ural region of the former Soviet Union, following a northward course over the Taymyr Peninsula and then straight across the pole to the North American Arctic. As spring approaches, however, this cross-polar flow is blocked by the development of a strong high-pressure area and Alaska receives pollutants from a pathway that runs westward from the former Soviet Union past the Norwegian Arctic, where it picks up pollutants of European origin before proceeding over Greenland and across the North American Arctic.[17] Little of the haze originates in North America because precipitation cleanses the air flowing northward over the Atlantic Ocean.[18] By one calculation, the Eurasian region contributes 94 percent of the sul-

---

16. This signature reflects the relative concentrations of trace elements in the pollution that the air contains. Comparing the signatures of the air found over Arctic locations in winter with the distinctive signatures from other regions offers a clue about the origins of the haze-causing pollutants. One such test developed by Rahn in the early 1980s measures the ratio of manganese to vanadium in the atmospheric aerosols. See Rahn, "Who's Polluting the Arctic," 37–38.

High ratios of manganese indicate that the pollutants originated in coal-burning and metal-processing regions such as the Soviet Union and Europe, whereas a greater presence of vanadium can be traced to areas where heavy oil is burned such as eastern North America. See Kerr, "Pollution in the Atmosphere Confirmed," 1014; also Rahn and Shaw, "Sources and Transport," 14.

Several other trace elements, including arsenic, selenium, antimony, zinc, and indium, are also used in reading chemical signatures (see Rahn, "Who's Polluting the Arctic," 37–38), as is the isotopic composition of sulfur in the haze (Jerome O. Nriagu, Robert D. Coker, and Leonard A. Barrie, "Origin of Sulphur in Canadian Arctic Haze from Isotope Measurements," *Nature* 349 [10 January 1991]: 142–145).

17. Wolfgang E. Raatz, "Meteorological Conditions over Eurasia and the Arctic Contributing to the March 1983 Arctic Haze Episode," *Atmospheric Environment* 19 (1985): 2121–2126; also Rahn and Shaw, "Sources and Transport."

18. Rahn, "Who's Polluting the Arctic," 30.

fate in the Arctic, and the remaining 6 percent comes from North America.[19]

Many questions remain to be answered about the impact of Arctic haze on the natural environment. Scientific evidence does not indicate that the haze has yet had serious environmental consequences. The impact of the haze would probably be greater if winds did not carry a large proportion of the pollutants away from the region.[20] Nevertheless, there are reasons for concern that the haze may have significant long-term implications of both regional and global scope.[21]

Much of the speculation on the consequences of Arctic haze focuses on the possibility that the presence of graphitic carbon may modify the radiation balance of the atmosphere, which could trigger complex climate changes resulting in a significant warming of the lower levels of the atmosphere in the Arctic region. If substantial warming in the Arctic region is observed in future decades, it will be difficult, however, to determine how much of it is owing to Arctic haze rather than to the more general global warming trends that scientists are concerned will result from the buildup of carbon dioxide and other "greenhouse" gases in the atmosphere.

The environmental changes that would be generated by a warming of the atmosphere over the Arctic are even more difficult to foresee. If a substantial melting of polar ice and snow were to occur, sea levels would probably rise globally, with major consequences for coastal regions. In the Arctic region, shipping might be more treacherous because of the accelerated calving of icebergs, but the reduced extent of pack ice would extend the season during which vessels could ply Arctic routes.[22]

A significant warming of the Arctic climate would have other implications for the regional ecosystem. The permafrost line would recede, altering the habitat of the fauna and flora inhabiting these areas and perhaps also allowing an immigration of plants and animals whose range was previously limited by the harsh Arctic conditions. The Arctic region might also become more amenable both to human communities

---

19. Leonard A. Barrie, M. P. Olson, and K. K. Oikawa, "The Flux of Anthropogenic Sulphur into the Arctic from Mid-Latitudes in 1979/80," *Atmospheric Environment* 25 (1989): 2510.

20. Barrie et al., "Arctic Contaminants."

21. Carey, "Peering into the Mystery," 28.

22. J. Barrie Maxwell and Leonard A. Barrie, "Atmospheric and Climatic Change in the Arctic and Antarctic," *Ambio* 8 (16 March 1989): 48.

and to resource exploitation, which could further disrupt the fragile environment or the way of life of the Native peoples.[23]

Another environmental concern is the biogeochemical impact of pollutants that fall on the fragile tundra ecosystem. Of particular concern are the acids formed when sulfur constituents, the most concentrated haze component, combine with moisture either in the air or on the Earth's surface. Aquatic life in lakes can be especially vulnerable to acidification. It is also believed that acid precipitation causes a sharp decline in the growth rate of lichens that reindeer depend upon for nourishment.[24]

Research on the consequences of Arctic haze is still in its infancy. Scientists have been hampered in their ability to analyze long-term trends by the lack of systematic observations before 1976.[25] Ice core samples indicate a 75 percent increase in Arctic pollution between 1952 and 1977.[26] Readings taken over the past decade, however, do not indicate a significant thickening of haze over the Arctic, and it is possible that national and international regulations limiting emissions of air pollutants have begun to lessen the problem.[27] Because of the complexity of ecosystems and the natural and human forces that are operating on them, however, there may well be unanticipated ramifications that could reverberate in unexpected ways through the regional and planetary ecosystems.

ANALYSIS AND HYPOTHESIS TESTING

This section applies various theories regarding the circumstances favorable to the creation of international regimes to the case of Arctic haze. It tests specific hypotheses drawn from these theories by considering whether they offer a plausible explanation for why the states of the Arctic region have not yet created a regime that explicitly addresses the Arctic haze problem, in contrast with the emergence of the LRTAP

---

23. Ibid.

24. Helen K. Søbye, "Arctic Nature under Threat," *Acid News* 1 (February 1989): 14.

25. Carey, "Peering into the Mystery," 28.

26. Gail Osherenko and Oran R. Young, *The Age of the Arctic: Hot Conflicts and Cold Realities* (Cambridge: Cambridge University Press, 1989), 123.

27. Glenn E. Shaw, "Introduction: International Symposium on Arctic Air Pollution," in *Arctic Air Pollution*, ed. Bernard Stonehouse (Cambridge: Cambridge University Press, 1986), xvi; Carey, "Peering into the Mystery," 28.

regime that addresses the problem of acid precipitation in Europe and North America. The hypotheses are confirmed to the extent that the conditions that would favor regime creation have been absent in the more narrow Arctic regional context but were present while the LRTAP regime evolved.

Power-Based Hypotheses

The cause of reducing Arctic haze has not had the benefit of a single hegemonic actor because both superpowers are among the Arctic rim states and have been dominant players in the political affairs of the region. Thus each superpower precludes the other from acting as a hegemon. Furthermore, neither of the two superpowers has shown much inclination to take a leadership role, much less act as a hegemon, in the creation of regimes dealing with environmental matters in the region. Their willingness to play such a role would undoubtedly be greater if they were primarily victims of the haze problem, but both contribute to the problem, particularly the former Soviet Union. What limited impetus there has been for regime creation on problems such as Arctic air pollution has come largely from the Nordic countries and Canada.[28]

Likewise, because both superpowers were participants, there was no single hegemonic actor in the Economic Commission for Europe when it took up the problem of LRTAP. The Soviet Union did play a pivotal role in placing environmental issues on the agenda of the ECE in the late 1970s for reasons that will be explained below in analyzing contextual variables. Although the Soviet leader Leonid Brezhnev took advantage of his country's status as a superpower to force the issue and get serious negotiations started on the LRTAP problem, the Soviet Union was not in a position to play a hegemonic role in determining the character of the regime that was eventually created, nor did it attempt to do so.[29] The United States has given little support to international efforts to regulate transboundary air pollution through the ECE and at times, especially during the Reagan administration, actively attempted to thwart an agreement on targeted reductions of emissions. The United States ratified the 1979 framework convention but not the 1985 protocol on sulfur emissions.

---

28. Oran R. Young, "Global Commons: The Arctic in World Affairs," *Technology Review* 92 (January–February 1990): 61.

29. C. Ian Jackson, "A Tenth Anniversary Review of the ECE Convention on Long-Range Transboundary Air Pollution," *International Environmental Affairs* 2 (Summer 1990): 218–220.

Thus the emergence of the LRTAP regime would seem to indicate that a single hegemonic actor is not a necessary condition for the formation of international regimes, as was hypothesized. Factors other than the lack of a hegemon could explain the failure to create an Arctic haze regime.

Is a bipolar distribution of power favorable to the creation of international regimes, in view of the fact that the two superpowers are leading actors in both the narrowly defined Arctic grouping and the broader ECE community? To the extent that bipolarity led to intense political conflict and military rivalry between the United States and the former Soviet Union, it was clearly a major obstacle to multilateral cooperation on Arctic matters. National strategic concerns led to large regions of the Arctic being set off-limits for environmental monitoring and scientific research. Scientists were not only denied access to the territory of foreign countries but also were limited in what they could do in regions deemed sensitive in their own countries. Much of the scientific research that did take place was done under military sponsorship, and the results were classified.[30]

The substantial easing of Cold War tensions coincided with the blossoming of efforts to move toward an Arctic environmental regime. The former Soviet Union has become much more open in supplying information on emissions of air pollutants and the condition of the Arctic environment within its boundaries, as well as an enthusiastic supporter of international scientific cooperation on Arctic problems.[31] The transition to democracy in Eastern Europe has led to an acknowledgment of the severity of air pollution and other environmental problems in the region.

The establishment of the LRTAP regime in the late 1970s suggests, however, that bipolarity does not necessarily preclude the creation of regimes that involve both superpowers. It illustrates how bilateral or multilateral cooperation on significant but tangential matters may become part of a larger strategy for lessening tensions between competing poles of power. Cooperation on LRTAP became a test of whether beneficial but not critical cooperation could defuse Cold War tensions be-

---

30. Juan G. Roederer, "International Scientific Cooperation in the Arctic: Problems, Opportunities and US Responsibilities," in *Arctic Air Pollution*, ed. Stonehouse, 291; Willy Østreng, "Polar Science and Politics: Close Twins or Opposite Poles in International Cooperation," in *International Resource Management: The Role of Science and Politics*, ed. Steinar Andresen and Willy Østreng (London: Belhaven Press, 1989), 102–103.

31. Østreng, "Polar Science and Politics," 104; Alexei Yu Roginko, "Arctic Environmental Cooperation: Prospects and Possibilities," *Current Research on Peace and Violence* 12 (1989): 136.

tween the Eastern and Western blocs, as will be elaborated further in discussing contextual factors.

On balance, bipolarity would seem to be a hindrance to the creation of international regimes, as was the case in regard to a solution to the Arctic haze problem. The LRTAP case indicates, however, that bipolarity does not preclude the formation of a regime and under unusual circumstances may actually enhance the prospects for a regime.

The power structure among the states of the Arctic region differs from the ECE in one significant way that may at least in part account for contrasting achievements in regime formation. Aside from the superpowers, the Arctic group is populated by states that rank low on most measures of power, with Canada being the only example of what could be described as a major middle power. The larger membership of the ECE includes several other middle powers and more substantial ones such as France, the Federal Republic of Germany, Italy, the United Kingdom, and Poland.

Much of the initial impetus for both Arctic environmental regimes and the LRTAP regime has come from the Nordic states and Canada. Being among the lesser middle powers of the region, however, these Nordic states lacked the economic size and political standing to have much influence over states primarily responsible for large transboundary fluxes of air pollutants. Thus the prospects for proceeding beyond the general framework convention of 1979 to specific international regulations on the reduction of acid-forming pollutants were dim until the Federal Republic of Germany, a leading middle power, abruptly shifted from an opponent to a supporter of the cause in 1982. Germany then played an instrumental role in the negotiations that led to the 1985 protocol on sulfur emissions. The Netherlands, Switzerland, and Austria are other non-Arctic members of the ECE that have been advocates of deeper reductions in emissions of sulfur and nitrogen oxides.

The preceding analysis leads to the conclusion that power-based theories do not offer a very compelling explanation for the absence of an Arctic environmental regime in contrast to the earlier emergence of LRTAP. The success in creating the LRTAP regime suggests that a hegemon is not a necessary condition for regime formation. Bipolarity has been a hindrance to multilateral cooperation on environmental matters among the Arctic states, largely because of the strategic sensitivities of the superpowers, but was not a significant obstacle to the creation of the LRTAP regime. Paradoxically, the desire to lessen Cold War tensions was a stimulus for the negotiations that led up to the LRTAP framework treaty in 1979. The role that West Germany played in the follow-up protocol on sulfur emissions suggests that major middle powers have acted as significant facilitators of regime development in the absence of strong support from the superpowers.

Interest-Based Hypotheses

The hypotheses considered in this section address the question of why parties in bargaining and negotiation reap joint gains in some instances but not in others. The formation of international regimes that address air pollution, such as the Arctic haze phenomenon, must reconcile two basic interests, first, those of polluters in having a convenient and inexpensive sink for disposing of the substances and, second, those of victims who must bear the consequences of the pollution.

Several interest-based hypotheses assert that international regimes are more likely to emerge when negotiations are integrative as opposed to distributive in character. Negotiators engaged in integrative bargaining seek to identify ways to further their common interests, whereas those inclined to engage in distributive bargaining pursue agreements that promote their narrow national interests.[32]

The circumstances do not favor an integrative mode of bargaining on Arctic haze if the problem is taken up separately. The pollutants that cause the haze are transported thousands of kilometers by wind currents from the industrialized states in the midlatitudes of Europe to the distant Arctic expanse where the consequences are manifest. Thus a clear-cut division exists between states that are the cause of the haze problem and those that are the victims of it, aside from the former Soviet Union, which fits into both categories and so could potentially play a leadership role in the creation of a regime.

For this reason, the upwind states apparently have not perceived an important enough shared interest in mitigating the haze problem to enter into serious integrative negotiations with the Arctic rim states. They can be expected to approach the haze problem in a distributive manner, concluding that they are being asked to make a costly commitment to address a problem that has a much greater impact on other states than it does on them. Because there is little or no contract zone between the polluter and victim states, bargaining is also bound to fail unless the issue can be linked to another matter of concern to the emitter. It is also possible that seriously affected downwind states may see it in their in-

---

32. Richard Walton and Robert B. McKersie, *A Behavioral Theory of Negotiations* (New York: McGraw-Hill, 1965); Oran R. Young, "The Politics of International Regime Formation: Managing Natural Resources and the Environment," *International Organization* 43 (Summer 1989): 361.

terests to offer to share the expense of reducing the emissions of the upwind state, as is the case in Finland's agreement to help the Soviet Union reduce pollutants from its smelters on the Kola Peninsula.[33]

The prospects for integrative bargaining on the Arctic haze problem might be given a boost if compelling scientific evidence suggested that haze has significant global implications, such as an acceleration of climate change, that would affect the upwind states as well.

The larger problem of LRTAP in the European region has been more conducive to integrative negotiation. Because of their geographical proximity, the continental European countries share a common airshed in which pollutants intermingle across many national boundaries. Most of these states are the recipients of significant volumes of transboundary fluxes causing acid precipitation, although there is considerable variation in the ratio of air pollutants that leave or enter their air spaces. Austria, France, the Netherlands, West Germany, Norway, Switzerland, and Sweden all "exported" more than 50 percent of their sulfur emissions, while more than half of the sulfur deposited in each one of them was "imported" from foreign sources.[34] Thus integrative bargaining can take place because such states have a shared interest in regionwide restrictions on air pollutants, even if it means limiting their own emissions that drift into other countries.

Not all ECE members, however, have consistently perceived a common interest in regulating transboundary pollution. The three principal upwind states—the United States, the United Kingdom, and Ireland—have refrained from accepting the 1985 protocol mandating a 30 percent reduction in sulfur emissions by 1993. As upwind states they have relatively little to gain from the emission reductions by downwind states relative to the costs that would be entailed in complying with the reductions specified in the protocol. The United Kingdom, for example, exported 71 percent of its sulfur emissions, but only 15 percent of its sulfur deposition was imported.[35] Such states are unlikely to take decisive action on air pollution until the domestic impacts of their pollutants provoke strong political demands to reduce emissions.[36]

---

33. Tapani Vaahtoranta, "Environmental Protection in Finnish-Soviet Relations: The Case of the Nickel Smelters in the Kola Peninsula" (paper presented at annual meeting of the International Studies Association, Vancouver, British Columbia, March 1991).

34. Hilary F. French, "Clearing the Air," in Lester R. Brown et al., *State of the World 1990* (New York: Norton, 1990), 115.

35. Ibid.

36. Sonja Boehmer-Christiansen, "Black Mist and Acid Rain—Science as a Fig Leaf of Policy," *Political Quarterly* 5 (1988): 153.

Thus this analysis suggests that the distribution of interests generally favored the pursuit of common interests through integrative bargaining in the case of LRTAP but not in regard to the Arctic haze problem, a finding that is consistent with the hypothesis that integrative bargaining is an important condition for the successful creation of regimes.

Another hypothesis states that uncertainties about the distribution of costs and benefits that would result from a proposed regime, or what has become known as a veil of uncertainty, enhance the likelihood that integrative bargaining will take place and lead to substantive agreements.

The basic nature of the Arctic haze problem suggests that the states responsible for the problem can anticipate the obligations they would be asked to incur in negotiating an Arctic haze regime. But continuing scientific uncertainty regarding the potential global impacts of Arctic haze, such as accelerated climate change and a rising sea level, could contribute to the veil of uncertainty, causing non-Arctic states to perceive a possible stake in addressing the problem in an integrative way. The veil of uncertainty would also be thicker if the problem of Arctic haze were to be taken up in the context of a more comprehensive regime on the Arctic environment.

The evolution of the LRTAP regime tends to confirm the hypothesis. The veil of uncertainty is thick in the case of the framework convention which has been ratified by most of the ECE members. The primary thrust of the convention was to facilitate cooperation on research on sulfur compounds and other major air pollutants, which would provide the basis for later decisions on specific strategies for mitigating the problem. Thus the veil of uncertainty on the ultimate impact of the emerging regime on specific actors is especially thick, which may account in part for its widespread acceptance.

Conversely, the follow-up sulfur and nitrogen protocols are much more specific about the emission reductions expected of the states. Thus the veil of uncertainty was thinner in the negotiations on these protocols because potential parties could calculate the costs of the obligations they would incur. The contentiousness of the negotiations on these protocols and the failure of some major polluting states to accept them bear out the hypothesis that a thick veil of uncertainty enhances the prospects for agreements.

The next hypothesis suggests that regimes are more likely to be created when the goal of reaching an agreement that is perceived to be equitable to the parties involved is not sacrificed to the often conflicting dictate of achieving an outcome that fosters efficiency.

Proposals designed to achieve economic efficiency in reducing air pollutants are usually based on a market mechanism, such as auctioning "rights" to pollute to the highest bidder or imposing taxes on pollution, which would have the result of concentrating emissions in those activities that have the greatest economic value. Such a strategy may be perceived as inequitable to poor countries that could find themselves priced out the market for pollution rights.

International discussions on Arctic haze have not gotten to the point of considering any options that can be evaluated for achieving equity or efficiency. In the case of LRTAP, equity has been the overriding consideration. Negotiations on the sulfur and nitrogen protocols centered at an early stage on percentage reductions or freezes that would be the same for all countries. Market mechanisms were never given serious consideration.

Although the mandate that all countries will achieve an equal percentage reduction of emissions has the appearance of equity, numerous questions of fairness arise. For example, is it just to expect states that historically have relatively low emission rates to achieve the same percentage reduction as those that have high ones? Likewise, should the same percentage reduction be expected of states that have already invested in reducing pollutants as of states that have done much less to curb emissions? Is it fair to expect the same percentage reductions for states lacking technological and economic means comparable to those of states that are more advanced? Difficulties in resolving these equity issues account in large part for the failure to write reductions into the 1988 nitrogen protocol.

In one respect, however, the approach of percentage reductions is a concession to efficiency in permitting countries the flexibility to select the least costly strategy for achieving the required reductions. An alternative of mandating the use of certain pollution abatement technologies such as smokestack scrubbers may stifle the search for more effective and cost-efficient methods of reducing emissions. Nevertheless, the overriding conclusion to be drawn from the creation and evolution of the LRTAP regime is that reaching an agreement that will be regarded as equitable by the potential parties is more critical to regime formation than arriving at one that ranks high on efficiency. Thus the hypothesis is confirmed in the case of the LRTAP regime.

The next hypothesis asserts that the presence of a salient solution to the problem at hand enhances success in negotiation of an international regime. A variety of strategies could be adopted to address transboundary air pollution, such as rules on the volume of air pollutants, requirements on the use of antipollution technologies, or economic penalties for pollution. In proceeding beyond the 1979 framework convention to address the specific problem of sulfur pollutants, negotiations among the ECE members quickly focused on the option of specifying percentage reductions. This mechanism has the advantage of flexibility because percentages and dates can be adjusted to take into account changing circumstances.

After determining the general approach, several specific issues needed to be resolved: whether reductions should limit levels of air pollutants within a country or the amount that flows across international boundaries, how big a percentage reduction would be expected, the baseline from which the percentages would be calculated, and the target date for achievement of reductions. On the most critical of these issues, proposals coalesced at the 1983 meetings of the Executive Body of the LRTAP convention on an arbitrary figure of 30 percent for reductions of *either* emissions *or* transboundary fluxes. Some states, however, argued strongly for higher percentage reductions, while a few others balked at specifying reductions. The status of the 30 percent figure as a salient solution was reinforced at the International Conference of Ministers on Acid Rain in Ottawa in March 1984, which convened representatives from ten countries favoring a reduction at least this large. These states became the original members of what became known as the 30% Club, which grew to twenty-one member states by April 1985.[37]

To summarize, the availability of a salient solution in the form of percentage reduction appears to have facilitated agreement on the 1985 sulfur protocol, which in turn was adopted as the approach for the Montreal Protocol to address the ozone depletion problem (see Chapter 5). These international agreements on air pollutants suggest a salient solution for mitigating the Arctic haze phenomenon, but there has not been enough diplomatic movement on the haze issue to determine what significance the salient solution may have.

In the case of Arctic haze, there has not been the stimulus of a perceived shock or crisis such as the sense of alarm triggered by the rapid growth of the ozone hole observed over Antarctica during the mid-

---

37. John McCormick, *Acid Earth: The Global Threat of Acid Pollution* (London: Earthscan, 1985), 64–65. The tendency for percentage reductions by specified dates to be the salient solution for international air pollution problems was also bolstered by the 1987 Montreal Protocol on Substances That Deplete the Ozone Layer, which specifically mandates a 50 percent reduction in use of several types of CFCs by 1998. In the case of the 1988 LRTAP nitrogen protocol, five countries proposed a 30 percent reduction in NO_x emissions from 1985 levels by 1995, but only a freeze on emissions at 1987 levels by 1994 was agreed upon. These figures are from Christer Ågren, "The NO_x Debacle," *Acid News* 2 (May 1988): 1–2.

1980s. In the haze case, there was no shocking event, although there was the surprising revelation of Glenn Shaw in 1972 that the atmosphere over the Arctic is not as pristine as commonly presumed. The scientific findings following that discovery contain no truly startling evidence on the severity or the consequences of the problem.

By contrast, the LRTAP protocols on sulfur and nitrogen oxide emissions were in part a response to the dramatic spread in Europe during the early 1980s of a phenomenon known as the "forest death syndrome," or—in German—*Waldsterben*.[38] Air pollution and acid precipitation have been generally believed to be the cause of this readily observable affliction of the forests, although scientists have been unable to determine definitively the complex processes that cause it.[39] As the magnitude of the problem became apparent, West Germany abruptly changed in 1982 from being a foe to being a strong supporter of international air pollution regulations, a key development leading up to the 1985 protocol on sulfur emissions.[40]

Thus the experiences with Arctic haze and LRTAP are consistent with the hypothesis that a highly publicized shock or crisis may be a precondition for, or at least a factor favorable to, the establishment of a regime.

Arctic haze clearly has not been a high-priority problem. Other environmental problems such as ozone depletion, climate change, deforestation, marine pollution, and toxic waste disposal have received much more attention. Furthermore, environmental problems have had much less priority than problems in other realms such as military security and economics. The Arctic rim countries that are victimized by the haze, in particular the Nordic states, give the problem a higher priority, but they cannot expect to stimulate international action while the problem is of little concern in the states outside the region that are major sources of the pollutants. It is significant that the United States has not given the haze problem much priority even though Alaska has been one of the areas victimized by the pollutants.

One reason why the haze problem has received so little priority is that it is concentrated over an area that, with the exception of the Kola Peninsula in Russia, is sparsely populated and remote from the regions that are largely responsible for the aerosol-forming pollutants. These

---

38. Don Hinrichsen, "Waldsterben: Forest Death Syndrome," *Amicus Journal* 7 (Spring 1986): 23–27; Peter H. Sand, "Air Pollution in Europe: International Policy Responses," *Environment* 29 (1987): 16.

39. Bernhard Prinz, "Causes of Forest Damage in Europe: Major Hypotheses and Factors," *Environment* 29 (1987): 11–15, 30–37.

40. Derek Elsom, *Atmospheric Pollution: Causes, Effects, and Control Policies* (New York: Basil Blackwell, 1987), 263.

small populations are not able to mount much political pressure for policies that would address the haze problem. The lack of a shock or crisis is another factor that keeps the haze problem in the background.

By contrast, for the past two decades in Europe and North America LRTAP has been a much more prominent issue, even in high governmental circles. In the 1970s, the priority of LRTAP was boosted by virtue of being selected as the first substantive issue in the 1975 Helsinki Accord to be used to demonstrate the potential for East-West cooperation. In the 1980s, political leaders found it necessary to respond to public alarm over the apparent severity of damage to lakes, forests, crops, and human health. The states in which the public was becoming the most alarmed, such as Norway, Sweden, Canada, West Germany, Austria, Switzerland, and the Netherlands, pushed strongly for the protocols on sulfur and nitrogen emissions. It is noteworthy that Western leaders attending the 1984 Economic Summit agreed on the need to identify environmental problems requiring international cooperation. In December 1984, at a follow-up meeting of the environmental ministers of the summit countries, the problem of acid deposition was put at the top of the agenda. The European Community has also given significant attention to curbing acid-forming pollutants.

Thus the hypothesis suggesting that a regime will be created only if an issue has high priority in the minds of relevant actors, including high-level officials, was well supported by this case.

Is the promise of effective compliance mechanisms that are not viewed as intrusive to participating states an important factor in regime creation? Such mechanisms would provide not only the means for monitoring the performance of states to detect whether they are following through on their commitments to comply with international regulations and standards but also the capacity to induce or facilitate a higher level of compliance from states that have fallen short in fulfilling their treaty obligations.

The OECD set up a network for monitoring air pollutants and transboundary fluxes in 1972. It was succeeded in 1977 by a monitoring network established by the ECE—the Cooperative Programme for Monitoring and Evaluation of the Long-Range Transmission of Air Pollutants in Europe (otherwise referred to by the acronym EMEP). Thus a mechanism that could be adapted to monitoring compliance on regional international regulations on air pollution was already in place when the 1979 framework LRTAP convention was adopted. EMEP has undergone further development during the 1980s, and the ECE adopted a protocol providing for its long-term financing in 1984, which enhances its capacity to support the sulfur and nitrogen protocols.

Although EMEP was tailored to service the needs of the LRTAP regime for data on air pollutants, in particular on levels of sulfur and nitrogen, it could be adapted to monitor compliance with agreements that may be negotiated to limit emissions of the pollutants responsible for Arctic haze. The techniques developed by scientists to detect the chemical signature of air pollutants for purposes of determining their sources could also be of use for monitoring compliance.

With the existence of an effective international monitoring system, states cannot assume that their failure to live up to international obligations to limit air pollutants will go unnoticed. This prospect alone may be a strong incentive for states to take seriously their obligations so as to maintain their reputations as responsible members of their regional community and to induce reciprocal actions by other parties to the agreement. Beyond that, the ECE does not have the authority or the means for sanctioning determined violators of its rules.

The probability of compliance also depends on the technological and financial means of states to conform to international standards. Unfortunately, Russia and several of the Eastern European countries, which are major sources of industrial air pollutants, face the immense challenge of rebuilding and restructuring their economies while undergoing fundamental political changes. The environmental problems of the region are now openly acknowledged, but the pressure to address other priorities will limit what can be done to reduce air pollution with the modest resources that are available.[41] Thus a significant shortcoming of the LRTAP regime is its failure to provide technological or financial assistance that would enhance the capacity of the economically strained countries to achieve the mandated reductions in emissions.

Thus the willingness of wealthier, more technologically advanced countries to provide international environmental assistance is a critical factor in the creation and success of environmental regimes, as was notably the case in gaining acceptance of the 1990 London Amendments to the Montreal Protocol by a large number of Third World states, in particular China and India. A 1990 agreement through which the Finnish firm Outokumpu will assist Russia in modernizing nickel foundries on the Kola Peninsula illustrates the type of assistance that will be needed to make compliance possible for some states.[42]

The record of international efforts to address Arctic haze and LRTAP does not offer a clear-cut test of the hypothesis that the availability of com-

---

41. Hilary F. French, "Industrial Wasteland," *World Watch* 1 (1988): 21–30.

42. Outokumpu, "Update on Kola Nickel Project," press release, 20 November 1990.

pliance mechanisms facilitates regime formation. Essentially the same capacities for monitoring air pollutants that were available to the LRTAP regime could be made available to an Arctic haze regime through an
expanded EMEP network. Furthermore, neither the absence of institutional sanctions to induce compliance nor the limited economic and technical resources of the USSR and Eastern European countries seemed to be
a significant impediment to the creation of the LRTAP regime, although
these factors may significantly affect their performance.

Two individuals are especially noteworthy for the key roles they
played in the formation of the LRTAP regime. The first is Soviet general secretary Leonid Brezhnev, who, in the aftermath of the Conference on Security and Cooperation in Europe in Helsinki in 1975, proposed following up on the Final Act by convening separate high-level
ministerial conferences on the topics of energy, transport, and the environment. Without his persistence in following through on environmental cooperation in the face of resistance from the West, it is unlikely
that the process would have been set in motion that led to the high-level
meeting of the ECE which adopted the LRTAP framework convention.[43] Brezhnev's influence can be characterized as structural in nature
because it was derived from his stature as head of state of a superpower.

The executive director of the ECE, Janos Stanovnik of Yugoslavia, also
performed a critical leadership role in the evolution of the LRTAP regime,
but his contributions were of an entrepreneurial variety. The impressive
role that Stanovnik played can be appreciated by a reading of Evgeny
Chossudovsky's detailed account of the conference diplomacy that led
to the adoption and implementation of the 1979 LRTAP convention.[44]
Stanovnik's organizational savvy, skillful presentation of proposals, adroit
diplomacy, and determination to achieve an environmental agreement
overcame numerous obstacles to reaching a significant accord on how to
address the increasingly severe problem of transboundary air pollution.

The cause of a narrowly focused Arctic haze regime has not yet had the
benefit of influential leadership. On the larger topic of preserving the Arctic environment, Soviet president Mikhail Gorbachev offered some structural leadership. Gorbachev's speech in Murmansk in October 1987
marked the beginning of a new era of international cooperation on the
Arctic environment in which the Soviet Union would be a more willing re-

---

43. Jackson, "Tenth Anniversary Review," 219–220.

44. Evgeny Chossudovsky, *East-West Diplomacy for the Environment in the United Nations: The
High-Level Meeting with the Framework of the ECE on the Protection of the Environment* (New
York: United Nations Institute for Training and Research, 1988).

gional partner.[45] Finnish ambassador Esko Rajakoski displayed considerable entrepreneurial leadership in his use of personal diplomacy to push the eight Arctic states to negotiate an agreement on the Arctic environment in hosting the 1989 Rovaniemi conference.[46] Canadian negotiator Garth Banguey provided competent entrepreneurial leadership in the follow-up sessions that facilitated the refinement of, and eventual agreement on, the Arctic Environmental Protection Strategy.[47]

The hypothesis on leadership, in particular structural and entrepreneurial, was confirmed. Brezhnev's structural leadership was the necessary impetus for getting the bargaining progress started in the ECE. The entrepreneurial leadership of the executive director of the ECE then became a necessary condition for keeping negotiations from getting off track in the face of the innumerable political issues that inevitably arise on matters of such importance. Such leadership has not materialized on a sustained basis in the limited efforts that have been made on behalf of international cooperation on Arctic haze, although it has emerged to a limited extent in the broader negotiations on the protection of the Arctic environment in the context of the Rovaniemi process.

Interest-based theory offers several plausible explanations for the creation of the LRTAP regime and the continuing absence of one for the Arctic environment, Arctic haze in particular. Among the factors that favored the creation of the LRTAP regime but did not characterize the more narrowly defined Arctic haze case were circumstances that favored integrative bargaining, a relatively thick veil of uncertainty, priority given to equity over efficiency in negotiating agreements, a sense of shock and urgency, high priority from leaders, and the exercise of structural and entrepreneurial leadership. Salient solutions and compliance mechanisms were present in both cases and thus not grounds for distinguishing between success and failure in regime creation.

Knowledge-Based Hypotheses

Cold War tensions were a major obstacle to Arctic research. Nevertheless, a substantial base of knowledge on Arctic haze was generated, stimulated by the pioneering research of scientists Glenn E. Shaw and Kenneth A. Rahn in conjunction with the Arctic Haze Program of the U.S.

---

45. Pertti Joenniemi, "Competing Images of the Arctic: A Policy Perspective," *Current Research on Peace and Violence* 12 (1989): 111–122.

46. Debora MacKenzie, "Environmental Issues Surface at the Summit of the World," *New Scientist* 121 (25 February 1989): 29.

47. Raymond V. Arnaudo, telephone interviews with the author, May 16, 1991.

Office of Naval Research (ONR).[48] Every third year the Arctic Gas and Aerosol Sampling Project, sponsored by the National Oceanic and Atmospheric Administration, has conducted a sampling program of Arctic air with international participation. Research on Arctic haze had its heyday in the early to mid-1980s. Since then haze monitoring and research has been cut back—especially in the United States but also in other countries—as the principal funding agencies, including the ONR, shifted their priorities. Heightened concern over climate change diverted attention and resources that otherwise might have supported research on Arctic haze.[49]

The research on Arctic haze led to a general agreement on key aspects of the phenomenon, in particular its composition and density, the causes for the substantial seasonal variations, and the origin of the pollutants outside of the Arctic region. One scientist suggests that the most significant outcome of the research effort on Arctic haze may have been to demonstrate how far air pollution is transported by air currents under certain conditions.[50]

Scientists are still uncertain about the nature and severity of the consequences of the haze aerosols for the atmospheric radiation balance in the region or for deposition on terrestrial inland and aquatic or marine ecosystems. Some believe that haze is a significant problem that should be addressed, others are yet to be persuaded that it is has more than a minor impact on the environment. It remains to be seen how much the intergovernmental Arctic Environmental Protection Strategy or the nongovernmental International Arctic Science Committee will do to stimulate scientific research that will address these remaining uncertainties.[51]

---

48. Rahn and Shaw, "Sources and Transport."

49. Kenneth A. Rahn, telephone interview with the author, 1991.

50. Ibid.

51. The International Arctic Science Committee (IASC) was founded in August 1990 at a conference in Resolute, Canada, following a series of meetings in San Diego (1986), Oslo (1987), Stockholm (1988), Leningrad (1988), and Helsinki (1989). An organizational meeting of the IASC Council was held in Oslo in January 1991. Among the projects under consideration are an inventory of major Arctic scientific activities, a plan for increasing the comparability and compatibility of Arctic data, social scientific research on the inhabitants of Arctic regions, and an Arctic climate research program. See Østreng, "Polar Science and Politics," 104; Elena Nikitina, "International Mechanisms and Arctic Environmental Research," *Current Research on Peace and Violence* 12 (1989): 128; Young, "Global Commons," 56; "The International Arctic Science Committee: From Conception to Birth," *Arctic Research of the United States* 4 (Fall 1991): 65–69; Sherburne Abbott, "Trip Report, First Meeting of IASC Council," supplement B (unpublished memorandum, 1991).

The evolution of the ECE's LRTAP regime can be attributed in part to the earlier development of a base of scientific information on acid precipitation and the transboundary flow of pollutants that contribute to the problem. Characteristics of acid rain were first observed in the mid-nineteenth century by Robert Angus Smith, an English chemist who conducted studies and issued reports on the air chemistry in and around Manchester, England. Unfortunately, more than a century passed before much notice was taken of Smith's observations.[52]

In the 1940s, Swedish scientist Hans Egnér established in his country the first network for the collection and chemical analysis of precipitation. Developed further during the 1950s by the Stockholm-based International Meteorological Institute, the network became known as the European Air Chemistry Network, with stations in the Nordic countries and most of western and central Europe and eventually in Poland and parts of the Soviet Union.[53] In the late 1960s, Swedish soil scientist Svante Odén called attention to an "insidious chemical warfare" taking place among the European countries. To back up his contention, he presented evidence that air pollutants from sources as distant as the British Isles and central Europe were a significant cause of the acidification of freshwater lakes in Scandinavia.[54] Although Odén's revelations were received with skepticism at first, Sweden and Norway became sufficiently concerned by 1972 to raise the issue of transboundary air pollution at the United Nations Conference on the Human Environment.[55]

Two major scientific projects on the acid rain phenomenon were undertaken during the 1970s. One was the Norwegian Interdisciplinary Research Programme, entitled Acid Precipitation: Effects on Forests and Fish. Numerous reports and two important conferences—in Telemark in 1976 and Sandefjord in 1980—led to the conclusion that fish populations had been eliminated in half of the lakes in southern

---

52. Robert A. Smith, *Air and Rain: The Beginnings of Chemical Climatology* (London: Longmans, Green, 1872); Ellis B. Cowling, "Acid Rain in Historical Perspective," *Environmental Science & Technology* 16 (February 1982): 111a.

53. Cowling, "Acid Rain in Historical Perspective," 113a.

54. Svante Odén, *The Acidification of Air and Precipitation and Its Consequences in the Natural Environment*, Ecology Committee Bulletin No. 1 (Stockholm: Swedish National Science Research Council, 1968).

55. Bertil Bolin et al., *Sweden's Case Study for the United Nations Conference on the Human Environment: Air Pollution across National Boundaries* (Stockholm: Norstadt & Sons, 1972); Gregory S. Wetstone, "A History of the Acid Rain Issue," in *Science for Public Policy*, ed. Harvey Brooks and Chester L. Cooper (New York: Pergamon Press, 1987), 165.

Norway.[56] The second project, a 1974 OECD study entitled the Cooperative Technical Program to Measure Long-Range Transport of Air Pollutants, collected data on the sulfur content of air and precipitation at seventy-six ground stations in eleven European countries. Based on this study, a report listing the percentages of each country's sulfur deposition that could be attributed to domestic and foreign sources was issued in 1977 (revised in 1979). Offering the first independent verification of the Scandinavian allegations that air pollutants were coming from distant places, the study found that in five of the eleven countries more than half of the sulfur deposition was attributable to foreign sources.[57]

The ECE established a more permanent atmospheric monitoring program in the form of the EMEP network in 1977. Also supported by the United Nations Environment Programme and the World Meteorological Organization, EMEP has grown to ninety-four stations in twenty-four countries that report data to the Chemical Coordinating Center in Lilleström, Norway.[58] Four international cooperative programs were established to monitor and evaluate the impact of air pollution on forests, rivers and lakes, historical and cultural monuments, and agricultural crops.[59]

Thus extensive scientific monitoring and research had been conducted on transboundary air pollution and the problem of acidification by the mid-1980s, but to what extent was there a convergence of scientific opinion upon which negotiations could be based? Over time, scientists from a growing number of European and North American countries were persuaded of the seriousness and causes of the acidification problem that were first asserted by Swedish scientists in the 1960s. The 1982 Stockholm Conference on Acidification of the Environment, attended by parties to the 1979 LRTAP framework convention, was a significant turning point in the emergence of this consensus.

---

56. D. Drablös and A. Tollan, eds., *Ecological Impact of Acid Precipitation: Proceedings of an International Conference*, held in Sandefjord, Norway, 11–14 March 1980; Cowling, "Acid Rain in Historical Perspective," 116a.

57. See Organization for Economic Cooperation and Development, *The State of the Environment in OECD Member Countries* (Paris: OECD, 1979), 77–93; Gregory S. Wetstone and Armin Rosencranz, *Acid Rain in Europe and North America: National Responses to an International Problem* (Washington, D.C.: Environmental Law Institute, 1983), 135–137.

58. Harald Dovland, "Monitoring European Transboundary Air Pollution," *Environment* 29 (December 1987): 13.

59. See United Nations Environment Programme, *Environmental Data Report*, 2d ed. (Cambridge, Mass.: Basil Blackwell, 1989), 42–47.

The first stage of the conference was a meeting of experts at which more than one hundred scientists, engineers, and pollution control officials from twenty countries summarized the existing knowledge on the problem. Their report concluded that man-made sulfur and nitrogen compounds were largely responsible for acid deposition and that acidification was causing significant damage, particularly to aquatic life and forests in Europe and North America.[60] An ECE report issued in 1984 concluded that "among scientists from different schools there is wide agreement that recent forest damages are predominantly to be ascribed to anthropogenic air pollutants."[61]

A convergence of scientific opinion on the seriousness of the acid rain problem has been slower to develop in the United Kingdom and the United States. Many scientists in both countries accept the dominant European and Canadian views that a serious problem exists and that steps should be taken to reduce the emissions of gases such as sulfur and nitrogen oxides, despite the expense. For example, in 1984 a group of leading English scientists spelled out their concerns about the impact of acid deposition on lakes and forests to government scientists and ministers, including Margaret Thatcher. These apprehensions have also been expressed in reports of authoritative groups such as the U.S. National Academy of Sciences and a select committee of the British House of Commons.[62] Nevertheless, scientists affiliated with the politically conservative administrations of Thatcher and Ronald Reagan or with industries responsible for much of the pollutants, such as the British Central Electricity Generating Board (CEGB) and the National Coal Board, persisted in arguing that international standards mandating the reduction of pollution emissions should not be adopted until scientific findings were more conclusive.[63]

To be sure, not all scientific questions had been answered definitively. By 1986 there was general agreement on the aquatic effects of acidification, but major uncertainties remained about the complex processes through which specific air pollutants were causing the forest damage reported in Europe and North America.[64] But critics of the American and British position contended that policy makers were simply trying to

---

60. Wetstone and Rosencranz, *Acid Rain in Europe and North America*, 146–147.

61. Quoted in Boehmer-Christiansen, "Black Mist and Acid Rain," 151.

62. Chris C. Park, *Acid Rain: Rhetoric and Reality* (London: Methuen, 1987), 230–231.

63. John McCormick, *Acid Earth: The Global Threat of Air Pollution*, new enlarged ed. (London: Earthscan, 1989), 101.

64. Prinz, "Causes of Forest Damage in Europe."

delay and obstruct the creation of international rules that they believe would have greater costs than benefits for their countries, given that they are significant net exporters of air pollutants.[65]

Official British thinking on the acidification problem underwent a transformation in the late 1980s, much as had occurred in West Germany five years earlier. In 1986, the CEGB conceded that its emissions were responsible for part of the acid rain falling over the British Isles and Norway.[66] This change was reinforced by growing evidence of damage to British forests, including the shocking revelation in an EMEP report issued in 1987 that the United Kingdom had the highest proportion of damaged forests in Europe, with 76 percent of conifers showing slight to severe damage and 28.9 percent showing moderate to severe damage.[67] The Thatcher government in 1988 approved a European Community directive for a 57 percent (from 1980 levels) reduction in SO_2 emissions from existing power plants by the year 2003 and a 30 percent reduction in NO_x emissions by 1998, but it still has not ratified the 1985 ECE sulfur protocol.[68]

Scientific controversy on the effects of acid rain continues to rage in the United States, where monitoring and research on acidification got a later start than in Europe. Disagreements within the scientific community were not resolved by recent reports from the National Acid Precipitation Assessment Program (NAPAP), which was conducted during the 1980s with $500 million of federal support. The interim and draft reports, released in 1987 and 1990 respectively, suggested that the consequences of acid rain were less than had generally been believed: damage to lakes and rivers was less widespread than had been believed, and, with the exception of the red spruce trees at high elevations in the eastern mountains, there was no evidence that acid rain had caused a general decline of forests in the United States.[69] Strong criticisms of the NAPAP report from numerous scientists, environmentalists, and Canadian officials, some alleging that the conclusions had been distorted by political considerations, are indicative of the continuing lack of consen-

65. Boehmer-Christiansen, "Black Mist and Acid Rain."

66. McCormick, *Acid Earth*, 106.

67. United Nations Economic Commission for Europe, *National Strategies and Policies for Air Pollution Abatement* (New York: United Nations, 1987).

68. French, "Clearing the Air," 116.

69. Philip Shabecoff, "Study Discounts Immediate Peril from Acid Rain," *New York Times*, 18 September 1987, p. 1; William K. Stevens, "Worst Fears on Acid Rain Unrealized," *New York Times*, 20 February 1990, p. C4.

sus among American scientists.[70] Despite this lack of a meeting of the minds on the seriousness of the acidification problem, the United States adopted a major Clean Air Act amendment in 1990 that will significantly reduce emissions of SO_2 and NO_x.

To summarize, the negotiations leading to the LRTAP framework convention and subsequent protocols were informed by an extensive body of scientific monitoring, research, and assessment, conducted over three decades, which linked specific pollutants to acidification and quantified flows of transboundary air pollutants. There has by no means been a consensus of scientific opinion on the nature and consequences of the problem and the need for international regulations, but gradually a geographical zone of general agreement has expanded from Sweden, Norway, and Canada in the 1970s to encompass West Germany and the continental European countries in the early 1980s and later the United Kingdom, but not yet the United States.

The more advanced state of scientific knowledge on transboundary pollution and acidification and gradual convergence of scientific opinion appears to be at least part of the reason why more progress has been made on the LRTAP regime than on a more specific Arctic haze one. The lack of agreement among scientists in the United Kingdom and United States has been a factor in their reluctance to accept the ECE protocol on sulfur emissions. Thus the hypothesis about the importance of a convergence of scientific opinion for regime formation is confirmed.

A related question is whether the existence of an epistemic community is a necessary condition for the formation of a regime. Such a community consists of an established network of scientists and government officials who have both a common understanding of a problem and similar normative preferences and policy orientations. An epistemic community can play a critical role in persuading governmental policy makers of the need for international cooperation to address the problems of concern to scientists.[71]

Has an epistemic community addressed the problem of Arctic haze? A relatively small international network of atmospheric chemists—primarily from the United States, Canada, Norway, and Denmark—has

---

70. Philip Shabecoff, "Acid Rain Report Unleashes a Torrent of Criticism," *New York Times*, 20 March 1990, p. C4. See also Leslie Roberts, "Learning from the Acid Rain Program," *Science* 251 (15 March 1991): 1302–1305.

71. See Peter M. Haas, "Do Regimes Matter? Epistemic Communities and the Mediterranean Pollution Control," *International Organization* 43 (1989): 377–404; also Haas, *Saving the Mediterranean: The Politics of International Cooperation* (New York: Columbia University Press, 1990).

been conducting research on the phenomenon. Among the more prominent participants in the network have been Glenn Shaw and Kenneth Rahn of the United States, Jost Heintzenberg of Sweden, Leonard A. Barrie of Canada, Niels Heidam of Denmark, and Brynjulf Ottar and Jozef Pacyna of Norway.

This group of scientists has communicated through an informal organization known as the Arctic Chemical Network that was set up at a small international conference held in Oslo in May 1977. Subsequent conferences on Arctic air chemistry at which data and research findings were shared took place at the University of Rhode Island (1980), in Toronto (1984), in Hurdal, Norway (1987), and in Copenhagen (1991).[72] The state of Alaska sponsored a major International Symposium on Arctic Air Pollution that was held at the Scott Polar Research Institute in Cambridge, England, in September 1985, which assessed the state of scientific knowledge on the haze and its potential implications.[73]

This network of scientists does not, however, appear to be a full-fledged epistemic community. Its members have been concerned almost exclusively with expanding scientific knowledge about the phenomenon, although there was an awareness that its findings could have policy implications. Without a consensus on the consequences of the phenomenon—in part because of the lack of attention to such questions as the impact of acidification on the Arctic environment—there has been no prevailing view on what if anything should be done to address the problem, although on a few occasions some scientists have called for international action to control pollutants.[74] This lack of consensus in part explains why the scientists do not have the ties with public officials that would be indicative of an epistemic community. The International Arctic Science Committee created in 1990 may facilitate the evolution of an epistemic community on the more general subject of the Arctic environment.

The role played by the scientific community in the evolution of the LRTAP regime is much more complicated. Has there been an epistemic community? The answer is clearly yes. It is a community that grew from a core group of scientists concentrated in Norway, Sweden, and slightly later Canada in the late 1960s and 1970s to one that by the mid-1980s

---

72. The papers from the Rhode Island, Toronto, and Hurdal conferences were published as special issues of *Atmospheric Environment*, Arctic Symposium II, 15 (1981); Arctic Symposium III, 19 (1985); Special Issue on Arctic Air Chemistry, 23 (1989).

73. The papers from this conference were published in Stonehouse, ed., *Arctic Air Pollution*.

74. "Scientists Ask for Efforts to Cut Air Pollution," *New York Times*, 7 October 1984, p. 24.

had significant representation from most ECE countries and from the United States, including scientists active in the NAPAP program. The primary disciplines represented are atmospheric chemistry and a variety of specialties within the more general field of aquatic and terrestrial ecology. Among the more prominent members of the community are Lars Overrein of Norway, Goran Persson of Sweden, Bernard Ulrich of West Germany, Lester Reed of the United Kingdom, Thomas Bridges of Canada, and Lester Machta, Arthur Johnson, and R. A. Linthurst of the United States.[75]

It is only since the late 1980s that scientists from Eastern Europe and the former Soviet Union became involved in the epistemic community as glasnost increased opportunities for contact with Western scientists. In Eastern Europe scientists have been more concerned with high, localized concentrations of airborne SO_2 that were destroying forests near major emission sources than with the long-range pollutants that have caused more selective damage on forests over a large region. While Western scientists have seen the solution in reducing acidic deposition, many of their Eastern counterparts were looking into the possibility of developing heartier trees that could withstand high levels of pollution as their governments single-mindedly pushed for industrial growth.[76]

Networking has taken place in numerous ways. One organizing mechanism has been the LRTAP working groups and EMEP. Members of the community have gathered at major scientific conferences held at five-year intervals since the 1972 Stockholm conference to share their ideas and research findings. These conferences were held at Columbus, Ohio (1975), Sandefjord, Norway (1980), Miskoko, Ontario (1986), and Glasgow, Scotland (1990). The next one will be held in Sweden in 1995. The scientific symposium held as part of the 1982 Stockholm Conference on Acidification was also an important gathering of members of the epistemic community. Finally, a series of unofficial Meetings of Acid Rain Coordinators have been held annually since 1986, which are attended by one or two representatives of each country, usually the director of the national research program on acid rain, if a country has one, the director of the government agency with responsibility for the problem, or both. The purpose of these sessions is to exchange information both on scientific and technical matters and on pertinent legislation. The countries represented are primarily the Western ones, but efforts

---

75. Ellis B. Cowling interview with the author, May 10, 1991.
76. Ibid.

are being made to involve the former Soviet Union and Eastern European countries.[77]

Has the epistemic community played a critical role in the creation and development of the LRTAP regime? In the case of the 1979 framework convention, the answer would seem to be no. The agreement was an outgrowth of efforts to dampen East-West tensions. What epistemic community existed at the time was still concentrated in Scandinavia and was not very well developed in many of the other countries that signed the agreement. The framework convention, with its emphasis on facilitating international cooperation on research on acid precipitation, perhaps has done more to expand and strengthen an epistemic community than it is the product of one.

The epistemic community was better able to play a role in the sulfur and nitrogen protocols of 1985 and 1988, but it is not apparent that it had a critical impact on the process of reaching agreement. The community's most significant contribution may have been in persuading governments of several countries to institute national monitoring and research programs.[78] Political pressure triggered in part by media publicity and activities of environmental action groups may have been more of a factor in persuading governments to pursue international agreements on transboundary air pollution.[79] Environmental political groups sought scientific opinion to support the positions they were espousing, much to the discomfort of many scientists. Furthermore, the impact of the epistemic community was diminished by determined officials and scientists, especially in the United Kingdom and the United States, who openly challenged their views. During the 1980s, the most persistent skepticism of the prevailing views of the epistemic community, and in particular of the claims of Scandinavian scientists about the source of acidification in their countries, came from British scientists working for the Central Electricity Generating Board headed by the outspoken Lord Marshall of Goring.[80]

The failure of the relatively small, informal network of Arctic haze scientists to become an epistemic community would seem to be at least part of the reason why there is no regime to address the problem, which is consistent with the hypothesis about the importance of such groups in regime formation. The LRTAP case is more complicated. An

---

77. Patricia Irving, telephone interview with the author, May 23, 1991.

78. Cowling interview, May 16, 1991.

79. Park, *Acid Rain*, 184–185.

80. McCormick, *Acid Earth*.

epistemic community gradually evolved but does not appear to have been much of a factor in the adoption of the 1979 framework convention on transboundary air pollution. By the mid-1980s, when serious discussions began on the supplementary protocols, the acid rain epistemic community had matured sufficiently that it could have a significant impact on international negotiations. By then, however, public concern and political activism over the all too apparent deterioration of the environment had become a more significant factor in motivating government action to address the problem. Thus the hypothesis about the role of epistemic communities is only partially supported by the LRTAP case.

Scientific knowledge alone will not stimulate a response to a problem. Another necessary condition for the creation of an international regime would presumably be an awareness and concern on the part of government policy makers and those who influence them, including advocacy groups and the general public. The media play a critical role in informing the larger public of the environmental dangers revealed by scientific research.

The Arctic haze phenomenon is not well known outside of the circles of atmospheric or Arctic scientists. Published overviews of international environmental problems, even those specifically on atmospheric pollution, rarely mention it. Coverage in the news media has at best been sparse and fleeting. Nor has the cause of Arctic haze been taken up in a significant way by the nongovernmental environmental organizations that lobby strongly, and often effectively, on other issues. It is thus not surprising that public awareness of the haze problem is slight outside the Arctic region, and within the region, population densities are too low to generate much political pressure.

By contrast, the problem of acid precipitation has been a major concern of publics in Europe and North America for decades. Extensive media coverage has drawn attention to the consequences of acidification, such as the damage to forests, disappearance of aquatic life, and deterioration of stone and metallic surfaces, problems that can be readily observed by the untrained observer.[81] Public opinion polls revealing a high level of concern about the environment and the growing electoral strength of Green parties in Western Europe have put pressure on public officials and mainline parties to address the acid rain problem through the LRTAP process.[82]

---

81. See United Nations Environment Programme, *The Public and the Environment* (Nairobi: UNEP, 1988).

82. Chossudovsky, *East-West Diplomacy*, 162.

Two instances in which the media had an effect are particularly noteworthy. In the late 1960s, the media in Sweden publicized Odén's findings, triggering a public reaction that pressured the Swedish government to take up the cause of transboundary air pollution at the 1972 Stockholm conference.[83] Likewise, a major report on the impact of air pollution on woodlands in West Germany released in 1979 received a skeptical response from the government until a dramatic cover story in *Der Spiegel* in 1981 aroused public concern about the problem, leading to the government's reversal in 1982 on the need for international regulations of transboundary pollution, which was announced at the Stockholm Conference on Acidification.[84]

Environmentally oriented nongovernmental organizations have been persistent advocates of much steeper reductions of emissions than governments have been willing to accept. For example, twenty-one environmental protection organizations meeting in Stockholm in 1986 called for an 80 percent reduction in sulfur emissions in Europe by 1993 and a 75 percent reduction of nitrogen emissions by 1995. Although such reductions are probably too drastic to be politically feasible, they expand the parameters of public debate and make the lesser reductions proposed in intergovernmental negotiations appear to be timid and inadequate by contrast.[85]

The stark contrast between the obscurity of the Arctic haze phenomenon and the widespread and intensifying concern over acid precipitation offers convincing support for a hypothesis that international regimes will be created when problems are widely recognized as being serious by governmental policy makers and their constituencies. This case study indicates that knowledge-based theory is helpful in explaining the development of international regimes. A convergence of scientific opinion on the seriousness of the problem and its causes appears to favor creation of a regime as does a heightened awareness in the general public. The findings were not as clear-cut on the role of epistemic communities.

Contextual Factors

Until the mid-1980s, the dominant contextual factor in the Arctic region was the confrontational, geopolitical relationship between the

---

83. Wetstone, "History of the Acid Rain Issue," 165.

84. B. Ulrich, R. Mayer, and P. K. Khanna, *Deposition of Air Pollutants and Their Effects on the Wooded Ecosystems in Solling* (Göttingen: University of Göttingen, 1979); Wetstone, "History of the Acid Rain Issue," 189.

85. "How the Nations Stand," *Acid News* 3 (October 1987): 10.

Eastern and Western blocs led by the Soviet Union and the United States. Multilateral cooperation on a wide range of Arctic issues was for decades the hostage of Cold War rivalries, although there were periods of detente when agreements on specific topics were possible—in the early 1970s, for example, when SALT I, the Polar Bear Agreement, and a bilateral agreement on environmental cooperation were concluded.

Acute distrust between the superpowers became a major impediment to the development of the scientific knowledge on the Arctic environment problems needed to inform the creation of international regimes. Large parts of the region, most notably the Soviet Arctic, were off-limits to Western scientists; and with a few exceptions such as the Polar Bear Specialist Group, Soviet scientists were not allowed to participate in international organizations involved in Arctic studies. Much of the Arctic research of the superpowers was guided by military priorities and the results classified for reasons of national security. Because of the strategic sensitivities of the superpowers in the region, other Arctic states limited most of their research efforts to their own territory.[86]

The relative progress since 1959 in developing an Antarctic regime offers an indication of the cooperation that might have been achieved in the Arctic region had it not been for Cold War concerns about security. Because of its remote location, the superpowers did not consider the Antarctic region to have enough strategic importance to justify restricting research activities, and the area became one of the principal sites for international collaborative research during the International Geophysical Year of 1957–1958.[87] The access of scientists to the region, the openness with which they have conducted their research and disseminated the results, and the level of international collaboration facilitated the development of a scientific base of knowledge that has informed negotiations leading to international agreements on the conservation of Antarctic seals (1972), Antarctic marine living resources (1980), and most recently Antarctic environmental issues (1991).

The demise of the Cold War significantly altered the context for international cooperation on preserving the Arctic environment. Indicative of the changing atmosphere was Soviet General Secretary Mikhail Gorbachev's speech in Murmansk in October 1987 in which he proposed regional cooperation between the Nordic and Arctic states on an Arctic "zone of peace" that might entail nuclear-free zones and re-

---

86. Østreng, "Polar Science and Politics," 102–103.

87. See Wallace W. Atwood, Jr., "The International Geophysical Year in Retrospect," *Department of State Bulletin* 40 (11 May 1959): 682–689.

stricted naval activities as well as cooperation in developing resources, coordination of science, and a comprehensive plan for protecting the Arctic environment.[88] The steps taken toward the creation of the International Arctic Science Committee and the Rovaniemi process leading to the Arctic Environmental Protection Strategy took advantage of the improving international political climate, in particular, the increased willingness of the Soviet Union to cooperate on matters pertaining to the Arctic environment.[89]

The broader East-West political context was also an important factor in creation of the LRTAP regime. The process that led to the 1979 framework treaty was set in motion at the Conference on Security and Cooperation in Europe (CSCE) in Helsinki in 1975, which was the culmination of efforts that began in the late 1960s to further the cause of peace and stability in the region. What is known as Basket II of the resulting Final Act of the conference, otherwise referred to as the Helsinki Accord, called for East-West cooperation in economics, science and technology, and the environment. The Final Act identified several more specific possibilities for cooperation on environmental matters, one of which was "an extensive programme for the monitoring and evaluation of the long-range transport of air pollutants, starting with sulphur dioxide and with possible extensions to other pollutants."[90]

Soviet general secretary Leonid Brezhnev followed up on the Final Act by proposing separate all-European ministerial-level conferences on the topics of energy, transport, and environment. Despite an initial cool reception from Western governments, Brezhnev's proposal eventually led to the high-level meeting of the ECE in November 1979 at which the framework convention on LRTAP was adopted. Six weeks later, the Soviet military intervention in Afghanistan brought an end to the era of detente and squelched prospects for East-West agreements on other subjects mentioned in the Final Act.[91] Little did the negotiators of the LRTAP convention realize how soon the window of opportunity for reaching an accord might close. Once in place, however, the LRTAP convention withstood the more hostile East-West atmosphere of the early 1980s, as evidenced by the continuing negotiations on reduction of sulfur emissions.[92]

---

88. Joenniemi, "Competing Images of the Arctic," 118.

89. Arnaudo, telephone interviews, May 23, 1991; "International Collaboration," *Arctic Research* 5 (Spring 1991): 9–10.

90. See Jackson, "Tenth Anniversary Review," 218.

91. See Chossudovsky, *East-West Diplomacy*, 23–30.

92. Jackson, "Tenth Anniversary Review," 220–222.

Thus, at least for the Soviet Union, it appears that the desire to establish examples of continuing cooperation between East and West was at least as much a motivation for creating the LRTAP regime in the late 1970s as the seriousness of the environmental problems it addressed. The specific focus of the cooperation did not appear to be as important as the fact that it was taking place. The environment was chosen as a suitable subject for cooperation presumably because it was less politicized than other issues that might have been selected. Brezhnev's desire for accommodations on Basket II issues, which included the environment, was perhaps motivated by a desire to divert Western pressure on human rights, freedom of information, and other topics included in Basket III of the Helsinki Accord.[93]

This interpretation of the events can be taken a step further to suggest that continued progress on environmental cooperation through the development of the LRTAP regime assumed greater significance as relations deteriorated between East and West, which was the case in 1978–1979. In the aftermath of the East-West tensions aroused by the decision of NATO to deploy a new generation of intermediate-range missiles in central Europe, a signal from the Soviet Union that it desired to keep at least one forum open for East-West communication was one of the factors prompting West Germany to call a Multinational Conference on the Causes and Prevention of Damage to Forests and Waters by Air Pollution in Europe in Munich in June 1984. The conference was a key step in negotiations leading up to the 1985 sulfur protocol.[94]

Thus the international political climate is one contextual factor that has had a bearing on whether international regimes are created to address environmental problems such as Arctic haze and LRTAP. Cold War geopolitics was clearly an obstacle to cooperation on the Arctic haze problem, in part because it hampered scientific research. The ending of the Cold War gave a boost to the prospects for multilateral agreements on the Arctic environment. Likewise, detente and the CSCE process leading up to the Helsinki Accord of 1975 offered new possibilities for East-West cooperation in a variety of sectors without which the LRTAP regime might never have come into existence. It is paradoxical however, that the demise of detente in the late 1970s and early 1980s may have also worked to the advantage of the regime because both sides

---

93. Lars Björkbom, "Resolution of International Problems: The Use of Diplomacy," in *International Environmental Diplomacy: The Management and Resolution of Transfrontier Environmental Problems*, ed. John E. Carroll (Cambridge: Cambridge University Press, 1988), 130.

94. Ibid., 130–31.

were anxious for interbloc dialogue and cooperation on a subject that was not highly contentious.

CONCLUSIONS

Arctic haze is a significant air pollution phenomenon about which little was known until the 1970s, although its presence was reported by one scientist as early as 1957. Thus far, no significant multinational diplomacy has addressed the haze problem, although the initial steps have been taken to create a more general regime for protecting the Arctic environment. The haze is part of a larger problem of long-range transboundary air pollution responsible for acid precipitation, which is being addressed by a well-developed international regime that came into being in 1979 upon adoption of a framework treaty by the members of the Economic Commission for Europe. Although the LRTAP regime does not directly address the Arctic haze problem, the limits on air pollutants incorporated into existing and future protocols may lessen the haze problem.

The marked contrast between the fledgling efforts to create regional regimes that address specific Arctic environmental problems and the substantial progress that has been made on creating the LRTAP regime was the basis for a comparative analysis of theories of regime formation. The study confirmed several interest-based hypotheses, in particular that the existence of integrative bargaining, a thick veil of uncertainty, a commitment to equitable policies, a sense of shock and urgency, a high priority for decision makers, and structural and entrepreneurial leadership are factors that favor the creation of regimes and may be necessary conditions.

Knowledge-based theory with such independent variables as the existence of a scientific consensus, public awareness and concern, active nongovernmental organizations, and extensive media coverage was also confirmed. Questions remain, however, on the role of epistemic communities. Furthermore, the study revealed that the larger political context, such as the state of superpower relations, can also be a significant factor in the creation of regimes. Power-based hypotheses that take into account whether a hegemonic actor was present or the existence of a bipolar distribution of power had less explanatory value, although there was some evidence that middle powers may play a role in regime formation.

Further analysis may establish interesting relationships between the three types of hypotheses that were generally confirmed. Knowledge of a problem both within and outside of the scientific community may have significant implications for how interests are perceived and accordingly the prospects for integrative bargaining. Contextual factors such as the general political climate may also contribute to the possibility of integrative bargaining. On the latter point, negotiations on the LRTAP agreement became a test of the feasibility of significant East-West cooperation and the ultimate sustainability of the CSCE process as a mechanism for reducing tensions between the Cold War blocs. These political considerations added substantially to the thickness of the veil of uncertainty regarding the advantages and disadvantages that would accrue to each state from a LRTAP agreement. Thus the broader political context enhanced the possibilities for integrative bargaining, which in turn favored the successful creation of a regime.

CHAPTER SEVEN

International Regime Formation: Findings, Research Priorities, and Applications

ORAN R. YOUNG AND GAIL OSHERENKO

What have we learned about the determinants of regime formation in international society? Are we now in a better position to explain both successes and failures in efforts to establish international regimes or to make predictions about prospects for success in current efforts to forge agreement on the terms of regimes to deal with such issues as climate change and the loss of biological diversity? Can we identify research priorities for those desiring to push forward the frontiers of knowledge regarding regime formation during the foreseeable future? Do we have useful lessons to offer practitioners endeavoring to reach closure on the terms of new regimes in a variety of issue areas? In this final chapter, we take stock of the progress made during the course of our project on the politics of international regime formation, seeking in the process not only to provide answers to these questions but also to convey a sense of the vitality of regime formation as a field of study.

REGIME FORMATION: THE UNIVERSE OF CASES

The cases we have examined convey a strong sense of both the richness and the diversity of the institutional arrangements belonging to the category of international regimes. The arrangement for the

Svalbard Archipelago, a stewardship regime in which a single member plays the role of trustee for the concerns of the broader community, stands as testimony to the proposition that the absence of a centralized structure of authority in international society does not preclude the development of mechanisms that serve to promote the common good.[1] The polar bear agreement establishes a coordination regime that commits its members to acting in accordance with a set of common rules and procedures, while leaving each member free to implement these rules and procedures in its own way.[2] The fur seal regime and the protection system for stratospheric ozone involve more complex arrangements. The regime for fur seals, articulated initially in the 1911 treaty, evolved into a users' club coupled with a cooperative mechanism for arriving at collective decisions regarding the consumptive use of seals. The ozone regime, which began as a coordination arrangement, has developed into a cooperative management system with the addition of the 1990 London Amendments to the Montreal Protocol.

Nonetheless, we have found ourselves dealing in each case with a process of regime formation that features more or less extensive efforts to reach agreement on explicit, though not necessarily legally binding, statements setting forth the major provisions of regimes.[3] In some cases, the process has been long and drawn out—it took more than twenty years of intermittent negotiations to produce the four-party treaty of 1911 on fur seals. Sometimes the provisions included in the final agreement differ dramatically from those under consideration in earlier phases of the negotiations—the pre–World War I deliberations on Svalbard, for example, centered on the idea of *terra nullius* coupled with a proposal for the establishment of an international administrative apparatus. In other cases, the outcome is an open agreement to which

1. On the decentralized character of international society see Hedley Bull, *The Anarchical Society: A Study of Order in World Politics* (New York: Columbia University Press, 1977).

2. The significance of coordination regimes in international society raises questions about Keohane's observation that "regimes are usually accompanied by organizations" (Robert O. Keohane, "Multilateralism: An Agenda for Research," *International Journal* 45 [Autumn 1990]: 733).

3. There is a rapidly growing literature on "soft law" in international society or, in other words, prescriptions that take the form of legal rules but that are not expressed in the form of treaties or conventions. For a discussion of soft law regimes see Peter S. Thacher, *Global Security and Risk Management* (Geneva: World Federation of United Nations Associations, n.d.). Some effective international agreements are even more informal. For a discussion of conditions under which actors are likely to prefer informal prescriptions see Charles Lipson, "Why Are Some International Agreements Informal?" *International Organization* 45 (Autumn 1991): 495–538.

additional members accede as they see fit—the LRTAP protocols on sulfur dioxide, nitrogen oxide, and volatile organic compounds fit this model. In still other cases, a regime develops in stages through a continuing series of negotiations punctuated by partial or interim agreements—the ozone regime evolved from the framework provisions of the 1985 Vienna Convention to the substantive arrangements set forth in the 1987 Montreal Protocol and the 1990 London Amendments.

In every case, however, the process of regime formation centered on efforts to negotiate the terms of a package of mutually acceptable provisions to be set forth in a constitutional contract.[4] We are now convinced that this pattern of negotiation eventuating in one or more explicit agreements constitutes the normal process of regime formation in international society. To be sure, there are instances in which social conventions have arisen and become operative through the sort of informal convergence of expectations that Thomas C. Schelling and George W. Downs and David M. Rocke have analyzed in their work on tacit bargaining.[5] Robert Axelrod's account of the live-and-let-live system in the trenches of World War I offers a particularly striking example of this sort of convergence.[6] There is, as well, a natural tendency for informal interpretations or supplementary understandings to evolve over time in connection with regimes. This is true in the case of the Svalbard regime, in which technological advances and geopolitics have raised issues that could not have been foreseen by the negotiators who labored to craft the provisions of the regime in Paris during the summer of 1919. Similar observations apply to the ozone regime, in which our scientific understanding of the problem is evolving so rapidly that there is general agreement on the need to achieve flexibility by allowing for informal interpretations of the constitutive agreements.[7] Yet the fact remains that those regimes that loom large as sources of governance in international society and therefore occupy the

---

4. A constitutional contract is an explicit agreement setting forth the rules of the game for a given social practice. Such contracts may, but need not, be codified in legally binding instruments such as treaties or conventions. For a well-known account of constitutional contracts by a nonlawyer see James M. Buchanan, *The Limits of Liberty: Between Anarchy and Leviathan* (Chicago: University of Chicago Press, 1975), esp. chap. 4.

5. Thomas C. Schelling, *The Strategy of Conflict* (Cambridge, Mass.: Harvard University Press, 1960), esp. chap. 3; and George W. Downs and David M. Rocke, *Tacit Bargaining, Arms Races, and Arms Control* (Ann Arbor: University of Michigan Press, 1990), esp. chap. 1.

6. Robert Axelrod, *The Evolution of Cooperation* (New York: Basic Books, 1984), chap. 4.

7. See Richard E. Benedick, *Ozone Diplomacy: New Directions in Safeguarding the Planet* (Cambridge, Mass.: Harvard University Press, 1991).

attention of students of international relations normally take the form of constitutional contracts emerging from some recognizable bargaining process.[8]

Does this mean that institutional arrangements in international society can be treated, for the most part, as negotiated regimes, in contrast to imposed or spontaneous regimes?[9] Admittedly, our choice of cases (which we do not assert constitutes a representative sample of the overall universe of regimes) influenced the conclusions we have reached regarding this question. On the basis of our own research supplemented by discussions with others engaged in research on regime formation, however, we are now prepared to argue that the formation of international regimes ordinarily involves a process of institutional bargaining. Negotiation is clearly a prominent feature of this process, even in the presence of a dominant party such as the United States in the negotiations that produced the international monetary and trade regimes in the aftermath of World War II. But we would add immediately that exercises of power in the form of efforts to translate the possession of material resources into bargaining leverage occur frequently in institutional bargaining. So also do spontaneous developments that take the form of tacit bargaining or the convergence of expectations around common formulas in the absence of explicit offers and counteroffers.[10]

Accordingly, we have come to regard the categories of negotiated, imposed, and spontaneous regimes as elements in a typology founded on analytic as opposed to concrete distinctions. In other words, these distinctions identify differentiable aspects of a single phenomenon rather than three different phenomena that are separable in the sense that actual cases can be allocated meaningfully to one category or another. Purely negotiated, imposed, or spontaneous regimes are extreme types that seldom, if ever, occur in connection with actual processes of regime formation. Although the mix undoubtedly varies from one case to another, the institutional bargaining giving rise to international regimes ordinarily involves some combina-

---

8. On the idea of governance in international society see James N. Rosenau, ed., *Governance without Government: Change and Order in World Politics* (Cambridge: Cambridge University Press, 1992).

9. For a discussion of the distinctions among spontaneous, negotiated, and imposed regimes see Oran R. Young, *International Cooperation: Building Regimes for Natural Resources and the Environment* (Ithaca: Cornell University Press, 1989), chap. 4.

10. The seminal account of tacit bargaining is contained in Schelling, *Strategy of Conflict*. For a discussion of recent developments in this field see Downs and Rocke, *Tacit Bargaining*.

tion of conventional negotiation, efforts to exercise power, and tacit bargaining.

Because institutional bargaining looms large both in our case studies and in our conclusions, we turn now to a brief account of the distinctive features of this process in contrast to bargaining of the sort envisioned in mainstream theories of the bargaining process.[11] Those engaging in institutional bargaining in international society normally operate under consensus rather than majoritarian rules. That is, once the problem to be addressed is formulated and the identity of the participants established (both matters that may give rise to complex negotiations and hard preliminary bargaining), actors endeavoring to agree on provisions to be incorporated in a constitutional contract make a concerted effort to devise packages of component elements that as many of the participants as possible can accept.

Two additional features of institutional bargaining save the resultant interactions from yielding nothing but broad formulas containing little content or eventuating in outright failure. Those engaged in regime formation in international society rarely begin with a fully specified (much less mutually understood) picture of the locus and shape of a welfare frontier or contract curve, a fact that serves to soften the distributive aspect of the process of regime formation. Because regimes ordinarily encompass a number of issues and are expected to remain in place indefinitely, moreover, it is difficult for those negotiating on behalf of individual participants to make confident predictions about the distributive consequences of the operation of alternative institutional options over time. This, too, serves to mute the positional or distributive (in contrast to integrative) aspect of institutional bargaining.

Faced with such a bargaining environment, parties endeavoring to reach agreement on provisions to be included in a constitutional contract rarely make a sustained effort to perfect the information at their disposal concerning the locus and shape of the contract curve before embarking on serious bargaining. Instead, they normally single out a few key problems and seek to work out approaches to these problems that each of the participants can accept as a package rather than as a set of discrete elements. The resultant process affords ample opportunity for efforts to make use of bargaining leverage, for the

11. For a more extensive account of institutional bargaining and the differences between this type of bargaining and the situations envisioned in conventional models see Oran R. Young, "The Politics of International Regime Formation: Managing Natural Resources and the Environment," *International Organization* 43 (Summer 1989): 349–375.

indirect initiatives characteristic of tacit bargaining, as well as for negotiation in the more traditional sense of conscious efforts to formulate
and reformulate key provisions of a draft treaty or convention. Above
all, the process reflects perspectives or systems of thought dominant at
the time and constitutes an ideal setting for the activities of individuals
who operate as what we have termed structural and entrepreneurial
leaders.

Institutional bargaining is a difficult process in social settings of
the sort prevailing in international society. To the classic array of collective-action problems that occur in all interactive relationships, we must
add complications that regularly arise in reaching consensus on the
formulation of the problem at the outset (including the issues to cover,
the actors to participate, and the product to seek), avoiding the pit-
falls implicit in the fact that each of the parties is a complex collective
entity, and coping with intrusions of exogenous factors that threaten
to divert the attention of participants or sap their political will.[12] Yet as
our cases demonstrate, those engaged in institutional bargaining in
international society not only succeed in reaching closure on the
terms of constitutional contracts in some cases but they also manage
from time to time to form regimes that prove effective and persistent.
Our task, then, is to pinpoint the determinants of success or failure in
such endeavors so that we can respond with some assurance to those
who ask why, for example, an international regime emerged in 1911
rather than in the 1890s for fur seals or why no regime has emerged
to deal with Arctic haze in contrast to transboundary air pollution in
Europe.

Given this conception of regime formation, it will come as no surprise
that the process is typically a protracted one in international society.
The regimes we have examined in this project took years (in several
cases decades) to devise, even after the problem had been clearly
defined and the process of institutional bargaining had begun.[13]
Though the need for international cooperation to manage the human
use of fur seals was evident at least from the time of the arbitration
tribunal's decision in 1893, for example, the four participants were un-

---

12. For additional insights see Jessica T. Mathews et al., *Greenhouse Warming: Negotiating a
Global Regime* (Washington, D.C.: World Resources Institute, 1991); and Robert D. Putnam, "Diplomacy and Domestic Politics: The Logic of Two-Level Games," *International Organization* 42 (Summer 1988): 427–460.

13. Though regime formation in domestic society normally occurs under a majoritarian
(rather than a consensus) rule, it is a mistake to overemphasize the consequences of this
difference with regard to timing. The process of regime formation can be just as protracted in domestic society as it is in international society.

able to reach closure on the treaty setting forth the terms of the regime until 1911. Even the ozone regime, regarded by many as a model for dealing with future environmental issues, emerged in stages over the course of a period spanning almost a decade.[14] It follows, we believe, that a satisfactory account of regime formation must approach the subject as a dynamic process unfolding over time rather than as a yes-or-no proposition without consideration of the dimension of time. It is not sufficient to confine our attention as students of regime formation to the simple question of whether or not a regime forms. Both scholars and practitioners seek answers as well to questions about why institutional bargaining is a more protracted process in some cases than in others and why the final product often looks quite different from the formulas presented and debated during the early stages of the process.

SINGLE-FACTOR ACCOUNTS

Considered separately, the case studies presented in this volume cannot confirm the hypotheses outlined in Chapter 1 and presented in summary form in the Appendix. But taken together, the results of these studies enable us to identify with some confidence hypotheses that are disconfirmed and to focus on those that have received sufficient support to make them interesting as subjects for further investigation. Tables 7.1 to 7.4 summarize the conclusions from the five cases for each of the hypotheses. In the course of the empirical phase of the project, the research team made some adjustments and elaborations to the hypotheses. These are discussed in the text and account for minor differences between the Appendix and Tables 7.1–7.4.

Power-Based Hypotheses

None of the cases offers strong support for the proposition that success in regime formation requires the participation of a single dominant party or, in other words, a hegemon (see Table 7.1). In four of the cases, researchers found no evidence of a single state making use of superior material resources to obtain or impose its preferred outcome. Power was important in each of the cases, but it is more easily understood as a source of bargaining strength in the interactive

---

14. Benedick, *Ozone Diplomacy.*

Table 7.1 Power-based hypotheses

Hypotheses	Fur seals	Svalbard	Polar bears	Ozone	Haze/ LRTAP	Summary
Hegemony	D	D	D	M	D	4D/1M
Middle powers play key role			C		C	2C
Other configurations of power		C	C		C	3C

An empty cell indicates that the hypothesis is not addressed in the case study.
C = consistent with hypothesis
D = tends to disconfirm hypothesis
M = results mixed

processes highlighted by the interest-based hypotheses. Power in the material sense may even come to be regarded as an obstacle, as in the polar bear case when American negotiators took care to avoid derailing negotiations by any display of dominance.[15]

Only in the case of ozone is there evidence of a single state playing a hegemonic role and then only during the middle stage (the development of the 1987 Montreal Protocol) of regime formation. Haas treats this as an instance of issue-specific hegemony, in which American negotiators were able to use the dominance of the United States in scientific research, diplomatic competence, and both production and consumption of CFCs to impose its preferred outcome. There is some evidence that the threat of unilateral action by Congress was effective in this context. Yet hegemony appears to have played little or no role during the first stage of this process (eventuating in the framework provisions of the 1985 Vienna Convention), in which the United States was unable to achieve agreement on its own terms. As Haas points out, hegemonic stability theory does not account for the ability of European producer and consumer states to temper the terms of both the 1987 and 1990 agreements to serve their interests. What is more, the United States made significant concessions in the stage of regime formation that produced the London Amend-

15. Our findings parallel those of a well-known group of European scholars working at the University of Tübingen. See Volker Rittberger and Michael Zürn, "Regime Theory: Findings from the Study of 'East-West Regimes' " (paper presented at the convention of the International Studies Association, Vancouver, British Columbia, March 1991), esp. 21–22.

ments of 1990 to satisfy the concerns of key developing countries such as China and India, whose bargaining strength arose from their growing demand for CFCs in refrigeration and other uses.

Haas would also modify the theory of hegemonic stability by turning to an analysis of domestic factors to explain the timing and reasoning behind the decision of the hegemon to exercise its superior resources in a particular issue area. He explains that although the power of the United States did not change during the 1980s, it was only in 1986 (when Du Pont broke ranks with the rest of the industry) that the United States was able to exercise its superior resources at the bargaining table. Taken as a whole, this discussion suggests the virtue of paying more attention to the distribution of power in specific issue areas in future research on regime formation.

After rejecting hegemonic stability theory, at least in its pure form, the authors of the other case studies searched for different configurations of power that may have come into play (although we had no explicit hypotheses to guide this inquiry). Several of the cases suggest that middle powers can assume key roles in regime formation. Germany played a central part in negotiating the 1985 SO_2 protocol to LRTAP; Canada played a pivotal role in creating the polar bear regime and may do so again in the future with regard to a regime to deal with Arctic haze. Soroos notes that the absence of strong support for a regime by the superpowers may enhance the role of middle powers. Furthermore, middle powers such as the Nordic states, acting individually or as a group, may offer to host and chair meetings (as Norway did in the final negotiation of the polar bear regime), thereby enabling the superpowers to avoid appearing too dominant or assertive. Future students of regime formation might examine further the potential roles of middle powers and compare the activities of those states that are middle powers by virtue of their military capability with those included in this category for economic reasons.

Soroos pays considerable attention to bipolarity in his analysis of Arctic haze, finding that bipolar relations (East-West conflict) in the world may hinder cooperation in a strategically significant area such as the Arctic. In our view, however, it is more likely that the strategic sensitivity of the region rather than bipolarity has impeded the formation of an Arctic haze regime. The strategic significance of the Arctic blocked most cooperation in Arctic scientific research until recently. Yet bipolarity was not a hindrance to formation of either the transboundary air pollution regime or the polar bear regime. In fact, there is evidence that a desire to find areas in which East and West could cooperate encouraged formation of these regimes.

One of the most provocative results of our study with regard to power arises from the role of surrogate negotiators in the Svalbard case. There, the Great Powers, the victors of World War I, were able to assert their authority to forge a regime in which they themselves had no intense interest. These surrogates used their position as victors—having fought a costly war, they were not particularly dominant in material terms at the time—to legitimize their role in deciding the fate of Svalbard. Is the role of surrogates a mere aberration occurring only in the unusual circumstances following the Great War? Or does the case of Svalbard offer a useful model for the future? These questions are certainly relevant today as the United Nations Security Council assumes a higher profile in handling international problems.

Interest-Based Hypotheses

Among the four central sets of ideas we tested (those pertaining to power, interests, knowledge, and context), the case studies consistently emphasized factors affecting interest-based behavior in the context of interactive decision making. With regard to the specific hypotheses tested, the role of individual leaders received such strong support that we now believe it may constitute a necessary condition for regime formation. A second group of hypotheses received enough support to suggest that they tap important (though not strictly necessary) conditions for the formation of regimes. Our cases tended to disconfirm a third group of hypotheses. In Table 7.2, these three groups of hypotheses are separated by extra space with the necessary condition at the top and the disconfirmed hypotheses at the bottom.

Table 7.2 Interest-based hypotheses

Hypotheses	Fur seals	Svalbard	Polar bears	Ozone	Haze/ LRTAP	Summary
Individual leadership	C	C	C	C	C	5C
Equity (more important than efficiency)	C	M	C	C	C	4C/1M
Salient solutions	C	C	C	M	C	4C/1M

Table 7.2 — continued

Hypotheses	Fur seals	Svalbard	Polar bears	Ozone	Haze/ LRTAP	Summary
Availability of effective compliance mechanisms	C	C	C	C	N	4C/1N
Integrative bargaining	M	C	C	C	C	4C/1M
Veil of uncertainty	M	C	C	D	C	3C/1M/1D
Exogenous shock or crisis	M	D	C	C	C	3C/1M/1D
All parties participate	C	D	C	D		2C/2D
Common good prevails		D	M	D		1M/2D
High priority on all agendas	D	D	D	D	M	1M/4D
Low priority on all agendas		D	D	D	D	4D
Technical over political issues	D	D	D	D		4D

An empty cell indicates that the hypothesis is not addressed in the case study.
C = consistent with hypothesis
D = tends to disconfirm hypothesis
M = results mixed
N = no clear test

One or more individuals emerged as leaders in each of the five cases, and the leadership they provided proved to be important in the formation of the regime. In addition, both the lack of strong and consistent leadership in earlier attempts to form a regime for Svalbard and the absence of leaders to push for a regime to deal with Arctic haze strengthen the case for leadership as a necessary condition for regime formation.[16]

16. We encountered some difficulty in assessing the personalities of players and the dynamics of the negotiations in the older cases because individual participants are no longer

As the project evolved, we came to understand that leadership on the part of individuals—not amorphous leadership exercised by governments on behalf of states—plays a key role in regime formation. One of the clearest and strongest findings of the project is that leadership is a crosscutting factor. Leadership is both affected by and affects power relationships. It also shapes the values and ideas discussed in connection with knowledge-based hypotheses.

The authors of the case studies found the typology of leadership—encompassing structural, entrepreneurial, and intellectual leadership—useful. All five case studies identify one or more individuals as entrepreneurial leaders (Stanovnik of the ECE in the transboundary air pollution case; Tolba, Lang, and Benedick in the ozone case; numerous individuals in the polar bear case; Jordan in the fur seal case; and Wedel-Jarlsberg in the case of Svalbard). Sometimes an individual identified as an entrepreneurial leader also played a role as a structural leader (for example, Benedick, Bohlen, and Wedel-Jarlsberg). An individual with exceptional entrepreneurial skills (such as Bohlen in the final negotiation of the polar bear agreement) may head the delegation of a powerful state engaged in institutional bargaining. In other cases, heads of delegations are properly regarded as structural leaders (for example, Clemenceau in the Svalbard case).

Although intellectual leadership surfaced in the fur seal and ozone cases and was provided by a group of individuals (the Polar Bear Specialist Group) in a third case, it was not a significant factor in three of the five cases (Svalbard, transboundary air pollution, and ozone). We suspect that this absence does not signify that such leadership was unimportant but suggests instead that the role of intellectual leadership is more central in earlier stages of regime formation, usually before ex-

---

living. Although we found extensive biographical and autobiographical material on individual leaders such as Georges Clémenceau (Svalbard) and David Starr Jordan (fur seals), our cases played minor roles in their careers. Thus the material relevant to our cases was insufficient to answer some key questions. We are unsure, for example, why Clemenceau decided that the status of Svalbard should be dealt with in Paris soon after the war as opposed to becoming an early agenda item for the anticipated League of Nations to decide.

We also encountered problems in recent cases whose actors are not only alive but still active in international policy circles. Their own accounts of events sometimes differ from the accounts our research teams have compiled. With due respect to the closeness of participants to events at the time, we believe outside researchers have the advantage of access to inside information from many actors present at the negotiation and, therefore, may reconstruct a more accurate picture. In the polar bear case, for example, the authors were able to read the records of each of the foreign ministries and gain insights not always apparent to any single individual present at the time.

234

plicit or public negotiations begin.[17] In the section on knowledge-based hypotheses, we discuss the role of science, scientists, and networks of scientists in generating knowledge and ideas relevant to regime formation. For now, we can state that the presence of intellectual leaders during the phase of institutional bargaining is not a precondition for regime formation.

Our examination of leadership not only suggests to us that leadership exercised by individuals is a necessary condition for regime formation, but it also allows us to formulate a more specific hypothesis for further examination, namely that the presence of one or more individuals acting as entrepreneurial leaders is necessary for regime formation to occur. In the absence of such leadership, attempts to form a regime will fail. The same individual may play more than one leadership role, and several individuals may play the same leadership role in the course of regime formation.

Members of the research team had difficulty testing the original version of the hypothesis in which we juxtaposed efficiency and equity rather than addressing the presence and importance of equity as distinct from efficiency. In several of the cases, the analysts considered both equity and efficiency important; it is fair to say that they concluded that the fur seal, Svalbard, and polar bear cases all produced regimes that are both equitable and efficient. These findings do not contradict the hypothesis. But when no trade-off between efficiency and equity is required, it is not possible to determine the relative importance of these factors.

The issue at stake here, we now believe, arises precisely when it is necessary to make trade-offs between the pursuit of efficiency and the achievement of equity. To be specific, the hypothesis should state that institutional bargaining cannot succeed unless it produces an outcome that participants can accept as equitable, even when the adoption of equitable formulas requires some sacrifice in efficiency. In this connec-

---

17. But see the discussion of Robert Lansing's role in the Svalbard case for an example of intellectual leadership at work during the actual negotiations. Also, on occasion a change in leadership in a particular state or a change in key officials can lead to alteration of a state's position enabling alternative ideas and values to emerge during the final phases of negotiation. Note, for example, the shift in Bush administration officials coinciding with a change of positions on amending the ozone protocol or the change in the American position regarding mining in Antarctica in response both to congressional action and the appointment of Bohlen as the assistant secretary of state responsible for this issue.

tion, the ozone and LRTAP cases are particularly interesting because they eventuated in regimes only when parties were willing to accept some reduction in efficiency to obtain equity. Efficiency alone would dictate arrangements encouraging deeper cuts in the consumption of CFCs or in SO_2 emissions on the part of those able to make such cuts at the least cost. But formulas featuring across-the-board or equal cuts on the part of the participants proved (with a few exceptions) more defensible on grounds of equity, and it seems apparent that a willingness to accept such formulas played an important role in producing successful outcomes.

In all the case studies, the authors found evidence that a salient solution broke through potential blockages in the negotiating process. In the case of the ozone regime (whose formation took place in three stages), however, Haas concludes that a salient solution was important only in the final stage when the emergent regime was strengthened through the adoption of the London Amendments.

The common factor in what we have termed salient solutions is simplicity in the sense of uncomplicated formulas that advocates can explain to policy makers in straightforward terms and that journalists can encapsulate in headlines for public consumption.[18] Frequently, the salient solution is also a formulation that breaks an impasse over a tricky distributive issue. Sometimes this involves avoiding the issue altogether, as in the polar bear and Svalbard cases. The salient solution in the polar bear case was one that avoided jurisdictional questions and defined the geographical coverage of the regime's rules in historical terms, thereby avoiding the complications of legalistic terminology. In the Svalbard case, the entire agreement is contained in ten short articles, compared with the fifteen chapters and seventy-five articles of the 1912–1914 drafts. The complexities of administration are eliminated by the simple device of assigning sovereignty to Norway and delegating to Norway the tasks allocated in earlier drafts to a more cumbersome tripartite commission.

In other cases, the salient solution is distributive in nature, but it offers a formula that is easy for policy makers to grasp and that is intuitively appealing to the general public. In the fur seal case, the salient solution involved the coupling of a total ban on pelagic sealing with a simple formula for sharing the proceeds of the harvest in a way that satisfied all the parties. The transboundary air pollution regime employs two different focal points that can be explained simply (though implementation is not so simple). The first is across-the-board percent-

---

18. For a seminal account of salience or prominence see Schelling, *Strategy of Conflict.*

age reductions. Thus a group of states built a coalition around the concept of 30 percent reductions in SO_2 emissions or transboundary fluxes by a set date; the group became known as the 30% Club. A different formulation is used in the 1988 nitrogen protocol in which the salient solution was a freeze on emissions by a specified date. Both these formulas have the advantage of flexibility, allowing parties to adjust either the percentages or the implementation schedule as new information becomes available or circumstances change.

Authors of four of the five case studies found evidence of the availability of compliance mechanisms which the parties at the time regarded as clear-cut and likely to be effective. These cases tend to confirm our hypothesis because they found that the availability of such mechanisms played an important role in institutional bargaining. The Arctic haze/LRTAP case offered no clear test of the hypothesis. Despite near unanimity regarding the need for compliance mechanisms, the specific methods used to obtain compliance differ substantially.

Negotiators of the Spitsbergen Treaty designated a single state as administrator of the regime, consolidating the issuance of regulations, monitoring, and enforcement under the auspices of Norway. In the fur seal case, by contrast, the fact that all seal skins were processed in London at the time reduced incentives to cheat by making verification of compliance relatively easy. The parties to the regime agreed to exclude nonauthenticated seal skins from their ports. Because northern fur seal skins are easily identifiable and not likely to be confused with skins of other seal species, the parties expected any illegal trade to be easy to prevent. All legal taking and processing of seals and seal skins would be conducted by central government authorities in the United States and in Russia, which further increased the likelihood of compliance.

The polar bear regime, the transboundary air pollution regime, and the ozone regime all rely on decentralized systems of implementation and compliance. These cases suggest that it is important not only to identify a compliance mechanism that parties regard as likely to be effective but also to handle compliance in the least intrusive way possible. The LRTAP regime, for example, relies on a monitoring system known as EMEP to increase the transparency of the behavior of members and, in the process, to reduce incentives to cheat. The ozone regime avoids intrusive measures by computing a party's consumption of CFCs as total production minus exports plus imports. The Montreal Protocol also bans imports from nonparties. These controls on trade, combined with reporting and distribution of data on CFC production, constitute the compliance mechanisms of the ozone regime.

Four of the cases produced evidence consistent with the hypothesis that integrative or productive bargaining plays a prominent role in successful institutional bargaining. Three of these cases also confirmed that a veil of uncertainty contributed to the process by making it difficult for individual participants to foresee how the operation of particular provisions would affect their interests over time. The mixed results of the fur seal case show that institutional bargaining is seldom wholly integrative or distributive but rather constitutes a hybrid involving both types of bargaining.

The cases show that deemphasizing or avoiding distributive issues enhances the ability of the participants to engage in a search for mutually beneficial solutions. By designating Norway as the administrative authority for Svalbard, for example, those negotiating in Paris in 1919 were able to circumvent numerous divisive issues that had plagued earlier attempts to forge agreement on membership and duties of a tripartite commission as well as the details of civil and criminal administration. Negotiators of the polar bear regime avoided a jurisdictional approach to defining the area within which polar bears would be protected and, in the process, arrived at a definition that would not produce winners and losers in the ongoing dispute over jurisdictional claims in Arctic waters. The ozone negotiators made the bargain struck more integrative by expanding the contract zone through the inclusion of a provision exempting developing countries from compliance with certain of the requirements for a ten-year period, as well as the establishment of a fund to assist these countries during the transition period.

Only three of the cases lend support to the hypothesis regarding the importance of a veil of uncertainty. In these cases, those engaged in regime formation sought to make the most of the veil of uncertainty by lengthening the time the regime was expected to operate (the polar bear case), leaving the arrangement open to accession by additional states in the future (Svalbard), and including ambiguous provisions subject to a variety of subsequent interpretations (the polar bear case). The transboundary air pollution case indicates that when the veil of uncertainty is thin, international cooperation is less likely to occur or participation in the regime may be limited. Note, in this connection, the inability to devise a regime for Arctic haze and the failure of some of the major polluters to ratify the SO_2 and NO_x protocols to LRTAP, both situations in which the costs and benefits of participating are relatively easy to compute.

In the ozone case, the veil of uncertainty present during the negotiations leading to the 1985 Vienna Convention became thinner by late 1986, when scientific models showed that inclusion of developing countries was not critical to starting up the regime. The increased ability to calculate costs and benefits enabled negotiators to agree to a ten-year exemption from compliance. Despite this exemption and the relatively small fund for technology transfer, developing countries were able to see that the costs of complying with the regime could be greater than the benefits to them. Thus, though the thinning of the veil of uncertainty may have helped to produce success in negotiating the Montreal Protocol in 1987 by making the benefits of participation clearer to the signatories, it also served to limit participation in the arrangements established under the terms of the protocol.

We suspect that a measure of integrative bargaining is a necessary condition of regime formation, but the complexity associated with the presence of numerous distributive as well as integrative issues in specific cases makes it hard for researchers to reconstruct the level of effort directed toward handling each type of issue and to determine the relative importance of integrative as opposed to distributive bargaining. In evaluating the importance of a veil of uncertainty, it is also difficult to separate regime formation and regime effectiveness. The evidence suggests that regimes may emerge even when the veil of uncertainty is diminishing but that the resulting regimes are apt to be less effective.

Three of the five cases are consistent with the idea that shocks or crises exogenous to the negotiating process are important in the regime formation process. The polar bear case study examines a manufactured crisis in elucidating the role of nongovernmental organizations and the media in creating at least the appearance of crisis. In the ozone case, Haas notes that the discovery of the Antarctic ozone hole, along with other scientific alarms, "jump-started" stalled efforts to go beyond the general framework of the 1985 Vienna Convention. The Arctic haze chapter compares the evolution of the LRTAP regime following the publicization of forest death (*Waldsterben*) in Europe with the absence of any comparable sense of crisis or shock regarding Arctic haze.

Nonetheless, the authors of the Svalbard case study found no specific shock or crisis associated with formation of the regime (although the changes wrought by World War I surely played a role). The authors of the fur seal case study found a series of shocks—initial seizure of British vessels by the United States (dubbed by some observers the seal wars), drastic declines in the size of the fur seal herds, and the killing of Japanese poachers in the early 1900s. But they were troubled because an atmosphere of crisis over the issue pervaded a long period of attempts to establish a regime and no particular shock appears to have triggered the final settlement in 1911.

We can conclude that, although the occurrence of an exogenous shock or a crisis is not necessary for regime formation, it does help in some cases to promote agreement on the terms of a constitutional contract. The cases also suggest that further research to determine the effect of crisis on the substantive provisions of the regime would be fruitful. Evidence is mixed on whether crises do more than speed regime formation or, in other words, on whether the heightened attention by media and the public to the issues leads to stronger terms or a more effective regime.

We turn now to the five hypotheses for which our cases tended to disconfirm the proposed relationship or the record is sufficiently mixed to cast doubt on the value of the hypothesis. These include the ideas that a shared conception of the common good must prevail over national interests; the issue must achieve a high priority on the agendas of all key participants; conversely, low priority on all agendas enhances prospects for regime formation; concentration on technical (as opposed to political) concerns and an enhanced role for technical or scientific experts in the process increases the likelihood of regime formation; and all interested parties must be present for a regime to emerge.

Our cases did not provide support for the hypothesis that a shared conception of the common good must prevail over national interest perspectives for a regime to form. Limited evidence in the polar bear case suggests that such a shared conception may be useful in some cases. But the Svalbard and polar bear cases led to the conclusion that although the terms of the agreement may be said to have promoted the common good, they also satisfied the national interests of the parties. Both cases illustrate that prospects for regime formation may be enhanced when actors find ways to accommodate their most important national interests, while at the same time promoting the common good or a shared conception of what will benefit all parties. Advocates of transcendent goals may also persuade policy makers that what promotes the common good serves a state's national interest. As the ozone case suggests, moreover, conceptions of the common good are affected by material circumstances. Even when most northern countries came to share a concern for the protection of stratospheric ozone, the developing countries, especially China and India, did not concur.

In four of five cases, the issue did not become a high priority on the agendas of all the key actors, although it may have been high on the agenda of one or more of the parties. Thus we must reject the hypothesis that high priority on agendas of all the key players is a necessary condition for regime formation. The evidence in three of the five cases (Arctic haze, ozone, and polar bears) also disconfirms the converse hypothesis that a low priority on policy agendas may enhance prospects for regime formation. Results are mixed in the Svalbard case. For the states composing the Spitsbergen Commission in 1919, the issue was not a high priority. But for Norway, the party with the strongest interest, the issue was high on the national agenda. By contrast, the issue of transboundary air pollution appears to have become relatively high priority on the agendas of most key participants in the LRTAP case. And the absence of Arctic haze as a high-priority issue for any of the Arctic states leads to the suggestion that high-priority status for at least some parties can be a help in mobilizing support for regime formation. These observations lead us to conclude that situations in which the issue is a high priority for one or more parties but low priority for others may be conducive to regime formation.

Although the evidence in the fur seal and polar bear cases is consistent with the hypothesis that all parties with an interest in the problem must participate in institutional bargaining for a regime to emerge, Russia was absent from the Svalbard negotiations in 1919 and that absence facilitated regime formation. Thus the presence of all interested parties is not a necessary condition for regime formation. Further consideration of this hypothesis, however, has led us to give more thought to the stages of regime formation. The ozone case, for example, may offer a model for the negotiation of future global environmental regimes. China and India, which could become major users of CFCs in the future and whose participation is necessary to form an effective regime, were not active participants during the first two stages (Vienna 1985, Montreal 1987). But they became active in the negotiation of the London Amendments of 1990 and now seem willing to join the evolving ozone regime. The creation of the LRTAP regime exemplifies another pattern of regime formation in stages, with all key parties involved in the negotiation of the framework convention in 1979 but smaller groups forging the 1985 SO_2 and 1988 NO_x protocols. The idea of staged development of environmental regimes is not new. The International Union for the Conservation of Nature, for example, envisioned a two-step process for the protection of polar bears, in which the five states inhabited by bears would agree to a limited and temporary regime to be followed by a broader convention open to participation by all states.[19] Future research should focus on alternatives to negotiation including a large number of parties and assess the advantages and disadvantages of beginning negotiations with some subset of the interested players (perhaps even surrogates for some parties) and gradually drawing increased numbers of players into the process.

The last of this group of disconfirmed hypotheses deals with the interplay between technical and political issues and the relative importance of technical experts or scientists as opposed to those possessing political skills. In three of the five cases, the parties focused more on the political issues, and the role of those with political credentials was more important than the role of technical experts. The Arctic haze/LRTAP case study does not address this question. The ozone case study indicates that negotiators were keenly aware of economic and political issues as well as highly technical issues and focuses on the interplay between technical experts and diplomats in forging agreement.

We suspect that the failure of this hypothesis is attributable to the fact that scientific research usually suffices to resolve factual issues. As a result, these issues are often disposed of before institutional bargaining proper gets under way. Value conflicts, however, remain as the sticking points that may block regime formation, and those with experience in diplomacy and institutional bargaining are most likely to succeed in devising the formulas needed to resolve these problems.

Knowledge-Based Hypotheses

Four of the case studies found evidence consistent with the general proposition that values and scientific knowledge influence regime formation independently rather than simply contributing indirectly to the exercise of structural power or to the definition of the interests of state actors (see Table 7.3). Only the Svalbard case study found cognitive factors largely irrelevant to regime formation. The fact that the four cases confirming the importance of knowledge and values all deal with natural resources or environmental issues leads us to ask whether such regimes differ markedly from others with regard to the knowledge factors involved in institutional bargaining. Certainly, environmental

---

19. As Chapter 4 explains, the second stage never occurred. Instead, the temporary protocol became a permanent agreement with expanded rules applying to a larger geographic area.

regimes rely heavily on the development of science coupled with changing values regarding the human use of natural resources, whereas a regime designed to resolve jurisdictional questions, such as the Svalbard regime, is not so dependent on scientific knowledge.

Table 7.3 Knowledge-based hypotheses

Hypotheses	Fur seals	Svalbard	Polar bears	Ozone	Haze/ LRTAP	Summary
Values/ ideas matter	C		C	C	C	4C
Consensus emerges (Cooper)	C	D	D	N	M	1C/2D/ 1M/1N
Presence of epistemic community	D	D	C	M	1C/1M	2D

An empty cell indicates that the hypothesis is not addressed in the case study.
C = consistent with hypothesis
D = tends to disconfirm hypothesis
M = results mixed
N = no clear test

We suspect, however, that the role of scientific knowledge and values in forming regimes that do not deal with natural resources or the environment is not irrelevant but merely more subtle and difficult to trace. For example, where did the idea of forging a stewardship regime for Svalbard originate, following two attempts in the previous decade to employ the traditional concept of *terra nullius*? The idea of demilitarization, which became an important element of the Svalbard regime, may have owed something to the establishment of neutralized states in the cases of Switzerland in 1815 and Belgium in 1839.[20] But its application to an area that had previously been no-man's land was a unique adaptation of an idea borrowed from prior experience with different situations.[21] It seems unlikely, then, that the Svalbard regime

---

20. On the practice of neutralization in international society see Cyril E. Black, Richard A. Falk, Klaus Knorr, and Oran R. Young, *Neutralization and World Politics* (Princeton: Princeton University Press, 1968).

21. Many observers regard Antarctica as the first demilitarized zone. But the evidence suggests that the demilitarization of Svalbard provided a model for the Antarctic Treaty in this regard.

could have come into existence without the infusion of the ideas of restricted sovereignty and demilitarization, together with the values they embody.

The results for the specific knowledge-based hypotheses in our template are mixed. Two cases (haze/LRTAP and fur seals) offer some support for the hypothesis advanced by Cooper and others that international cooperation emerges easily and almost spontaneously once a common or widely shared understanding of the problem, its causes, and its solutions emerges and that no regime will emerge in the absence of consensual knowledge. But other cases tend to disconfirm this hypothesis. Though scientific convergence clearly helped in developing the polar bear regime, it did not eliminate the need for hard bargaining among the principals. Strikingly, the Montreal Protocol calling for sharp reductions in the production and consumption of chlorofluorocarbons emerged prior to the achievement of scientific consensus on several critical points. Yet scientific consensus did contribute substantially to the success of subsequent efforts to strengthen the regime through the adoption of the 1990 London Amendments.

Although the Svalbard and polar bear case studies note a rise in media attention and activity by nongovernmental organizations as factors promoting regime formation, both these cases and the fur seal case failed to confirm the presence of an epistemic community. In the Svalbard case, the attention of nongovernmental organizations appears to have had little effect on those negotiating the regime. In the polar bear case, advocacy organizations did enhance prospects for regime formation, and the scientist/managers of the Polar Bear Specialist Group greatly influenced the provisions of the regime. But these groups held considerably different views regarding the severity of the problem and the appropriate solutions. In contrast to the three earlier cases, however, our studies of the two more recent cases (transboundary air pollution and ozone) confirm the existence of epistemic communities. The ozone case study argues that an epistemic community played an important role in regime formation. The transboundary air pollution case is more equivocal on this point. Soroos explains that by the time the epistemic community matured, the general public's activism on LRTAP had become a more significant factor than the epistemic community in motivating governments to cooperate internationally on the issue.

Under the circumstances, we conclude that the development of an epistemic community is not a necessary condition for regime formation, even if we limit the hypothesis to environmental regimes in which scientific information plays a major role. Yet the creation of a transnational network of scientists and policy makers may prove to be an influential force in regime formation, especially in defining the form and range of options considered.

To summarize, the cases suggest that epistemic communities—when they arise—deal with the technical and scientific issues and that this effort precedes the main phase of institutional bargaining conducted by diplomats who confirm the work of the scientists and resolve remaining controversial issues. Media and advocacy groups may also play roles in increasing the prominence of issues and instigating substantial shifts in national policies that bring these policies into line with the views of the epistemic community.

Contextual Factors

One of the most striking findings of this project is the identification of a class of factors that appear to play a major role as determinants of regime formation but have not received much attention in the scholarly literature. Our cases strongly suggest that any explanation of regime formation will be incomplete in the absence of a discussion of the relevance of natural and human events unfolding outside the issue area to which the regime pertains (see Table 7.4). These contextual factors, as we call them, create windows of opportunity in which regimes may form.

Table 7.4 Contextual factors

Hypotheses	Fur seals	Svalbard	Polar bears	Ozone	HAZE/ LRTAP	Summary
Contextual factors	C	C	C	N	C	4C/1N

An empty cell indicates that the hypothesis is not addressed in the case study.
C = consistent with hypothesis
D = tends to disconfirm hypothesis
M = results mixed
N = no clear test

In the case of Svalbard, for example, war altered the configuration of power in international society and gave rise to a unique procedure for handling international disputes. World War I and the Russian Revolution together removed a major player from the negotiations, thus eliminating a potential obstacle to regime formation. At the same time, improvements in Norwegian-Swedish relations opened the door for a solution mutually acceptable to these two key parties. In other cases, analysts have concluded that the window of opportunity would have closed within a relatively short period. The negotiation of the polar bear regime, for example, occurred during a transient period of East-West detente; less than a year separated the signing of the 1979 LRTAP convention and the outbreak of the Afghan war with its chilling effect on East-West relations.

The range of contextual factors extends from broad shifts in values and ideas (for example, a growing environmental consciousness) to political trends (for instance, periods of thaw in the Cold War) and even to specific events (for example, the outbreak of war or changes of officials occupying key positions). Only in the ozone case did we find little evidence of contextual factors enhancing regime formation, though even in that case the electoral success of the Green Party in Germany during 1986 altered the German position on CFCs in a manner that increased prospects for success in regime formation. The strong evidence in four cases suggests that a more systematic analysis of contextual factors can make an important contribution to the explanation of regime formation and to our understanding of institutional bargaining more generally.

MULTIVARIATE ANALYSIS

There is an understandable tendency among students of regime formation to concentrate on formulating hypotheses that focus on bivariate relationships involved in the formation of international regimes. Especially when cast as necessary or sufficient conditions, these hypotheses are powerful in the sense that they direct attention to relationships that are invariant across an entire universe of cases. They can be stated in a clear and precise manner. Equally important, they are comparatively easy to test. Every case should conform to the expectations raised by such hypotheses, which makes it possible to engage in testing without resorting to the deployment of statistical techniques. Because the numbers of truly comparable cases are always small in dealing with international phenomena such as regime formation, the appeal of hypotheses stating necessary or sufficient conditions from the point of view of testing is not just understandable, it is almost irresistible.

Our research suggests that this way of thinking about the determinants of regime formation does have merit. Though we do not hold out great hope for the identification of conditions that by themselves are sufficient to bring about the formation of regimes, we continue to think

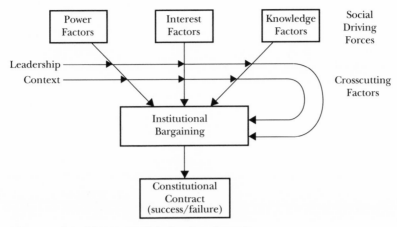

Figure 7.1 A multivariate model of regime formation

that some factors are so central to the process of regime formation that they can serve as a basis for propositions stated in the form of necessary conditions. The hypothesis concerning the role of individual leaders able to exercise entrepreneurial skills merits attention in this context. The hypotheses dealing with equity, salient solutions, and compliance mechanisms also received strong support from the case studies. Nonetheless, we are now convinced that it will not do to confine scholarly attention in this field to a search for bivariate relationships governing the process of regime formation. Those who proceed in this manner will not only find that most of their hypotheses are disconfirmed, but they will also fail to develop a clear picture of the complex process of regime formation. Surely, this is an unsatisfactory outcome; there are compelling reasons not to leave the study of regime formation here.

Reflecting on these epistemological concerns, we have concluded that the appropriate response is to construct a multivariate model of the process of regime formation in international society. Figure 7.1 depicts the key components and linkages of such a model. The independent variables or forcing functions in this model all feed into a process of institutional bargaining, which may or may not eventuate in success in the sense of agreement on a set of provisions that are articulated in the form of a constitutional contract. We have labeled the driving social forces in this model, any one of which may carry the bulk of the weight in specific cases of regime formation, power factors, interest factors, and knowledge factors. At the same time, several crosscutting factors, which we have named leadership and context, ordinarily come into play in directing or channeling the operation of the driving social forces in specific cases. That is, leadership and context exert their influence on the process of institutional bargaining not directly but indirectly through their capacity to determine how power is exercised, the mix of integrative and distributive bargaining, and the ability of participants to bring knowledge to bear on an issue.

A review of our case studies has led us to place strong emphasis on two sets of considerations arising in connection with this multivariate model: substitution effects and interaction effects.

There are, we now believe, several differentiable paths or routes along which institutional bargaining can move toward success. In other words, regime formation in international society can follow any of a number of tracks that are, in effect, substitutes for one another. Thus we do not dispute the view that the presence of a dominant power can on occasion be a critical factor in the process of regime formation. But our cases point to several other routes to success in international regime formation. In the case of Svalbard, the Big Four operating as surrogate negotiators through the mechanism of the Spitsbergen Commission played a critical role, although it would hardly be accurate to describe any one of them as a dominant power in this case. Progress in the fur seal case became possible when the participants acknowledged that the efforts of individual parties to exercise power in a process accentuating distributive bargaining to the exclusion of integrative bargaining could not succeed. As to polar bears, the efforts of the scientific community to reach consensus regarding the need to protect bears and their habitats undoubtedly played an important role in preparing the ground for the diplomats to agree on the provisions of the polar bear regime within the span of a few days at the Oslo meeting in November 1973.

That success in regime formation can occur along any of several paths helps to explain why those engaged in institutional bargaining frequently succeed in producing positive results despite the operation of an array of well-known collective-action problems that plague the bargaining process. At the same time, the existence of these distinct paths or tracks can become a source of complications in the politics of regime formation. There is room for misunderstanding among the participants concerning the nature of the track they are on, an occurrence that can slow or even block progress toward agreement on the provisions of a constitutional contract. Because bargaining is inherently a process in which parties seek to manipulate each other's perceptions and expectations, moreover, we can expect to encounter cases of strategic behavior or even self-deception with regard to the path toward regime formation prevailing in specific instances of institutional bargaining. Even with the benefit of hindsight, for example, there is a lively debate between those who emphasize the exercise of structural power in analyzing the process that eventuated in the 1987 Montreal Protocol and those who see the process as one of problem solving or integrative bargaining in the absence of pressure tactics.[22]

Even more interesting is the occurrence of interaction effects among the driving social forces and between these forces and the crosscutting factors. Whereas students of regime formation have often sought to demonstrate the primacy of power, interest, or knowledge factors in the formation of international regimes, we have become convinced that some of the most illuminating insights into the process of regime formation arise when we direct our attention to the interactions among these factors. The growth of knowledge and the emergence of epistemic communities can play a critical role both in identifying and framing the issues at stake and in shaping the way participants understand their interests, even when the actual process of regime formation is properly construed as a form of integrative bargaining. This, we now believe, is an important realization in making sense of the creation stories of the polar bear regime, the transboundary air pollution regime, and the regime for the protection of stratospheric ozone. In all three cases, scientific concerns played a key role in defining the problem and bringing it to the attention of policy makers and diplomats, who then proceeded to negotiate the terms of an international regime with their counterparts.

Contextual developments, to take another example, can stimulate the emergence of the political will needed to tackle an issue as an exercise in integrative bargaining or problem solving rather than as an exercise in bringing structural power to bear in the form of bargaining leverage. The rise of the conservation movement, with its emphasis on such ideas as managing resources scientifically to achieve maximum sustainable yield, made it much easier to come to terms with the fur seal problem in 1911 than it had been in the 1890s, when efforts to tackle the problem stalemated over jurisdictional issues. The window of opportunity created by improved relations between Norway and Sweden and Russia's incapacity at the end of World War I coupled with the existence of a political forum in the form of the Paris Peace Conference made it relatively easy to devise a pragmatic solution to the problem of governing Svalbard, which had proven intractable in the prewar era. The desire of several key players to demonstrate the feasibility of transcending the confines of the Cold War in the context of the Conference on Security

---

22. In this connection, compare the account set forth in Benedick, *Ozone Diplomacy*, with the analysis Haas develops in Chapter 5 of this volume.

and Cooperation in Europe process clearly facilitated efforts to reach agreement on the terms of the 1979 Geneva Convention on transboundary air pollution.

The simultaneous operation of several different types of leadership constitutes yet another mechanism through which the forcing functions involved in regime formation can interact. The case of transboundary air pollution, for example, highlights the interplay of structural leadership, in the form of Brezhnev's effort to propel the issue to the forefront as a means of breathing life into the CSCE process, and entrepreneurial leadership, in the form of Stanovnik's efforts to devise mutually agreeable formulas and to broker the interests of the various participants. Similar comments are in order regarding the case of the Montreal Protocol, in which Benedick wielded considerable influence as the chief negotiator for the United States, while Tolba played a crucial entrepreneurial role in articulating the emerging scientific consensus concerning ozone depletion and disseminating this consensus among the participants in the ozone negotiations.

In one sense, the prominence of these interaction effects poses difficulties for the analyst of regime formation. The methodological problems involved in separating out the contributing factors and assigning weights to each in an effort to explain or predict regime formation are formidable, especially because the available universe of cases is too small to support the use of techniques of multivariate statistics. Yet the study of these interaction effects not only offers the promise of a more accurate understanding of the process of regime formation, but it also provides opportunities for analysts to engage in intriguing detective work as they endeavor to understand the synergy generated by the interaction of two or more driving social forces and crosscutting factors. The importance of coming to terms with these interaction effects in the quest for an improved understanding of regime formation also reinforces our conviction that the use of comparative and focused case studies constitutes an appropriate methodology for the study of this subject. It is difficult to see how the complexities of these interactions can be grasped in the absence of the richness and detail that can be obtained from in-depth case studies.

What are the implications of this discussion of multivariate analysis for future research on regime formation in international society? In the first instance, we are convinced that major advances in our understanding of regime formation in the future will not come through studies that set out to prove the importance of single factors, much less through continuing debates about the relative importance of the presence of a hegemon, the emergence of an epistemic community, and so forth.

What we need instead is increased sophistication regarding the role of equifinality in regime formation (that is, the variety of distinct paths along which the goal of regime formation may be reached) and the operation of interaction effects that regularly undermine the persuasiveness of single-factor accounts as explanations of success or failure in processes of institutional bargaining. Of particular importance, we now believe, is an explicit effort to improve our understanding of the relationship between what we have called social driving forces (that is, power, interest, and knowledge) and crosscutting factors (that is, leadership and context).

These observations have clear implications as well for methodology in the narrow sense. They serve to reinforce the conviction, with which we began this project, that focused and comparative case studies constitute the most fruitful methodology for the study of regime formation in international society. Because we have concluded that hypotheses stating necessary—much less sufficient—conditions are sharply limited in the contribution they can make to our understanding of regime formation, a methodology emphasizing single case studies is not helpful to students of regime formation. What we need is systematic comparisons across cases to clarify the roles of substitution and interaction effects. Because we are interested in these multivariate relationships, moreover, research that focuses on isolated factors across a larger universe of cases also seems limited as a method of deepening our understanding of regime formation. Whatever the merits of this methodology in other areas of inquiry, it is not likely to shed much light on the complex and varied processes through which regimes form in international society. There is nothing simple or cut-and-dried about the use of comparative, focused case studies as a method of analysis. As we observed in Chapter 1, this method has limitations as well as strengths. Given what we now know about the process of regime formation in international society, however, we are convinced that this procedure has much to recommend it as a vehicle for taking the next steps toward an improved understanding of this important process.

ANALYSIS: RESEARCH PRIORITIES

If the argument we have presented is persuasive, where should students of regime formation in international society direct their attention in future research? In this section, we provide a brief account of issues needing further attention and areas that have struck us as good bets for additional research as we have reflected on preexisting theories of regime formation in the light of the sustained empirical research reported in this volume.

First and foremost, we need to ask whether the findings reported in this volume are artifacts of the set of cases examined in our project. These cases all deal with issues involving natural resources and the environment; even within this domain, we do not claim that our cases constitute a representative sample. It is therefore natural to inquire whether various forms of selection bias have colored our results. Do environmental cases differ from those involving issues of security or economics because they are more technical and less political in nature? Do our Arctic cases fail to tap some of the political difficulties posed by the North-South split in contemporary efforts to form regimes to deal with climate change or to protect biological diversity? The appropriate response to these questions is to conduct systematic studies of additional cases using the theoretical template we have devised. We are eager to see others pick up this challenge and prepared to revise our findings should the work of others make this necessary. For the moment, however, we believe that the burden of proof rests with those who assert that our findings are biased as a consequence of our choice of cases.

Turning to more substantive matters, there is much to be done to strengthen the analytic tools available for understanding the dynamics of institutional bargaining. Bargaining of this sort, which dominates the critical stages of the process of regime formation in international society, differs from the process envisioned in most formal models of bargaining both because it takes place in the absence of complete information regarding the contours of the contract zone and because it normally features efforts to reach consensus or to form coalitions of the whole in contrast to winning coalitions.[23]

Some of the consequences of these attributes are easy to identify. Integrative, in contrast to distributive, activities are more prominent in institutional bargaining than in the bargaining occurring in the world of economic or game-theoretic models.[24] Negotiating texts play a major role in institutional bargaining but not in the processes envisioned in

---

23. For an overview of the principal theoretical approaches to bargaining consult Oran R. Young, ed. and contributor, *Bargaining: Formal Theories of Negotiation* (Urbana: University of Illinois Press, 1975). An accessible survey of N-person game theory, in which the central concern is the search for winning coalitions, can be found in Anatol Rapoport, *N-Person Game Theory: Concepts and Applications* (Ann Arbor: University of Michigan Press, 1970).

24. As Schelling says in discussing game-theoretic work on bargaining, "We shall be concerned with what might be called the 'distributional' aspect of bargaining" (*Strategy of Conflict*, 21).

the formal models. Although leadership emerges as a phenomenon of great importance in institutional bargaining, there is no place for leadership in the economic and game-theoretic models. Nonetheless, we do not yet have a well-developed model of institutional bargaining in the sense of a logically interrelated set of propositions spelling out the links between the relevant dependent variables (for example, success or failure in regime formation, the timing of regime formation, and the content of regime provisions) and a set of clearly defined forcing functions. There are undoubtedly numerous opportunities to expand our understanding of institutional bargaining through analyses of individual factors in the absence of such a model. Yet we are convinced that efforts to construct a model should be accorded a high priority among those desiring to maximize our ability to explain or predict regime formation in international society.

The findings of our case studies also suggest research priorities relating to the principal clusters of explanatory variables we have examined. We have laid to rest the argument derived from hegemonic stability theory that the participation of a single actor dominant in the material sense is necessary for regimes to form in international society. Yet this certainly does not license the conclusion that power-based arguments are unimportant in explaining or predicting the process of regime formation. On the contrary, it frees us to return to a serious examination of the role of power without the blinders imposed by the idea of hegemony. The cases of Svalbard and transboundary air pollution, for example, suggest that progress toward regime formation is facilitated by the emergence of a small group of actors prepared to take action to forge the provisions of a constitutional contract. Perhaps these groups bear a resemblance to what students of collective action, following Schelling's lead, have called "k groups."[25]

The cases of fur seals and polar bears suggest that the process of regime formation goes more smoothly in the presence of a rough parity of power among the parties, at least in the issue area encompassing the prospective regime. The case of ozone, however, leads us to ask if and when initiatives on the part of an issue-specific hegemon (that is, an actor possessing exceptional material resources with regard to the issue at stake) are important in the process of regime formation. These are merely initial impressions that may merit further analysis in a nonhegemonic study of the role of power in the formation of international regimes. More systematic work in this area, we now believe, is likely to

---

25. Thomas C. Schelling, *Micromotives and Macrobehavior* (New York: Norton, 1978), chap. 7. See also Axelrod, *Evolution of Cooperation.*

turn up other relationships of interest to those desiring to understand the process of regime formation in international society.

It now seems clear, as well, that there is a need for a much more careful analysis of stages in processes of regime formation. Partly, this is a matter of clarifying the distinction between institutional bargaining as such and the stage of prenegotiation, including the emergence of an issue on the active policy agenda and the jockeying for position that occurs in connection with framing the issues and identifying the participants for an exercise in institutional bargaining.[26] In part, it is a matter of differentiating stages in the bargaining process itself, both in the sense of distinguishing unsuccessful stages from successful stages, as in the case of Svalbard, and in the sense of recognizing distinct phases in the evolution of a complex regime, as in the case of ozone. The development of these distinctions, we believe, will make it possible to sort out some of the differences that currently separate those who study regime formation. A reading of the polar bear, transboundary air pollution, and ozone cases, for instance, suggests to us that knowledge-based factors can and often do play a role of considerable significance in the early phases of regime formation but that they decline in importance as the negotiators begin to hammer out the actual provisions of a regime. It may even make sense to consider the role of hegemony in the cognitive or Gramscian sense in the formulation of the problem during the early stages of regime formation, despite the lack of support for arguments pointing to the role of hegemony in the material sense in connection with institutional bargaining as such.[27]

Our research has led us to believe also in the need to seek a better understanding of two factors that we did not grasp or only dimly perceived when we were formulating the hypotheses to be tested in this project. These are what we would now characterize as the crosscutting factors of leadership and context. Leadership in the sense of efforts on the part of individuals to circumvent or solve collective-action problems surfaced as an important consideration in all our case studies. Once we distinguish among structural, entrepreneurial, and intellectual leadership, moreover, it is easy to see how the actions of leaders can play a role in bringing power-based, interest-based, and knowledge-based factors

26. James K. Sebenius, "Negotiation Arithmetic: Adding and Subtracting Issues and Parties," *International Organization* 37 (Spring 1983): 281–316.

27. Robert W. Cox, "Gramsci, Hegemony, and International Relations: An Essay in Method," *Millennium* 12 (Summer 1983): 162–175.

to bear on the process of institutional bargaining.[28] Leaders are, in effect, transmitters who act to focus underlying social forces (that is, power, interest, and knowledge) on the issues at stake in specific instances of institutional bargaining and to guide the impact of these forces on the process of regime formation. Our cases have led us to think that leadership in one or more of its forms may well constitute a necessary condition for regime formation in international society. But there is clearly a need to devise more specific hypotheses about the role of leadership and to test them in the light of future case studies dealing with regime formation.

Turning to context, we have come to believe that institutional bargaining is a highly constrained process that occurs at the surface of the sea of international and transnational relations. Those engaged in institutional bargaining, and especially in its final stages, have strong incentives to distance themselves from the intrusions of contextual factors. But there are clear indications in our case studies that context can and often does impinge on all phases of the regime formation process. Sometimes the impact of context is direct and dramatic as in the case of Svalbard, where World War I broke out within weeks of the 1914 conference in Oslo and the Paris Peace Conference took up the issue in 1919 even though the question of Svalbard had not figured in any way in the war. At other times, the role of context is more subtle and harder to pinpoint, as in the case of fur seals when the independent emergence of the scientific conservation movement appears to have played a role in shifting the problem from a jurisdictional issue to a question of managing a shared resource.[29] Conventional models of bargaining either abstract away context or attempt to assimilate it in the process of specifying contract zones or payoff spaces. Our research suggests that this will not do for those seeking to understand institutional bargaining. We are greatly in need of more suitable ways to factor context into our efforts to explain and predict the course of regime formation in international society.

Drawing these threads together, we have concluded that those interested in regime formation should accord high priority to what we have labeled multivariate analysis. No doubt, there is much still to be gained

---

28. See also Oran R. Young, "Political Leadership and Regime Formation: On the Development of Institutions in International Society," *International Organization* 45 (Summer 1991): 281–308.

29. On the emergence of the conservation movement see Samuel P. Hays, *Conservation and the Gospel of Efficiency* (Cambridge, Mass.: Harvard University Press, 1968).

from efforts to clarify the role of individual factors such as leadership and context. But it now seems apparent that regime formation is a complex process that does not lend itself well to analyses that focus on single factors and seek to formulate propositions taking the form of necessary conditions. At this stage in our search for understanding, we need to devote considerable time and energy to what we called substitution effects and interaction effects in the preceding section of this chapter. Can we move beyond the recognition of equifinality to specify distinct tracks regarding regime formation and to say something about the factors that determine which of these tracks is likely to be followed in specific cases? Can we trace the linkages between knowledge and interests (for example, new knowledge may lead to the redefinition of interests) and between power and interests (for example, power may play a role in determining what gets treated as the national interest) as they affect processes of regime formation? It seems clear in this connection that the model depicted in Figure 7.1 is no more than a beginning in this realm. It identifies variables but says little about the linkages between or among them. The challenge now is to proceed step by step to specify the character of these linkages. There is an important sense in which progress toward a fuller understanding of regime formation in international society can be measured in terms of the development of this model from its present status as a simple "wiring diagram" toward a construct in which the nature of the relationships between variables is fully specified.

Praxis: Lessons for Practitioners

Does our research yield insights of interest to practitioners engaged in the give-and-take of institutional bargaining at the international level? Can we improve our understanding of the process of regime formation by cultivating a dialogue between practitioners, who have insights derived from direct experience but who often lack the perspective that comes from comparing and contrasting a variety of cases, and scholars, who have time for reflection and analysis but who have little opportunity to test their ideas in the light of direct experience? In this concluding section, we comment briefly on the implications of our research for those actively engaged in efforts to form international regimes, such as the ongoing negotiations concerning a global climate regime, in the hope of taking the first steps toward the initiation of such a dialogue.

As every experienced practitioner knows, institutional bargaining is a political process, a drama whose purpose is to foster convergence in the positions of autonomous players seeking to reach agreement on packages of provisions to be included in constitutional contracts. The process is not an exercise in rational planning or institutional design in which those with common goals employ their technical expertise to devise means of achieving these goals in an effective and efficient fashion. Still, this does not mean that all instances of institutional bargaining are the same, or that there is nothing to be done to improve the process or to maximize the likelihood that it will produce results that stand the test of time. On the contrary, the drama of institutional bargaining is far more productive in some cases than in others. On the basis of our study, we would now suggest the following lessons that may prove helpful to practitioners desiring to succeed in institutional bargaining not only in the sense of reaching agreement on the terms of international regimes that seem attractive to the actors they represent but also in the sense of producing results that prove effective over time.

Get the Problem Straight

Institutional bargaining constitutes a late stage in the overall process of regime formation. By the time the process reaches this stage, it is difficult (although not impossible) to alter the way in which the issues are framed or the identity of those who will participate in the bargaining process. Yet the formulation of the problem and the selection of participants is often an important determinant of the results produced by institutional bargaining.[30] During the 1890s, when the fur seal case was cast as a jurisdictional problem, for example, progress was painfully slow. Similarly, the pre–World War I treatment of Svalbard as a problem of managing *terra nullius* was not conducive to success in institutional bargaining. In both these cases, it took a major break in the process to allow for a recasting of the issue. It is easy to see, therefore, why it makes sense to invest the time and energy required to get the problem straight at the outset, rather than assuming that the process of institutional bargaining will serve as a natural corrective to faulty initial formulations.

Exercise Power with Care

In their accounts of institutional bargaining, practitioners often

---

30. Sebenius, "Negotiation Arithmetic."

downplay the role of power and depict the process as a form of problem solving.[31] Many scholars (especially those who describe themselves as realists or neorealists) go to the opposite extreme, arguing that the (re)formation of international regimes is fundamentally guided by the underlying structure of power in international society.[32] Our research suggests that power is one of many factors relevant to regime formation and that the role of power in the process is more complex than any simple analysis (for example, hegemonic stability theory) would lead one to believe. It indicates, as well, that blatant or unsophisticated attempts to bring power to bear in the course of institutional bargaining are apt to backfire. It follows, we believe, that participants should, at one and the same time, remain alert to the role of power in the bargaining process and strive to orchestrate their own efforts to exercise power with care.

Balance Integrative and Distributive Concerns

By its nature, bargaining is a process involving mixed motives. Certain features of institutional bargaining (for example, the absence of complete information regarding the shape of the contract zone and the operation of a consensus rule) serve to enhance the integrative potential of interactions relating to regime formation. Yet participants in efforts to form regimes exhibit a natural tendency to resort to the use of bargaining tactics to promote their preferred options, a development that directs attention toward distributive in contrast to integrative bargaining.[33] Accordingly, it is important to make the most of opportunities to accentuate the integrative potential of institutional bargaining, through conscious efforts to make use of such techniques as expanding the contract zone and thickening the veil of uncertainty.

Make the Most of Intellectual Capital

Institutional bargaining is constrained by the nature of the intellectual capital available to participants. All too often, those engaged in efforts to form regimes become prisoners of conventional perspectives

---

31. For a case in point, see the account of the ozone negotiations in Benedick, *Ozone Diplomacy*.

32. See, for example, Stephen D. Krasner, "Global Communications and National Power: Life on the Pareto Frontier," *World Politics* 43 (April 1991): 336–366.

33. This is partly a matter of bargaining cultures or of the way people are taught to think about bargaining. The widespread influence of the work of Schelling no doubt both reflects and reinforces the tendency in Western cultures to focus on bargaining tactics that place distributive concerns ahead of integrative concerns.

unable to embrace new ways of thinking. Yet the evidence suggests that one of the keys to success in institutional bargaining is an ability to introduce new ways of understanding the problem. The fur seal negotiations made progress when the precepts of scientific conservation began to take hold. The negotiation of the polar bear regime benefited from the rise of an ecosystems perspective with its emphasis on habitat protection. The evolving regime for ozone protection can be seen as a product of the intellectual movement centered on the notion of global change. Overall, then, there is much to be said for the proposition that success in regime formation generally goes to those who are able and willing to entertain new ideas.

Follow the Leader(s)

Given the importance of leadership in the process of regime formation, it is to be expected that numerous individuals will compete to become leaders in specific instances of institutional bargaining. To a point, this is a good thing; leaders often play key roles not only in inventing mutually acceptable formulas but also in mustering the political will needed to reach closure on the specific provisions of a constitutional contract. Yet leadership cannot succeed in the absence of followership. That is, leaders cannot produce results unless others are willing to back them by committing themselves to supporting the institutional designs worked out by leaders. Although leadership is undoubtedly more glamorous than followership, no one can expect to function as a leader in every situation. There is much to be said, therefore, for a policy of deliberately choosing the role of follower in some cases of institutional bargaining and learning to play this role in an effective manner.

Seize Windows of Opportunity

Contextual factors regularly influence the course of institutional bargaining both by creating conditions favorable to regime formation and by derailing ongoing efforts to form regimes. In the nature of things, however, it is difficult to predict when and how such factors will intrude on the course of regime formation. What this suggests is the importance of being prepared to make the most of windows of opportunity whenever they arise. Under the circumstances, it makes sense to invest sufficient time and energy in the design of institutional arrangements in a variety of issue areas to be ready with imaginative proposals when transient windows of opportunity open. The alternative is to fall back on routine formulas that are not carefully crafted to fit the problem at hand or to miss opportunities to form mutually beneficial regimes altogether.

Explore Alternative Routes

Nothing is more common than arguments that take the form of assertions that because a pattern of regime formation worked in a specific case, it should be applied to other cases as well. To take a current example, many are now touting the virtues of the framework convention/protocol approach in the wake of its apparent success in the formation of a regime to protect stratospheric ozone. Yet our study suggests that regime formation can follow any of a number of paths and that the choice of a particular path is best made in conjunction with an analysis of the circumstances surrounding specific instances of regime formation. What worked in the ozone case, for example, is not necessarily the best route to success in efforts to negotiate a global climate regime.[34] It follows that those responsible for working out the terms of any given regime should make a conscious effort to evaluate the pros and cons of alternative paths to regime formation rather than fixating on the alleged virtues of a single route.

Combine Forces

Above all, the process of regime formation typically involves interactions among driving social forces—power, interests, and knowledge—as well as crosscutting factors—leadership and context. Success is likely to go to those who are able to grasp these interaction effects in a sophisticated manner and to knit together the diverse forces that come into play in the course of institutional bargaining. Because our models of these interaction effects are not highly developed, it is difficult to formulate precise recommendations in this area of interest to those responsible for devising the terms of constitutional contracts. Yet it seems clear that the most successful players in processes of institutional bargaining have a sophisticated, though often intuitive, grasp of the interplay of power, interests, and knowledge in the formation of international regimes. This suggests to us another reason for improving the dialogue between scholars and practitioners in thinking about regime

---

34. James K. Sebenius, "Negotiating a Regime to Control Global Warming," in Mathews et al., *Greenhouse Warming*, 69–98. For an intriguing suggestion that we employ the GATT model (that is, a set of general principles that serve as a framework for a series of rounds of substantive negotiations) in thinking about climate change, see David G. Victor, "How to Slow Global Warming," *Nature* 349 (7 February 1991): 451–456.

formation. Just as scholars can focus on past cases to extract lessons of interest to practitioners, those who participate in processes of institutional bargaining can draw on their experiences to enrich the thinking of students of regime formation.

Template of Hypotheses to Be Tested

A. Power-based hypotheses

Basic premise: Institutions, including international regimes, are structured by and reflect the distribution and configuration of power in international society.

1. Hegemony. The most widely discussed hypothesis in this set, which arises from hegemonic stability theory, states that the presence of a hegemon (that is, an actor possessing a preponderance of material resources) is a necessary condition for regime formation in international society.
   a. Benign hegemony: the hegemon, functioning as the dominant member of a privileged group, supplies institutional arrangements to others as public goods.
   b. Coercive hegemony: the hegemon exercises structural power to impose institutional arrangements favorable to itself, regardless of the consequences for others.
2. Other power-based hypotheses are possible. Here are some examples to consider:
   a. A bipolar or bimodal distribution of power (producing a balance of power) is necessary for success in regime formation.
   b. The greater the degree of symmetry in the distribution of power, the more likely efforts to create regimes are to succeed.
   c. The existence of a small group of great powers in a given issue area (that is, a directorate) enhances prospects for regime formation.

B. Interest-based hypotheses

Basic premise: Social institutions, including international regimes, arise from the interaction of self-interested parties endeavoring to co-ordinate their behavior to reap joint gains that may but need not take the form of public goods. It follows that the availability of joint gains or, in other words, a contract zone or zone of agreement constitutes a nec-essary (though not sufficient) condition for the formation of interna-tional regimes. There is, however, no need to assume that the parties possess full or complete information regarding the extent or precise nature of the feasible joint gains at the outset. (In some situations par-ties dispute or disagree regarding the existence or scope of joint gains.)

Efforts to construct theories about the resultant interactions address the following question: Why do actors in international society succeed in forming international regimes to reap feasible joint gains in some cases but not in others? The processes leading to success or failure are ordinarily conceptualized as bargaining or negotiation; the hypotheses of interest to us identify determinants of success or failure in the result-ant institutional bargaining.

1. Integrative bargaining and a veil of uncertainty. Institutional bar-gaining can succeed only when the prominence of integrative bar-gaining and/or the presence of a veil of uncertainty make it easy for the parties to approach the problem under consideration in contractarian terms.
2. Equity. The availability of institutional options that all partici-pants can accept as equitable (rather than efficient) is necessary for institutional bargaining to succeed.
3. Salient solutions. The existence of a salient solution (or a focal point describable in simple terms) increases the probability of suc-cess in institutional bargaining.
4. Exogenous shocks or crises. Shocks or crises occurring outside the bargaining process increase the probability of success in ef-forts to negotiate the terms of international regimes.
5. Policy priority. (a) Success in regime formation can occur only when the issue at stake achieves high-priority status on the policy agenda of each of the participants. (b) Alternatively, it is easier to form a regime when the subject matter is not high on the political agendas of the parties.
6. Common good. A willingness to set aside narrow national inter-ests in favor of some broader conception of the common good is necessary to achieve success in regime formation.
7. Science and technology. (a) The greater the tendency for parties to concentrate on scientific or technical considerations as opposed

to political issues, the greater the likelihood of successful regime formation. (b) The greater the role of negotiators with scientific or technical competence in relation to those with political credentials, the greater the likelihood of successful regime formation. (c) It is easier to form a regime when the issues at stake are highly technical.

8. Relevant parties. All parties with an interest in the problem must participate in the negotiations for regime formation to succeed.
9. Compliance mechanisms. The probability of success in institutional bargaining rises when compliance mechanisms that the parties regard as clear-cut and effective are available.
10. Individuals as leaders. Institutional bargaining is likely to succeed when individual leadership emerges; it will fail in the absence of such leadership.

C. Knowledge-based hypotheses

Basic premise: Shared perceptions, beliefs, and understandings of causal mechanisms among the relevant parties as well as identifiable communities, including epistemic communities and advocacy organizations, that arise to propagate this knowledge are important determinants of regime formation. Some would argue that cognitive considerations—including ideas, values, and learning shared through transnational alliances, nongovernmental organizations, and groups of experts—constitute a more significant factor in regime formation than power or the interests of states.

Two alternative accounts of how cognitive concerns influence regime formation are identifiable in the literature.

1. Scientific convergence. Agreement or consensus within the scientific community regarding causal relations and appropriate responses is a prerequisite for regime formation. (Values are less important, though not irrelevant, to this hypothesis than to the next hypothesis.)
2. Epistemic communities. A group of individuals (whose membership usually transcends national boundaries and includes both scientists or experts and policy makers) who share a common view regarding causal mechanisms and appropriate responses and who have a common set of values emerges in conjunction with the issue in question. For a regime to form, some mechanism (possibly an international organization but in some cases a less formal network) arises to link the members of this group. The resulting

epistemic community is able not only to promote its own preferred arrangements but also to prevent opposing views and values from becoming influential or dominant at the domestic level
in each of the relevant states.

D. Contextual factors

National and world circumstances and events seemingly unrelated to
the issue area under consideration play a major role in determining if
and when international cooperation to address a particular problem or
issue area occurs and in shaping the content of any regime that forms.

Contributors

ALEXANDER ARIKAINEN is Professor of Economics and was Head of the Arctic Laboratory in the Institute for Systems Analysis, Russian Academy of Sciences, Moscow.

MARGARET CLARK is Visiting Assistant Professor of Political Science at the University of Oregon, Eugene.

ANNE FIKKAN is Head of the Secretariat for the Norwegian National Committee on Environmental Research in the Norwegian Research Council for Science and the Humanities. She was previously Head of the Polar Division and the Planning and Research Division in the Norwegian Ministry of Environment.

PETER M. HAAS is Associate Professor of Political Science at the University of Massachusetts, Amherst.

NATALIA S. MIROVITSKAYA is Senior Researcher at the Institute of World Economy and International Relations, Russian Academy of Sciences, Moscow.

GAIL OSHERENKO is an environmental lawyer and Senior Fellow of the Institute of Arctic Studies at Dartmouth College, Hanover, New Hampshire.

RONALD G. PURVER was a Senior Research Fellow at the Canadian Institute for International Peace and Security in Ottawa.

ARTEMY A. SAGUIRIAN is Senior Researcher at the Institute of World Economy and International Relations, Russian Academy of Science, Moscow.

267

ELEN C. SINGH is Professor of Political Science in the Department of Social Science at Mississippi Valley State University, Itta Bena.

MARVIN S. SOROOS is Professor and Head, Department of Political Science and Public Administration, North Carolina State University, Raleigh.

ORAN R. YOUNG is Director of the Institute of Arctic Studies at Dartmouth College, Hanover, New Hampshire.

Index

269

Cornell Studies in Political Economy

Edited by Peter J. Katzenstein

Library of Congress Cataloging-in-Publication Data

Polar politics : creating international environmental regimes / edited
  by Oran R. Young and Gail Osherenko.
      p.   cm. — (Cornell studies in political economy)
   Includes bibliographical references and index.
   ISBN 0-8014-2793-2 (alk. paper : cloth). — ISBN 0-8014-8069-8
(alk. paper : paper)
    1. Arctic regions—International status.   2. Environmental law—
Arctic regions.   3. Environmental law, International.
4. Environmental policy—Arctic regions—International cooperation.
I. Young, Oran R.   II. Osherenko, Gail.   III. Series.
JX4084.A68P64   1993
341.2'9'0998—dc20   92-54972